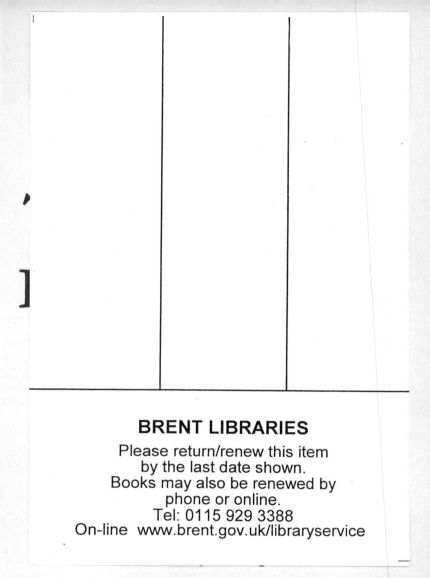

BRENT LIBRARIES

Please return/renew this item
by the last date shown.
Books may also be renewed by
phone or online.
Tel: 0115 929 3388
On-line www.brent.gov.uk/libraryservice

Dedica[...] [...]Bishop Spring to Stan Crowley [...] 'that in these Papers my name and Mr Crowley's name shall be read together for posterity'.

First published in 2014 by Gibson Square Books

www.gibsonsquare.com

ISBN: 9781908096654

Printed by CPI Mackay.

CONTENTS

Please note that all spellings have been modernized and dates are given in modern form.

THE JERMYNS OF RUSHBROOK

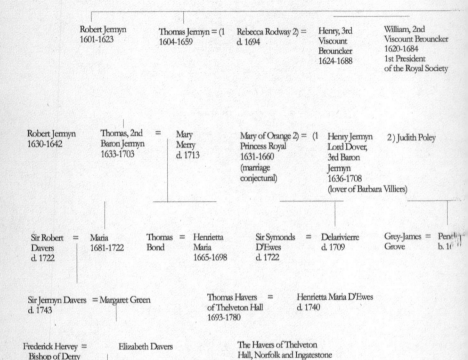

Robert Jermyn
1601-1623

Thomas Jermyn = (1
1604-1659

Rebecca Rodway 2) =
d. 1694

Henry, 3rd
Viscount
Brouncker
1624-1688

William, 2nd
Viscount Brouncker
1620-1684
1st President
of the Royal Society

Robert Jermyn
1630-1642

Thomas, 2nd
Baron Jermyn
1633-1703

=

Mary
Merry
d. 1713

Mary of Orange 2) = (1
Princess Royal
1631-1660
(marriage
conjectural)

Henry Jermyn
Lord Dover,
3rd Baron
Jermyn
1636-1708
(lover of Barbara Villiers)

2) Judith Poley

Sir Robert
Davers
d. 1722

=

Maria
1681-1722

Thomas
Bond

=

Henrietta
Maria
1665-1698

Sir Symonds
D'Ewes
d. 1722

=

Delarivierre
d. 1709

Grey-James
Grove

=

Penel[...]
b. 1[...]

Sir Jermyn Davers
d. 1743

= Margaret Green

Thomas Havers
of Thelveton Hall
1693-1780

=

Henrietta Maria D'Ewes
d. 1740

Frederick Hervey =
Bishop of Derry
Earl of Bristol
1730-1803

Elizabeth Davers

The Havers of Thelveton
Hall, Norfolk and Ingatestone
Hall, Essex

The Hervey Marquises of
Bristol and Earls Jermyn

Sir Robert Jermyn = Judith Blagge
1540-1614   d. 1615

Catherine Killigrew = (1   Sir Thomas Jermyn 2) =   Mary Barber
                            1573-1645   d. 1679

HENRY JERMYN   x   Eleanor   Robert   Elizabeth = (1   Sir Cyril Wyche
1st Baron Jermyn   Villiers   Jermyn   b. 1644   d. 1707
EARL OF ST ALBAN   d. 1685   d. 1660   2) = Mary,
1605-1684   niece
(rumoured husband of   of John Evelyn
Queen Henrietta Maria   the diarist
and father of her children)

Charles Jermyn   Katherine   Elizabeth   Judith   Henrietta   (conjectural)
d. 1660   1635-1668   b.1638   1636-1701   = Henry   Eleanor
                  = Sir Edward   = Mr Hacon   = George Raleigh Gage   1633-1694
                  Walpole   = Philip
                                                                           DAKINS
                                                                           of Jamaica

Sir Thomas = (1 Merelina   2) = Sir William
Spring   1673-1727   Gage

KEY

= married
x unmarried union

THE KILLIGREWS OF ARWENACK

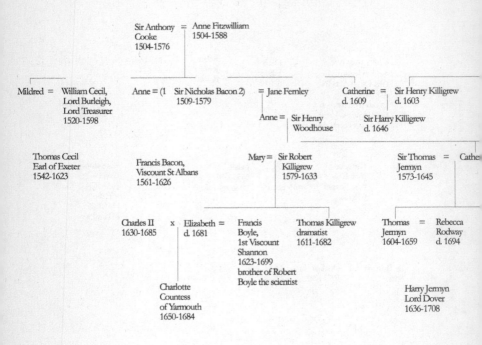

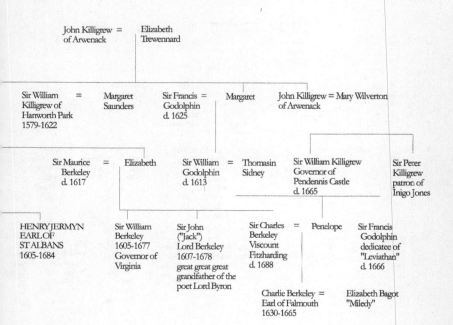

John Killigrew = Elizabeth
of Arwenack   Trewennard

Sir William = Margaret   Sir Francis = Margaret   John Killigrew = Mary Wilverton
Killigrew of   Saunders   Godolphin   of Arwenack
Hanworth Park   d. 1625
1579-1622

Sir Maurice = Elizabeth   Sir William = Thomasin   Sir William Killigrew   Sir Peter
Berkeley   Godolphin   Sidney   Governor of   Killigrew
d. 1617   d. 1613   Pendennis Castle   patron of
                                                      d. 1665   Inigo Jones

HENRY JERMYN   Sir William   Sir John   Sir Charles = Penelope   Sir Francis
EARL OF   Berkeley   ("Jack")   Berkeley   Godolphin
ST ALBANS   1605-1677   Lord Berkeley   Viscount   dedicatee of
1605-1684   Governor of   1607-1678   Fitzharding   "Leviathan"
                    Virginia   great great great d. 1688   d. 1666
                                      grandfather of the
                                      poet Lord Byron
                                                        Charlie Berkeley = Elizabeth Bagot
                                                        Earl of Falmouth   "Miledy"
                                                        1630-1665

STUARTS AND BOURBONS

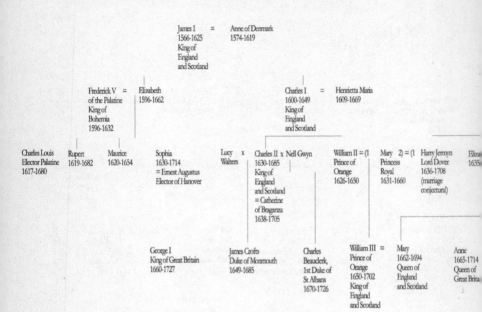

James I = Anne of Denmark
1566-1625   1574-1619
King of
England
and Scotland

Frederick V = Elizabeth   Charles I = Henrietta Maria
of the Palatine 1596-1662   1600-1649   1609-1669
King of   King of
Bohemia   England
1596-1632   and Scotland

Charles Louis   Rupert   Maurice   Sophia   Lucy x Charles II x Nell Gwyn   William II = (1   Mary 2) = (1 Harry Jermyn   Eliza
Elector Palatine 1619-1682 1620-1654 1630-1714   Walters 1630-1685   Prince of   Princess   Lord Dover   1635
1617-1680   = Ernest Augustus   King of   Orange   Royal   1636-1708
                                       Elector of Hanover   England   1626-1650   1631-1660   (marriage
                                                                 and Scotland   conjectural)
                                                                 = Catherine
                                                                 of Braganza
                                                                 1638-1705

                            George I   James Crofts   Charles   William III =   Mary   Anne
                            King of Great Britain Duke of Monmouth Beauclerk,   Prince of   1662-1694   1665-1714
                            1660-1727   1649-1685   1st Duke of   Orange   Queen of   Queen of
                                                                 St Albans   1650-1702   England   Great Brita
                                                                 1670-1726   King of   and Scotland
                                                                                 England
                                                                                 and Scotland

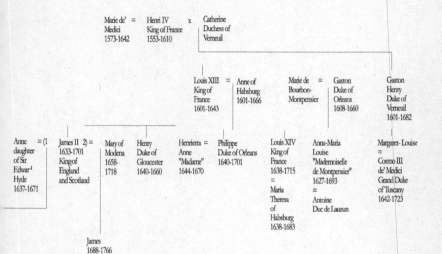

Marie de'
Medici
1573-1642
= Henri IV
King of France
1553-1610
x Catherine
Duchess of
Verneuil

Louis XIII
King of
France
1601-1643
= Anne of
Habsburg
1601-1666

Marie de
Bourbon-
Montpensier
= Gaston
Duke of
Orleans
1608-1660

Gaston
Henry
Duke of
Verneuil
1601-1682

Anne
daughter
of Sir
Edwar¹
Hyde
1637-1671
= (1

James II 2) =
1633-1701
King of
England
and Scotland

Mary of
Modena
1658-
1718

Henry
Duke of
Gloucester
1640-1660

Henrietta =
Anne
"Madame"
1644-1670

Philippe
Duke of Orleans
1640-1701

Louis XIV
King of
France
1638-1715
=
Maria
Theresa
of
Habsburg
1638-1683

Anna-Maria
Louise
"Mademoiselle
de Montpensier"
1627-1693
=
Antoine
Duc de Lauzun

Margaret- Louise
=
Cosmo III
de' Medici
Grand Duke
of Tuscany
1642-1723

James
1688-1766
"James III"
in exile

FOREWORD

'But I (most righteously) am proud of thee.'
Sir William d'Avenant, 'To Henry Jermin'

The Great Fire ravaged the City of London at the start of September 1666. The stone walls of old St Paul's Cathedral exploded in the intense heat, and molten lead from its roof flowed through the nearby gutters like lava. Panic spread in waves among the terrified Londoners as the flames rampaged through their homes and shops.

Henry Jermyn, Earl of St Albans, heard news of the fire from mariners along the quayside at Calais, where he waited impatiently for the wind to change so that his ship could set sail and carry him home. Behind him in Paris fretted Henrietta Maria, the Queen Mother, whom he had served with such loyalty that most people assumed he was her secret husband and even the real father of her son the King, Charles II.

Around Jermyn, on either side of the Channel, spread a vast spider's web of informants and agents, Freemasons and Presbyterians, junior British courtiers in his pay and French officials who smuggled him news of the business of Louis XIV, the Sun King. But none of them now could speed him information on what he most wanted to know.

How far west had the fire spread, and how many Londoners had been killed? Had Whitehall perished, with its marbled Banqueting House where the previous king, Charles I, Henrietta-Maria's husband, had been beheaded in 1649? And what had happened to the embryonic new city he was building on the Queen's dower lands in St James's which, by a series of leases and freehold grants, were now his too?

Since the 1660 Restoration, which he had done so very much to bring about, Jermyn's masons had applied their set squares and compasses to the work of planning, levelling, squaring and civilizing the rough fields beyond the western edge of London. He had laid out the ground-plans of elegant straight streets of fine, classically-styled houses around one magisterial square, St James's Square, all so radically different to the old hotchpotch of the City.

Much of the City was indeed devoured by the fire. But at the same time Jermyn set sail, his new city was being saved both by the wind and the unstoppable energy of Charles II. The King fought the Great Fire like a military campaign, creating a successful firebreak beyond the Strand between old London, and the new London in the West End.

Over the heady Restoration years which followed, Jermyn's St James's continued to rise up, a new city whose broad, paved, clean, well-lit streets became the blueprint by which the City of London itself would be reconstructed. Inspired by Jermyn's vision for a new Rome, and for the new Empire which Britain's overseas colonies were soon to become, the fields spreading north and west of St James's blossomed under a new patchwork of squares, each vying with Jermyn's original to become ever more liveable, elegant and refined.

It is easy to find a single word or phrase to sum up the lives of the subjects of most biographies, because often they have only been one noteworthy thing: 'writer', 'prime minister', 'general', 'artist', and that says it all. Jermyn defies such an easy description. One of the many inspiring things about him is the way his career was so multifaceted, opening up many fresh windows into the riotous and turbulent world of Stuart Britain.

'Favourite of Queen Henrietta Maria' is one phrase sometimes used about Jermyn. From 1626, until he broke his wand of office over Henrietta Maria's open grave in 1669, Jermyn served continuously in the Queen's household. Unofficially, she had known and trusted him even longer, since they had first met in Paris in 1624 – ever since she had recognised in him what a poet described as 'a soul composed of the eagle and the dove'.

Henry Jermyn lived in an era in which Charles I was busy enforcing the Divine Right of Kings, excluding virtually all his subjects from power. Yet in doing so he created a situation in which a handful of royal favourites could exercise very real power of their own – as in France. Jermyn's contemporary and equivalent in France, Cardinal Richelieu, was nothing, after all, if not a royal favourite. In England, Henrietta Maria was one of the few with direct access to Charles's ear, and it is ironic that Jermyn, though he was only the younger son of a Suffolk squire, had access to hers, and thus found himself able to exercise ever greater power as Charles I's power became more absolute.

Much remains uncertain about Jermyn and Henrietta Maria's love life, but one thing is very obvious. Throughout his career, Henry Jermyn was close enough to the Queen of England for many stories to arise, to gain currency and to continue to buzz about the Stuart court long after all the main participants had died. Throughout seventeenth century Europe, too, Jermyn was widely believed to be Charles II's father, and both of them were aware of the gossip.

After the imprisonment and 1649 execution of Charles I, Jermyn was the closest thing Charles II had to a father-figure. Bearing this in mind, we can start at last to understand the exceptional manner in which Charles II acted towards this most loyal and resilient of Stuart courtiers. Because the King's interactions with his leading courtiers had such a major impact on England's history, it is of genuine importance to understand the peculiarly filial attitude lying at the heart of the King's complex feelings about Henry Jermyn.

Yet Jermyn was so much more than a royal favourite. A treatise could be written about Jermyn's role as a diplomat. That is a term which, in Jermyn's case, covers an extraordinary range of activities, from his junior role in the embassy which brought the young Princess Henrietta Maria over from France as a bride for Charles I, through to his covert negotiations with English Freemasons and Royalists, which were pivotal in the Restoration of Charles II in 1660, and then his obscure and secretive negoti- ations with the French which kept Charles II secure on his throne to the very end.

'Diplomat' also helps explain Jermyn's own self-deprecating style, for he maintained a diplomat's inscrutability right up to the end. Only now, once Jermyn's shadowy power-broking has been pieced together, can we appreciate how it preserved the Stuart monarchy, despite all the massive upheavals of the mid- seventeenth century.

Was Jermyn also a spymaster? He did not run an organization comparable to MI6 or the CIA, for the simple reason that structured organisations like these had not yet come into being. But he grew up in a court saturated with a culture of spying and intrigue, inherited from the time of Elizabeth I's great spymaster, Sir Francis Walsingham (c. 1532-1590). Everyone with their eye to preferment was both a spy for their patrons, and spymaster to their own *ad hoc* ring of underlings and informants.

John Cooper wrote of the success of Walsingham as a spymaster that

> ... his agents were his own servants and clients, operating
> as individuals rather than as cogs in a departmental
> machine. The gathering of intelligence was lubricated by

patronage and profit. Yet it is this absence of bureaucracy which makes Walsingham's achievement so remarkable. Success or failure depended on his ability to keep alert, to spot the connections in the avalanche of information and to keep his people loyal.

The same could easily be said of Jermyn, but his case was more remarkable still. Walsingham operated first as an underling of the great Lord Treasurer Lord Burleigh, and then as Secretary of State. Yet for the majority of Jermyn's career, during which his spy network was so pivotal to the cause of the Stuarts in the Civil War and Restoration, he held no official government positions at all. Jermyn's intelligence network was, nonetheless, just as important as Walsingham's, and his lack of any official position allowed him much freer reign to act in the king's interests.

Although the *modus operandi* of a man who was both Freemason and spymaster almost allowed Jermyn's fame to blow away into oblivion, his great spirit of Restoration confidence, of the new planning and building of London, has never left us. Before Jermyn, British towns and cities grew up randomly. Yet once Jermyn had envisaged St James's, an area with an overall, masterfully-planned effect – and once he had introduced the concept of planning regulations to ensure the effect he wanted was achieved – everyone started imitating him.

From Georgian Edinburgh to Regency Brighton; from elegant, well-planned additions to towns and cities right across the British Isles and the expanding British colonies, and right down history to the broad new squares of the King's Cross development in 21st-century London, the spark of architectural vision which Henry Jermyn ignited blazes on.

My own relationship with Henry Jermyn started with a surprise encounter whilst reading about Queen Henrietta Maria in Joseph Gillow's *Biographical Dictionary of the English Catholics* in my university library. My interest in the period had been fired by finding I had a family connection to Oliver Cromwell, the nemesis of Charles I. It did not take long to find Henrietta Maria working vigilantly to bring Cromwell down, and there by her side was the shadowy figure of Jermyn.

Gillow wrote that rumours of the Queen secretly marrying Jermyn could not be true, because in her funeral oration she was described as an exemplary, almost saintly woman. Even as a young history student I was aware that funeral eulogies are the last place you would expect to hear the truth about someone's past. I took Gillow's words as a challenge. I was determined to explore those rumours in more detail, and to discover the truth.

The task proved harder, and more stimulating, than I could possibly have imagined. Many books about the Stuart era mention Jermyn, but often only as a footnote, not an active protagonist. Another major obstacle – and the reason why nobody had attempted a full biography of Jermyn before – is that all his correspondence with Henrietta Maria has vanished. Out of the thousands of letters they must have written to each other, none are known to have survived. There might be some in a secret part of the Royal Archives at Windsor (the archivists there say there aren't) but, sadly, it is likely that Jermyn and Henrietta Maria destroyed their letters themselves. Much of what the Queen and her (rumoured) lover would have written about, both personal and diplomatic, was simply too sensitive. The repercussions for Charles II, had such letters been discovered soon after their deaths, could have been disastrous for him.

At the start of the twentieth century, an ancestral nephew of Jermyn's, the Reverend Sydenham Hervey, made an attempt to collect his letters to others, and any original references to him in reports and letters. But everything was scattered hopelessly throughout British and French archives. I was immensely lucky, working a century later, in having access to many more indexes, off- and on-line, in being able to obtain photocopies and print-outs of letters from microfilm, and also in having use of the invaluable inter-library loan system.

By such means I was able, over two decades, to piece together the story. It was a huge jigsaw puzzle, and slowly a picture of the lives which Jermyn and Henrietta Maria led together began to emerge. Back in 2004, I was invited to rewrite Henry Jermyn's entry in the new *Oxford Dictionary of National Biography*. Many aspects of their relationship could not be disclosed in a succinct entry. This book finally allows the space to lay their intimate and influential relationship before the reader.

Jermyn Street and the whole area which Jermyn developed around St James's Square remains a stunning, physical monument to the lives, cares, achievements, and love (of whatever kind) of Jermyn and Henrietta Maria for each other. I hope this book may serve as a similar monument to them, in words.

St James's Square today, seen from the garden at the centre of the square. The dark building in the middle of the picture is Chatham House, and stands on the site of Jermyn's second house, in which he died in 1684.

PRELUDE

THE GREAT COACH
– Thursday, 12 September 1678 –

'Paint then St Albans full of soup and gold.'
from *Last Instructions to a Painter* (1681),
attributed to Andrew Marvell (1621-1678)

Thursday, 12 September 1678.

The gates of Windsor Castle were thrown wide open with a deafening crash. Thrown into golden relief by the hazy sun, a great coach came clattering out. Street hawkers and pickpockets jostled fine gentlemen in long wigs, all desperate to flee the pounding hooves of the carriage's six enormous white horses.

The coachman cracked his whip. The pounding grew louder as the coach gathered speed and hurtled down the narrow streets. Some street-side gawpers rushed with crazy courage up close to the vehicle to try to catch a glimpse of which of the celebrities of Charles II's court might be sitting inside.

Was it debauched Prince Rupert of the Rhine? Could it possibly be the dashing Earl of Rochester, whose outrageous poems about courtesans and penises make everyone gasp? Or was it the glamorous Nell Gwyn, former orange-seller turned royal mistress? Or perhaps another of Charles II's many lovers, such as the aristocratic Barbara Villiers, whom the besotted king had made Duchess of Cleveland? Or even his latest French favourite, dark-eyed Hortense Mazarin?

The coach's dark interior yielded no secrets. But as the coach rumbled past, the unusually simple coat of arms painted on the carriage doors flashed before the crowd's eyes.

The shield was jet-black with three shining points of light against it. First was a five-pointed star, fierce in its blazing whiteness. Below was a crescent moon, lying on her back, her horns cradling her companion. Underneath the crescent was another star, also five-pointed. Supporting the arms were two greyhounds, their collars decorated with the fleur-de-lys emblems of the Bourbon dynasty.

As they swept off their hats, it was only the elegant gentlemen of Windsor, well-versed in decoding the esoteric mysteries of heraldry, who could comment on whom the coach concealed.

Inside the coach was Henry Jermyn, the Earl of St Albans. The young rakes of Windsor knew the Earl as the builder of the most modern and fashionable part of London including Jermyn Street and St James's Square. To much older men he was the formidable courtier who, right back in the 1640s, had almost managed to bring an army to London to close down Parliament, and who thus, almost, averted the Civil War.

More romantic souls knew of St Albans' long devotion to Charles I's queen, Henrietta Maria, whom he had served for forty-three years. The less romantic scoffed, recalling prolific tales that it was the Earl, not Charles I, who was the true father of Henrietta Maria's children, including Charles II himself.

Court insiders, furthermore, knew that the seventy-three-year-old Earl of St Albans had retired from his last position, as Charles II's Lord Chamberlain, four years ago.

Which made what happened next seem extremely peculiar indeed.

St Albans' carriage rumbled through the crowded streets of Windsor until the coachman pulled back on the reins outside the lodgings of the French ambassador. The footmen in their austere black and white liveries jumped down, one pounding on the ambassador's gate, another opening the carriage door, a third bringing down the Earl's special chair. Their strong hands supported the Earl's arms as he eased himself out of the carriage and into the chair. He was then borne swiftly out of sight into the dark interior of the house.

Hidden from the eyes and ears of the town gossips, St Albans' footmen set his chair down in the elaborately furnished drawing room, bowed to the gentleman they saw standing there, and departed neatly. Paul de Barillon, Louis XIV of France's ambassador to Charles II's court for the last year, made his own obeisance to the old man, who took off his broad-brimmed hat in return.

A long career in diplomacy and many nights in the gambling salons of London and Paris had made St Albans' appearance extremely familiar to Barillon. Age – helped along by three-quarters of a century of almost uninterrupted consumption of courtly delicacies: roast quails and partridges, stags' tongues and sirloin steaks, marrow patties and crayfish, meat jellies and custards, and all the other heavily-larded wonders of seventeenth-century high-living, and all washed down with what must have amounted to a shipful of the finest Bordeaux wines and brandies – had turned the once strikingly-handsome Cavalier into a barely recognisable shadow of his younger self.

The Earl's brown wig was so lustrous that you might almost forget the bristles of his real, white hair underneath, cropped short to deter lice. His bloated face seemed worn out by his many years' over-indulgence. The careworn eyes were framed and half-concealed between drooping eyelids and sagging bags, the pupils now white and almost sightless.

St Albans' full lips seemed pale compared to the maze of blood vessels mottling his nose. Below his face his chins rolled down into a thick lace neck-cloth, which in turn gave way to his long, and bulging, waistcoat.

Over this, on its blue ribbon, hung the glittering image of St George slaying the dragon, the insignia of the Most Noble Order of the Garter. Besides this and the blue Garter band strapped just below the knee of his swollen left leg, the Earl's attire was expensive but plain – black velvet and white satin. His fleshy right hand, with its brown patina of liver-spots, grasped a silver-topped cane. His black shoes with their white ribbons were disproportionately over-sized, padded with cotton to ease the perpetual pain of his gout.

The Earl of St Albans' appearance was extremely familiar to Barillon, as was his history. Indeed, knowing about the Earl of St Albans was near the top of the list of requirements for any prospective ambassador to the Court of St James. Very few but Lord St Albans knew both Charles II and Louis XIV equally on such intimate terms, nor understood so well the perplexing twists and turns of their minds.

Still, his sudden arrival in the French Ambassador's lodgings now must have filled the younger man with intense anticipation. The future of Britain and France lay in the gouty hands of this elderly, retired courtier, who had come to discuss a highly-secret plan for Europe – a plan which could prove explosive if the enemies of Louis XIV and Charles II ever caught scent of it.

So when the Earl began to speak in his fluent if somewhat old-fashioned French, the Ambassador listened with extreme attention. St Albans related how God, the Divine Architect of the Universe, had used his secret, sacred geometry to create the world. Two and a half thousand years ago, Brutus, great grandson of Aeneas, settled Albion's hills with descendants of survivors of the siege of Troy. After Brutus died, the land became miserably partitioned and remained so until Charles II's grandfather, the magnificent James VI of Scotland, had inherited the throne of England and Wales, and the Lordship of Ireland. Known thenceforth as James I, he had at last brought the entire British Isles under one glorious ruler.

The Earl enumerated Charles II's possessions in the East and West Indies including the rich jewels of Bombay and Barbados, the growing trading-stations clinging to the west coast of savage Africa, and all the colonies penetrating the wild forests up the eastern seaboard of North America, not least Jermyn's own vast estates in the Northern Neck of Virginia.

Then he spoke of France, whose people were descended from the Trojans, too, and whose kings derived their ancestry from Aeneas's cousin Priam, the last king of Troy. Once hopelessly divided into semi-autonomous fiefdoms, France was now, too, united under the centralising power of Louis XIV, the Sun King, and now, too, expanding into colonies around the world, often abutting and sometimes in conflict with those of Britain.

Barillon nodded politely at this tiny barb, knowing that the Earl would unfold his plan soon. But first, running his plump fingers through the air, St Albans traced a world map of Britain and France's friends and enemies. He told the ambassador of the powerful commercial empire of the Dutch Republic, rival to both Britain and France. Sweden and Denmark, he said, and the north German trading towns of the Hanseatic League, not to mention the multiplicity of German princedoms, disunited by religious denomination, were useful as allies, irritating as enemies, worth keeping an eye on, but seldom of very great consequence. The realms to the east were of even less consequence. There lay Poland, whose throne Louis XIV was planning to acquire for his family. Beyond lay the barbarous Russian Tsardom.

To the south, Portugal, clinging to the Iberian coast, with her own trading empire, was firmly allied to both France and Britain through Charles II's marriage to Queen Catherine. Out of all the Italian states, Savoy, Mantua, Naples, Rome and the rest, only Tuscany, ruled from Florence by St Albans's old drinking-companion Cosmo de Medici, was a genuine friend to France. The rest allied themselves to whichever greater European power they happened to be looking at when the wind changed.

The Earl sighed when speaking of Venice and the great struggle of the Doge and his heroic ally Prince Rákóczy in Transylvania against the galleys and scimitar-wielding armies of the Sultan, which pushed forth unchecked from the portals of Turkish Constantinople. The Sultan's only virtue, the Earl told Barillon, was the trouble he was causing the Hapsburgs – the greatest enemy of Louis XIV and Charles II.

He emphasised this point, colour rising in his cheeks as he delineated the territories of the Holy Roman Empire including Bohemia, the Protestant kingdom that had been so sorely crushed by the Hapsburg emperor when the Earl was still a boy.

His finger passed across the world to the other Hapsburg domain, Spain, with all her swathes of gold-bearing jungle in South America. Spain, the Earl repeated angrily, whose Inquisition aimed wipe out man's ability to think freely, just as her soldiers had annihilated the noble empire of the Incas.

Habsburg Spain, whose armies had been ejected from the Dutch provinces by the House of Orange and the English volunteer armies at the beginning of the century, still occupied the southern Netherlands from Antwerp right up to Lille with its ruthless armies, and remained the most pernicious thorn in the side of northern Europe.

As long as Parliament had the power to vote Charles II

money through taxation, the Earl said, it could continue its obstructive stance: opposing the Closer Union of the two crowns of England and France, against the Spanish. Both the Houses of Lords and Commons were packed full of men only too happy to drink French wine and follow French fashions. Yet the moment anyone suggested co-operating with France against the Hapsburgs, the politicians howled in protest, waving their ridiculous order-papers as if anywhere in their beer-addled brains they had the slightest idea how foreign policy worked. So deep-seated in their Anglican upbringing was the Francophobia of the majority of Members of Parliament, they would rather Britain became mediocre allies of the republican Dutch and the haughty Hapsburgs, than fight for future greatness by the side of France!

Barillon had a pretty good idea what the Earl would say next. If Louis XIV would send sufficient money, Charles II would not need to ask Parliament to grant him taxes. Free of Parliament, Charles could honour the promises he had already made, eight years earlier, to form a special relationship with Louis XIV.

Between them they could conquer and divide the Spanish Netherlands. The King of France's claims to the Habsburg throne of Spain could be made good, and South America would be theirs for the taking. Charles II's nephew, William of Orange, could be helped to overthrow the States General – the Dutch Republican government – and take up his place as sovereign in the Dutch provinces. Thus united and vastly increased in their joint power, the armed force and commercial weight of Louis and Charles would become invincible.

It was a brilliant and audacious plan that would promote Britain into a super power in Europe at the expense of the Habsburgs – and it was the Earl's own, secretly sanctioned by the King in private conversations. This was why, although Charles II had a host of ministers who would ordinarily have undertaken such work, the King had entrusted these incredibly sensitive negotiations to an old man, born a mere squire, who no longer held any official position whatsoever.

I

THE EDUCATION OF A COURTIER
1605 – 1622

You've lived in Court, where wit and language flow,
Where judgements thrive, and where true manners grow;
There great and good are seen in their first springs,
The breasts of Princes, and the minds of Kings;
Where beauty shines clothed in her brightest rays,
To gain all loves, all wonder, and all praise.

Thomas Killigrew,
The Prisoners and Claracilla, 1641, dedication

Late one afternoon towards the end of January 1605, seventy-three years before the September day when the Earl of St Albans' coach left Windsor Castle, England lay under a blanket of snow.

Villagers dragged what little firewood their lords had allowed them home to their cold, dank cottages. Farmers sat by warm hearths in village alehouses complaining about the weather. Young nobles, splendid in their thick beaver-fur hats and richly-braided doublets, admired the elegant spirals their sharp skates were carving on the frozen surfaces of lakes.

In the middle of a deer park by the Thames, three miles west of the market town of Twickenham, stood Hanworth House. Heavy velvet curtains were drawn across all the glazed windows of the Tudor mansion. Above, on the sharp-pointed roofs, a forest of corkscrew-shaped red brick chimneys belched out smoke from the well-stocked hearths beneath.

The house was full of noise. After racing hard across the

snowy deer park to beat the gathering dusk, a hunting party had arrived home. Wolfhounds and mastiffs pushed through the boots of servants and huntsmen, skidding over the reed-strewn floorboards of the icy hallway. The hunting party piled into the glowing warmth of the Great Parlour, where the largest of the mansion's hearths blazed.

The yelping of dogs and chattering of people drowned out the perpetual noise of the house's principal occupants.

As in every house in Stuart England, rats outnumbered humans many times over. Behind every panelled wainscot they scuttled about on their endless quest for smaller vermin and scraps of food left behind by men and dogs.

Every day the servants threw pieces of bread and butter laced with arsenic into the corners of the rooms. Yet nothing had ever stilled the scratching footfalls of the vermin.

Collapsing into the high-backed oak chair closest to the roaring fire, the head of the household, Sir William Killigrew, vied with his sons-in-law to relate the best tales of the day's carnage.

With a tight lace ruff round his red neck and a grey goatee beard and clipped moustache partially covering his rosy face, Sir William was the epitome of an Elizabethan courtier.

Like Sir Francis Drake and Sir Walter Raleigh, Sir William Killigrew's roots were planted deep in the iron-red soil of the West Country. He owed his advancement at court to his brother, who had married the sister-in-law of the Queen's First Minister, Lord Burleigh – a connection which might seem trivial to us today, but at that period meant everything.

As a result, Sir William had served Queen Elizabeth I as a Gentleman of her Privy Chamber. The complex ceremonials and codes of court behaviour that both baffled and excluded outsiders had become second nature to him. By 1605 Elizabeth had been dead for two years, and a new king, James VI of Scotland and I of England, sat on the throne, but her memory still loomed massively over the nation's consciousness.

Few could ever have presumed to call Elizabeth I a friend, but Sir William had rejoiced in the knowledge that his sovereign held him in high esteem.

While she was still young enough to enjoy vigorous exercise, Sir William had been one of those fortunate courtiers with whom she loved to ride, the hounds baying after a noble stag, the sun shining on her rosy cheeks. When she was old, with white makeup daubed thick over her harrowed face, she would sometimes bring her retinue of ministers and priests, scribes and poets, musicians and tumblers, cooks and ladies-in-waiting, to stay at Hanworth.

Here, Queen Elizabeth could sit with him and watch the herds of deer run through the bracken in the short, golden autumn afternoons. Her last visit had been four years ago. She had passed the time sitting for one of the last portraits ever painted of her. The visit coincided with the baptism of the daughter of Sir William's errant son-in-law, Sir Thomas Jermyn. The girl had been named after Elizabeth I. Though it was not recorded at the time, it is likely that the Queen was the child's godmother.

Now, little Elizabeth Jermyn was upstairs with the nurses, chasing about with her two brothers, Robert and Thomas, and all of her Killigrew and Berkeley cousins.

With Sir William in the warm parlour were the grandchildren's parents. These included Sir William's daughter, also called Elizabeth, and her husband Sir Maurice Berkeley, the scion of an ancient family whose pedigree stretched back to the Norman Conquest. Everyone hoped the baby she was carrying would turn out to be a boy – and in fact it did. The child would become Sir

William Berkeley, Governor of Virginia.

Also in the parlour was Sir William's daughter Catherine, a small woman with a sweet smile, blushing in the warmth of the room and of seven months' pregnancy. Her unborn child was destined to own a great swathe of Virginia, too, but his life and destiny were firmly rooted in Europe – just as Europe's destiny was rooted in him, perhaps, too.

Sir William looked up to see his other son-in-law, Sir Thomas Jermyn, the husband of Catherine and father of her unborn child.

Thirty two-year-old Sir Thomas was seldom seen without the thin stem of a clay pipe sticking out between his handsome goatee beard and thick, dark brown moustache. He was one of the first people to have enjoyed the thick, sweet smoke of the tobacco leaves that his friend Sir Walter Raleigh had brought back from the Americas. He would continue to indulge the hobby all his life, stating in the Commons once that 'he has long used it and finds no hurt'.

Although he was now a moderately successful courtier, his close friendship with Elizabeth's heart-throb favourite, Robert Devereux, Earl of Essex, had brought him perilously close to falling foul of Elizabeth I's spy network, that she had inherited from the days of Lord Burleigh (who was Sir William Killigrew's sister-in-law's brother-in-law) and his protégé Francis Walsingham.

Sir Thomas had served under Essex on three expeditions, fighting for the Protestant Henri of Navarre against the Catholic King of France, then attacking the Spanish in the Azores and, most recently, subduing Catholic rebels in Ireland. The latter two were expensive failures, and when Essex capped incompetence with flagrant disobedience to the Queen's orders, he found himself faced with disgrace.

Essex's solution was to blame everything on the Queen's counsellors, and tried to raise the citizens of London in a rebellion aimed at overthrowing them. This foolhardy escapade failed and Essex was arrested. Sir Thomas, who had acted as Essex's spokesman, was in danger of guilt by association, and only managed to distance himself from the Earl's circle just before the arrests began.

On Monday, 26 November 1599, while Essex awaited trial, Sir Thomas made a prudent marriage to Sir William Killigrew's daughter Catherine, thus bringing himself within the network that included the powerful family of the late Lord Burleigh.

Their first child, a daughter, was born in November 1600. Naming her after Elizabeth I was another step calculated to atone for Sir Thomas's past connections with Essex. Just as well, for a mere three months later, the Earl was beheaded.

On this snowy day at Hanworth, however, this family link to the old court, young Mistress Elizabeth Jermyn, the Virgin Queen's probable godchild, fell into a terrible fit.

Alerted by the screams of children and nurses, the family went hurrying upstairs. They found the child sweating and shivering violently. The bread and butter she had found on the floor had seemed appealing to her. She had forgotten the adults' continual warnings to keep away from it because it contained arsenic to kill the rats. Already, the chemical had started its terrible work, distending Elizabeth's stomach and causing her to vomit black bile in violent spasms from her contorted insides. Within minutes the little girl was dead.

Cradling the bump of her unborn child and choking back her tears, Lady Catherine told her father she could not bear to give birth in a house stained with such an appalling tragedy. Accompanied by their retinue of servants, she and Sir Thomas left a few days later, huddled in a carriage with furs piled over their knees for warmth.

A short journey through the snowy morning brought them to the north bank of the Thames. Here stood the sprawling complex of Hampton Court, which that ill-fated royal minister, Cardinal Wolsey, had built and given to Henry VIII three quarters of a century before.

At Hampton Court, they embarked in Sir William's barge, decked out in the Killigrew livery of a golden field emblazoned with magnificent black eagles.

With a splash of the watermen's oars the barge began its journey over the steely cold waters of the Thames. Huddled around the glowing brazier they watched as the snowy fields of Twickenham, Hammersmith and Fulham slipped past.

Around them, the river bristled with birdlife, from ruffian cormorants to great flotillas of mallard and teal. Recently a seal had been spotted in the river. The Jermyns did not see it that day, but otters and water voles ran among the dead reeds on the riverbanks and splashed into the icy water in search of trout and salmon.

Ahead of them, clearly visible even from Hampton Court, they could see the smoky haze which hung over London. Though the myth was now under fire from sceptical scholars, most people still believed that London had been founded over a thousand years before Christ by Trojan Brutus, and named Trinovantum, or 'new Troy', a name they still used occasionally. After a period of neglect, it was rebuilt just before the Romans came by Brutus's descendant, King Lud, whose statue still gazed imperiously down on Londoners passing to and fro through the city's Lud Gate. Lud's city, or 'London', was now home to 350,000 inhabitants. Throughout the world, only Naples, Paris, and colossal Constantinople could boast a larger number of denizens.

Many more barges like the Jermyns', rowed by the brightly-liveried watermen, conveyed passengers of all classes up and down the great highway of water. Between the barges pushed wherries with their single square spritsails and the vessels of the lightermen, the special class of boatmen who carried goods of all descriptions from the great galleons and galleasses moored in the Upper Pool, down-river on the eastern side of London Bridge.

Now they passed by the tall tower of Lambeth Palace standing almost alone amongst the snowy pasture-land on their right and saw the Privy Steps leading up to Whitehall Palace on their left. Lights shone out into the gloomy afternoon haze from Whitehall's jumble of narrow casements and Gothic arched windows. Inside, clustered round their blazing fires, King James I and his court transacted the daily business of eating and dancing, scheming and plotting.

Beyond Whitehall they passed by the ornamental gardens of the mansions in the Strand, over which they could just see the towers of the gatehouse of St James's Palace.

After the Strand came Temple Bar and the jumble of human dwellings which comprised the City of London itself. The boats were even more numerous here and by the shore women could be seen with their white arms plunged into the freezing water, washing clothes. Shivering horses stood knee-deep in the river while the buckets they carried were filled with water to be taken up through the narrow streets and sold to the wealthier citizens for drinking, cooking and, very rarely, for washing.

Over the whole scene loomed the crinkled Gothic towers of old St Paul's Cathedral, built, it was believed, over the site of Brutus's temple of Apollo. In its shadows, the inhabitants of the great city were alternately freezing for want of fuel or risking igniting their timber houses by the heat of their blazing fires.

Such a fog of smoke spewed forth from their teeming chimneys that it almost masked the dizzying stench of the sewage lying in the semi-frozen mud outside their bolted doors.

So closely packed were the wooden houses of pauper and merchant alike that sociable citizens from one side of a street could lean out of their top-floor windows and shake hands with neighbours living opposite.

Towards twilight, the Jermyns landed at one of the wooden quays that jutted out from the muddy banks of the river. Their carriage was waiting to convey them past Cornhill into the heart of the city, to Sir William's town house in the parish of St Margaret's Lothbury, near what is now the Bank of England.

Here Lady Catherine mourned her way through the last two months of her pregnancy whilst an anxious Sir Thomas fidgeted helplessly, puffing nervously at the long, thin stem of his clay pipe. Towards the end of March Lady Catherine went into labour.

Many women died giving birth or succumbed soon after to infections picked up whilst birthing their infants. But in the midst of the stench and squalor and rats and all the heaving, sweating human multitude outside her windows, Lady Catherine survived the childbirth, and produced a healthy baby boy.

They named him Henry, probably after the Protestant hero Henri of Navarre, although perhaps with a respectful nod as well to James I's son, Prince Henry.

The boy was baptised in the Anglican parish church of St Margaret's Lothbury, near Sir William's house, on Friday, 29 March 1605, which happened to be Good Friday, two days before Easter.

* * *

Lady Catherine Jermyn (née Killigrew), mother of Henry, painted by Marcus Gheeraerts the Younger.
(Yale Center for British Art, Paul Mellon Collection)

He was bound up securely in swaddling clothes, and would remain constricted until his wriggling limbs encouraged him to start toddling. Then, if God ordained he should live so long, he would be put into a dress with a lace cap on his head, just like a girl, until his seventh birthday. From then on Jermyn would dress like a miniature adult in hose and doublet, even including a padded codpiece to enable him to imitate the swaggering costume favoured by grown men at the time.

Although the Jermyns and their extended family rejoiced at the successful birth, little Henry's chances of surviving to the age of one were less than fifty per cent. Besides cot deaths from unknown causes, diseases such as smallpox and measles took their toll on numerous babies, and many adults as well.

The odds of him living beyond his first birthday were

decreased sharply by the mere fact of his being in London. The lice that roamed through most Londoners' hair carried typhus on their bloated bodies. As the spring days lengthened, the rotting piles of horse and human manure which lay outside the windows became nurseries for millions of flies which crawled over meat in the kitchens leaving lethal diarrhoea germs behind in their footsteps. When summer came the mosquitoes that swarmed over the banks of the Thames injected countless Londoners with malaria.

Yet more feared than any of these diseases were the bouts of bubonic plague. People thought it was borne by stale air, but in reality it was carried by the fleas who sucked the blood of the rats, and which allowed the pestilence to sweep in deadly, periodic waves through the City of London.

To give little Henry a better chance of survival, Lady Catherine took him on the first of many journeys of his eventful life. At some point after March, probably once the warmth of late spring had dried out the muddy roads, their carriage transported them out of the City and through Mile End, escorted by a retinue of servants wearing Sir Thomas's livery of black and silver, armed with pistols and halberds to defend them against the murderous robbers who lurked in Waltham Forest.

They proceeded north along the well-beaten road that led to Newmarket in the Cambridge fens, where the court loved to come to watch horse racing. At Newmarket the road divided and they took the easterly route, over the gentle hills of western Suffolk to the market town of Bury St Edmunds.

It was the duty of the mayor and aldermen of the town to turn out in their finest regalia to greet the arrival of the greatest landowners in the area, each ready with deferential words of congratulation for the proud parents.

From Bury, the route home led two miles south-east along a

lane so narrow that the flowering branches of hawthorn trees brushed against the sides of their carriages, and its musty smell made their hearts beat faster in expectation. At long last they rounded the last bend and Lady Catherine could hold her baby boy up so he could see for the first time his ancestral home: Rushbrook.

Rushbrook Hall, pictured here in the 18th century, but very much as Jermyn would have known it in his boyhood.

Rushbrook Hall was built on three sides of a square, open to the south to form a courtyard. Its walls were of small, locally-baked red bricks. The porch through which Lady Catherine carried her son was made of finely-cut Barnack stone plundered from the dissolved Abbey of St Edmund's in the decades following the Reformation.

Surrounding the house was a moat, a relic of earlier more troubled times, and one which would provide some comfort to the family later when the Civil War began. Beyond the Hall came the barking of hounds in the kennels, the whinnying of fine horses in the stables and the low murmur of doves in the cone-shaped dovecote.

Little Henry's ancestors had owned Rushbrook since the day, three and a half centuries before, when an earlier Sir Thomas Jermyn had married the heiress of the Medieval estate. But the family's roots were planted even deeper in the local soil.

Their very surname commemorated a distant ancestor who had prayed with all the Catholic fervour of the Middle Ages to St Germain, the saint whose relics had long been the most treasured possession of St Edmund's Abbey.

Henry's family tree had sprouted many branches, and through male and female lines he was related to much of the East Anglian nobility and gentry, and many more influential people further afield.

The Jermyns' involvement with the royal court had only begun quite recently. They had remained relatively obscure landowners until the time of Henry's great-great-grandfather Thomas Jermyn, who was knighted as a reward for escorting Henry VIII's fourth wife Anne of Cleves to London in 1539. Even since then, although they had served the Crown faithfully in war and peace, they had never really stood out as courtiers.

Near Rushbrook Hall stood St Nicholas' Church, rebuilt by Henry's great-great-grandfather in a far more simple, Protestant style than the elaborate Gothicism of the earlier, Catholic era. Inside the church, young Henry could touch the cold stone and engraved brasses of his family's tombs and monuments in the east chapel.

Instead of a chancel arch, the church had a stout beam bearing the royal motto, misspelled, *dieu et mon droiet* and the royal arms of Henry VII. God was above everyone, even wealthy landowners. And between God and man, acting as the divinely anointed intermediary between the two, was the King.

For religion, Henry was brought up under the influence of his grandfather, Sir Robert Jermyn, who belonged to the Puritan wing of the Anglican Church, dedicated to eradicating all traces of Catholicism from his worship. For schooling, Henry was most likely sent to Bury St Edmund's grammar school. This is not, however, known for certain – although his nephews certainly went there, the records of his own generation were destroyed by fire.

Doubtless Henry read, or was forced to read, the staple books of the time, first and foremost the Bible, perhaps in Myles Coverdale's first, 1535 English translation, or else the King James version, that was finished when Jermyn was six.

After this came, with almost equal importance, Homer's *Iliad*, about the fall of Troy, and Virgil's *Aeneid*, about Aeneas's escape from the burning ruins of Troy and his long journey to Italy, where he and his Trojan followers settled, and where his descendant Romulus later founded Rome. That staunch Christians read so much overtly pagan literature may seem strange to us, but the Church Fathers had long since established that humans, Trojans and all, were descendants of Noah, and the gods, if they had existed at all, were simply glorified kings of old.

After these stirring tales came the British sequel to the story, Geoffrey of Monmouth's twelfth century *History of the Kings of Britain*, that related how Aeneas's grandson Brutus left Italy and led a further party of displaced Trojans to Britain, where they killed the giants and founded London, though Henry is more likely to have read the story through its fifteenth century re-telling, John Hardinge's *Chronicle*, whilst the story of Brutus's eventual successor, Arthur, was best known through Sir Thomas Malory's *Morte D'Arthur*. And maybe, too, he struggled through *The Faerie Queene* of Edmund Spenser, first published only 15 years before Henry's birth, a complex retelling of these stories circling around an allegory of Elizabeth I herself.

In Henry's time, these stories were still read as popular literature and most people accepted them as being true. Only an intellectual minority had started to question them, and thus to start groping their way towards what would eventually coalesce into a new, scientific view of British and, more generally, of human origins.

The myths had played an important psychological role in Britain's consciousness, providing a mythical explanation for a significant reality – that Britain had once been a Roman colony, and continued to be the cultural inferior of Rome. The 1537 Reformation, however, when Henry VIII tore the English church out of the Pope's grasp, asserted that England could look Rome in the eye on spiritual matters. In Jermyn's time, the dream that Britain might rival Rome in terms of culture, civilisation and empire hardened into a genuine aspiration – and little did young Henry's tutors imagine that this tousle-headed boy fidgeting on his stool would one day stand at the forefront of this momentous shift in national identity.

Whilst Henry's imagination may have been fired by these stirring tales of Troy and ancient Britain, he had no burning desire to study for study's sake. He would have agreed with his future friend Saint-Évremond, who once remarked that life was 'too short to read all sorts of books, and to burden one's memory with a multitude of things, at the expense of one's judgment'.

Henry's talents lay in more practical matters. He learned to write, and thus to communicate, in clear, fluid handwriting, which compares favourably to the crabbed hands of his more academically orientated contemporaries, such as Sir Edward Hyde and Secretary of State Nicholas. His training in mathematics set him in good stead for understanding a little of geometry, and juggling debts and calculating interest both for himself and, as it turned out, for two generations of the Royal Family.

Tall elms shaded Rushbrook Hall in the summer and sheltered it from the buffeting winds that swept across Suffolk from the North Sea each winter. Beyond the elms lay the deer park where young Henry could watch his parents and their guests riding after their hounds. Clambering over the palisades of the deer park, Henry could run down through the water meadows to the willow-lined banks of the River Lark, the rushy brook which had given Henry's ancestral home its name.

He was never alone. He had two elder brothers, boisterous Robert and the shy, scarcely noticeable Thomas. Butterflies would rise up from the pollen-filled grasses every time they scampered through the meadows with their wooden swords, playing at Trojans versus Greeks, or English sailors attacking Spanish men-o'war. His grandfather's grazing sheep and cattle would start in alarm every time their youthful mouths emitted high-pitched 'booms' of cannon fire or shrieks of laughter as they tumbled together through the fragrant seas of thyme and marjoram.

Fortunately for the adolescent Henry Jermyn, his grandfather's Puritanism did not extend much beyond the heavy oak doors of St Nicholas's Church. Life at Rushbrook revolved around hunting parties, great feasts and extended visits from the neighbouring gentry. These included the Crofts family from nearby Little Saxham and the Bacons from Redgrave, a family that included one of the most interesting men of the age, Francis Bacon.

With his full, pointed beard and a perpetual twinkle in his eye,

Bacon, later to become Viscount St Albans, is sometimes credited with being the real author of the plays attributed to William Shakespeare. Beyond doubt is his authorship of a series of books defining and promoting Natural Science.

Bacon's notion of studying the world through direct observation, rather than simply dredging conclusions out of the comparison of other peoples' theories, was revolutionary. It enabled his followers in the seventeenth century to break away from the Medieval scholasticism which had prevailed since the Dark Ages, and led directly to the birth of modern science.

Bacon had known Sir Thomas through mutual association with the Earl of Essex. He was also a nephew by marriage of Sir William Killigrew's brother Henry, another connection that sounds obscure to modern ears, but was highly significant in an era when whole careers rose and fell on the basis of family ties. This opens the intriguing possibility that Francis Bacon himself may have been an early mentor of Jermyn's, walking by the Lark with him, explaining his polymath ideas of cities and architecture, of statesmanship, and of how best to influence people at court.

Jermyn's grandfather Sir Robert employed a composer, George Kirbye from Bury St Edmund's, who wrote madrigals for the family to sing and tunes to which they could dance. As it was one of the courtly arts, Jermyn practised hard at dancing, easily surpassing his father, who was well known as the clumsiest dancer at court.

Jermyn also learned to ride, to shoot with crossbows and pistols, and to play tennis. Skimming impatiently through the wordy fencing manuals that were so popular at the time, he would have parried and thrusted with his brothers, rapidly becoming adept at sword-play. This was another courtly skill that would stand the teenage Jermyn in very good stead.

He also had a great talent and enthusiasm for French. His obvious interest in the language made him stand out in an age when, just like today, few Englishmen bothered to master foreign languages to any great degree of fluency.

Most of James I's courtiers could speak a bit of French, but they were so bad at it that, when communicating with Frenchmen, they preferred to attempt speaking Latin instead. Most of the ambassadors representing the French and English kings in their respective courts had to rely on interpreters to make themselves properly understood.

Exactly how Jermyn came to be quite so proficient in French is unclear. We know that, in 1618, two of Sir Thomas's sons were given permission to travel abroad. These were probably his elder brothers, Robert and Thomas, leaving thirteen-year-old Jermyn behind, but when they came back, better-versed than before in foreign tongues, they and their tutors may have topped-up the basic learning he would have received at home. Later, as Jermyn evidently had some talent for French, he may have sought out French diplomats and their households at James I's court. What is important, however, is not so much what French he learned, but the fact that he had an easy and fluent talent for picking the language up. It was this talent, above all else, which would serve him so very well in the future.

To be at court, to inhabit that mysterious, dangerous, glamorous, sanctified world: this became Jermyn's sole ambition. It was the only world both sides of his family knew, and the only one for which he had been trained. It was his good fortune that the things courtiers had to do well – eating, drinking, dancing and flattering – were among his favourite occupations.

But to succeed at court and earn the trust of kings, Jermyn needed to serve his apprenticeship under a high-ranking courtier. In 1622, at the age of seventeen, his gift for languages secured just such an opportunity, as a Gentleman in Attendance on Lord Bristol's embassy to Spain.

Jermyn's star had started to rise at last.

II

THE MADRID EMBASSY
1622 – 1623

Travel, in the younger sort, is a part of education... things to be seen and observed are the courts of princes, specially when they give audience to ambassadors; the courts of justice, while they sit and hear causes; and so of consistories ecclesiastic, the churches and monasteries...
Francis Bacon, *Essays*: 'of travel' (1625)

Jermyn's patron in Spain, John Digby, the first Earl of Bristol, had a difficult task on his hands: to negotiate a marriage treaty between the King's Anglican son Prince Charles and the Catholic daughter of the Hapsburg King Philip III of Spain.

That was a tough job in itself, but there was more. James I's daughter Elizabeth was married to a German prince, Frederick of the Palatine of the Rhine, who had been elected King of Bohemia in 1619. Opposed to his election, the King of Spain's cousin the Hapsburg Emperor had ransacked Prague, defeated Frederick and expelled him from the Palatine. In negotiating the marriage alliance, Bristol was also expected to gain the King of Spain's agreement to help Frederick regain his lost German patrimony.

Young Jermyn's task was less complicated. Besides running necessary errands for Lord Bristol, his job was simply to augment Bristol's entourage, as befitted the ambassador of a monarch of the power and majesty of James I.

Just over a decade after the seventeen-year-old Jermyn arrived in Spain, he was painted by Van Dyck. The painting reveals a handsome young man with a straight nose, intelligent eyes and a small goatee beard sprouting fresh from his firm chin, all framed by lustrous auburn hair. His tall, imposing torso is depicted clad in a fine satin doublet embroidered with gold. The crisp expanse of his white lace collar emphasises the broadness of his shoulders.

At the Spanish court, Jermyn would have added to this appealing appearance a short cloak trimmed with fur and pearls, flung rakishly over his shoulder; a pair of baggy breeches of soft leather covering his muscular thighs down to the knee; white silk stockings stretched over the shapely, athletic curve of his calves; polished shoes fastened with golden buckles and, by his side, a state-of-the-art cup-hilted rapier dangled in a jeweled scabbard, adding extra panache to his precocious teenage swagger. He must have been an eye-catching spectacle for Spanish girls of noble blood, or of any blood, for that matter.

When not obliged to attend the endless ceremonial receptions, Jermyn could put on less ostentatious clothing to explore the streets of Madrid. His companions were the other boys on the embassy, including Bristol's ten-year-old son George Digby, an inquisitive boy with fair hair, large blue eyes and a long, straight nose.

They were joined sometimes by thirty-five-year-old Endymion Porter, a Gloucestershire squire turned court wit. Porter soon picked up on the Spanish pronunciation of 'Harry' and gave Jermyn his long-standing nickname, 'Arigo'. It was Endymion above all who took Jermyn under his wing and showed the teenager around.

Founded only sixty-three years earlier by the forward-looking King Philip II, Madrid was the new royal and administrative capital of Spain. The city was laid out around a series of squares, the greatest of which, the Plaza Major, had only just been finished.

Here, locals and visitors alike could watch matadors bating and killing bulls. On the corner of the square stood the house where Miguel de Cervantes, author of *Don Quixote*, had lived until his death, on the same date as Shakespeare, seven years earlier.

Like the town's layout, Madrid's heady mixture of Baroque and classical styles were completely unfamiliar to a boy used to Jacobean bricks and Tudor beams. Had he ever peered suspiciously into any of the city's numerous Catholic churches, Jermyn would have smelt the overpowering odour of incense and glimpsed the idolatrous statues of the saints, the Virgin and even of Christ himself.

Did Endymion also take the boys to watch with disgust mingled with boyish fascination while Jews and Protestants who had defied the Holy Inquisition were burned to death? Jermyn knew only too well that when his father was a boy, the Spanish Armada had only narrowly failed in bringing the same religious terror to England's shores.

Of equal fascination, no doubt, were the city's taverns, where it is not hard to imagine Endymion plying the boys with watery red wine, while they watched Spanish girls wandering past through the sultry afternoons.

If his later career is anything to go by, however, Jermyn would not have been too completely bored by the tedious nature of the marriage negotiations, and was probably rather entranced by the principal character with whom his master was negotiating.

In Spain it had become accepted that the King, whose burden of ruling was likened to that of Atlas supporting the world, should have a favourite – called a *privado* or *valido* – to share his toil. The privado's power was exercised not so much through high office, such as membership of the Council of State, but more through personal influence over the monarch, acquired through force of personality and free access to the royal person, which was acquired by the holding of seemingly trivial domestic positions, such as that of *caballerizo mayor* – Master of the Horse.

When Jermyn reached Madrid, the newly ascendant *privado* was Gaspar de Guzmán, Count of Olivares, soon to become Duke of San Lúcar la Mayor. Young and ambitious, Olivares had gained the Spanish King's friendship and seemed unstoppable in his pursuit of power. Here was a highly charismatic role model for young Jermyn to observe at close quarters.

On Friday, 7 March 1623, several months after Jermyn's arrival in Spain, there was a sharp knock on Lord Bristol's door. Jermyn dashed down to answer it. Two men stood on the doorstep, broad-brimmed hats pulled down over their faces and long cloaks concealing their bodies. In a suspiciously well-heeled English voice one of them demanded to see the ambassador. It was only once they had stepped in and swept off their hats that Jermyn realised he was in the presence of the two most powerful men in the whole of Britain besides the King himself.

The man who had spoken to him so sharply was George Villiers. Only slightly shorter than Jermyn, Villiers was a remarkably handsome man, normally to be seen sporting the most ostentatious clothes it was possible to buy. Aged thirty-one, he was also one of the most dangerously fickle products of the English court. King James I, obsessively in love with Villiers, had dismayed his counsellors and friends by promoting this son of a country squire up the social scale to become a marquess. Two months after his arrival in Madrid, Villiers was further promoted by James, to become Duke of Buckingham. Buckingham was fully to England what Olivares was to Spain – the *privado* – the royal favourite.

The second man whom Jermyn encountered at the door was much shorter, with a long, pale face; baleful pink-rimmed eyes; shoulder-length brown hair, and clean-shaven except for a thin moustache. He was James I's eldest surviving son, the twenty-three-year-old Charles, Prince of Wales and future King Charles I. The wan Prince looked awkward while Buckingham laughed at Jermyn's confused apologies at not having addressed them properly in the first place. The Prince then trotted meekly upstairs after the Duke of Buckingham, to make a surprise entrance on poor, unsuspecting Lord Bristol.

Like Essex before him, Buckingham was keen to manipulate foreign policy for his own aggrandisement. His purpose in coming to Madrid with the Prince – both *incognito* – was to speed up what he had decided was an ineptly conducted negotiation.

In fact, Buckingham could do no more to sever the Gordian Knot of Spanish court bureaucracy than Bristol. Even the subsequent arrival of a whole train of extra courtiers, including Lord Kensington and Jermyn's father Sir Thomas, could not help Buckingham inveigle the King of Spain into agreeing to England's impossible terms. Placing all the blame for this on Bristol himself, Buckingham swept the Prince back off to London in a huff.

Bristol returned to England in disgrace. Jermyn went with him, but was still too junior to share in any of his master's ignominy. Indeed, young Jermyn had conducted himself so well on the Spanish embassy that he was immediately assigned to another one, to Paris – and destiny.

III

COURTING THE LOUVRE
1624 – 1628

She is a lady of as much beauty and sweetness to deserve your affections, as any woman under heaven can be: in truth, she is the sweetest creature in France, and the loveliest thing in nature. Her growth is a little short of her age, and her wisdom infinitely beyond it. I heard her, the other day, discourse with her mother and the ladies about her with extraordinary discretion and quickness. She dances – the which I am witness of – as well as ever I saw any one: they say she sings most sweetly; I am sure she looks as if she did...

Lord Kensington on Princess Henrietta Maria, 1624
(*Memoir of Henrietta Maria*, 1671)

The failure of Prince Charles's marriage negotiations in Spain forced Buckingham to turn to the Hapsburgs' greatest rival, France.

In February 1624, a new embassy was dispatched to Paris to propose a marriage alliance between Charles and Princess Henrietta Maria de Bourbon, sister of Louis XIII, King of France.

To conduct these fresh negotiations, a new ambassador was chosen in the form of Henry Rich, Viscount Kensington, a handsome thirty-four-year-old, who epitomised the courtly grace and panache so beloved of the French court. And travelling with Kensington as a Gentleman in Attendance was a younger man well on his way to emulating such refined elegance – Henry Jermyn. But as he approached the gates of Paris for the first time, Jermyn had absolutely no idea what a momentous impact the coming weeks would have on the rest of his life.

That word, Paris, conjured up images of style and chic in the minds of the young people of the seventeenth century just as it does today. Admittedly, the Seine, like the Thames, was clogged with raw sewage, and swathes of its population were scythed down by the same plagues and diseases. But that did little to diminish the wonder that this great European capital inspired in the minds of its English visitors.

In the previous century, King Henri II of France had married Catherine de Medici, daughter of the Duke of Urbino, whose family epitomised the highest achievements of the Italian Renaissance.

Catherine had an inspired vision for Paris. Everyone still believed, then, that when the Trojan ancestors of the Franks came from France, they had founded Paris, naming it after Priam's wayward son, he whose abduction of Helen had caused the Trojan War. Now, she felt, it was time for the city to live up to its grand, mythical past. Under her influence, the decaying Medieval centre of Paris was cleared away to make room for the first classically-styled buildings and gardens ever built there, including the Tuileries Gardens, based on those at the Pitti Palace in Florence. Later, in 1600, Catherine's Florentine cousin Marie de Medici married Henri of Navarre, who had recently converted to Catholicism to become Henri IV of France. Marie and Henri continued Catherine's work, including finishing the Pont Neuf, whose twelve stone arches linked the Isle de Cité with both banks of the Seine.

On the triangular tip of the Isle, a visitor such as Jermyn could admire the elegant three-sided 'square' they had built there. In the centre of the square stood a life-size statue of Henri IV on horseback, standing on a pedestal describing the famous military victories that had earned him the epithet 'the Great'.

Among Henri and Marie's numerous other projects was the Cours la Reine, which was finished in 1616. On balmy summer evenings the most fashionable Parisians would be driven in their open carriages past the Louvre, and then up through the Cours la Reine's triple avenues of stately elms to the fields called the Champs Elysées, named after the Elysian Fields of classical mythology, where the great and good heroes of old went when they died. These were wonders that England could not even begin to match.

Although not as big as the great palace it is today, the Louvre that Jermyn and Lord Kensington entered was still one of the most impressive buildings then standing in the world.

While trumpets blasted out in welcome, their carriages and horses clattered noisily over the palace drawbridge, past liveried musketeers standing stiffly to attention. The enormous palace was in fact a string of interconnected buildings starting with the twelfth century Medieval fortress with arrow slit windows and imposing towers surmounted by pointed slate roofs.

The elegant Petite Gallerie connected its south-western tower to a long range of classical pavilions and salons full of carved columns, cornices and elegant marble staircases connected by airy galleries, all strung like a vast necklace along the banks of the Seine.

At the western end, the complex turned abruptly north through the Gallerie de Diane to connect with Catherine de Medici's Tuileries Palace, whose terraces ran directly into the sumptuous flowerbeds and tree-lined avenues of the Tuileries Gardens. Jermyn and his friends could walk awestruck over black and white marble floors past walls painted with bright frescos or hung with rich tapestries depicting heroic battles and the classical gods.

From the galleries they could gaze out through tall cypress

trees to the sparkling waters of the Seine. One gallery was lined on each side with pictures of all the kings and queens of France, right back to their mythical Trojan founders. In another salon Jermyn could have seen an inlaid globe of the world suspended from the ceiling by gilt chains.

Everywhere he could see classical statues including the terrifying presence of 'Diana of the Ephesians', said to be the very statue that had uttered oracles in her temple in Ephesus, to the south of Troy, in the long centuries before the coming of Christ.

As the doors to the great audience chamber were flung open, the hubbub of the assembled French nobility would have given way to fascinated silence as the English party entered. It was at that moment that Jermyn's eyes fell for the first time on the French royal family. First was Louis XIII sitting stiffly on his richly gilded throne, his cold face expressionless between two long dark curtains of lank hair. Next to him sat his tubby, blonde-haired young wife Anne of Hapsburg, another daughter of Philip III of Spain.

With them was enthroned the King's formidable mother Marie de Medici, with her double chin and penetrating brown eyes, her jewelled clothes reflecting a dazzling rainbow of colours in the light of the candelabras that shone overhead.

And then Jermyn's eyes fell on the girl who, if Kensington's negotiations were fruitful, would become the next Queen of England: Henrietta Maria.

Even if she was not a daughter of Henri IV, the fourteen-year-old princess would have stood out in her own right. 'Little Madame', wrote a delighted Lord Kensington, 'is the loveliest creature in France and the sweetest thing in nature'.

Her clear face, with its full cheeks and delicate nose and chin, was framed by dense ringlets of lustrous dark, Italianate hair. Diamonds sparkled from her hair, and her ears, and around her soft neck, white as alabaster, that curved down into the rich lace top of her silk dress. But what Jermyn must have noticed most is that which is most apparent from the portraits painted of Henrietta Maria as a girl – the glint of candlelight in her large, dark brown eyes, and the enigmatic smile that lingered shyly on her lips.

Henrietta Maria de Bourbon was born on Wednesday, 29 November 1609, daughter of the Catholic Henri IV and his second wife Marie de Medici. Henri IV had been the Protestant Henri of Navarre, but had abandoned his religion with the memorable words 'Paris is worth a mass', in order to inherit the French throne. When Henrietta Maria was only six months old, an assassin attacked King Henri in the streets of Paris and stabbed him to death. The French throne passed to his son, Henrietta Maria's brother Louis XIII, and their mother Marie became France's dominating Queen Regent.

Henrietta Maria lived with her siblings and nurses near Paris at the royal summer palace of Saint-Germain-en-Laye, which was named, entirely coincidentally, but perhaps rather fortuitously, after the saint who had given rise to Jermyn's surname. Here, Henrietta Maria spent a happy enough childhood, until she was seven. Her elder brother the King had by then become deeply resentful of his mother's power and ordered the murder of Marie's hated advisor Concini. Soon afterwards he sent his mother into virtual exile in the Castle of Blois.

Marie went off to Blois in the mother of all Italian huffs. She took her little daughter Henrietta Maria with her, but that turned out to be not such a bad thing. For it was due to their being forced to live together in the relatively cramped confines of the castle at Blois that Marie's tastes began to rub off on her daughter. Both were already devout Catholics, fervently devoted to the Pope, the Virgin Mary and the communion of saints. But now, from her mother, Henrietta Maria learned to understand and love classical architecture, and also to appreciate fine paintings: Rubens and Van Dyck, after all, were personal friends of Marie's.

Music was another delight, and dancing too. Two years' incarceration at Blois passed quickly enough, and then Marie was allowed to return to Paris, to share limited power with Louis. The Louvre became home and here Henrietta Maria's courtly education continued as she blossomed into a beautiful, young, and eminently marriageable princess.

Henrietta Maria. There are many portraits of Henrietta Maria, but this is a very special one. It is Jermyn's own copy of one of Van Dyck's portraits of the Queen: the face is probably by the artist himself, and the rest by his assistants. It hung in his house in St James's Square, and ended up at his ancestral home, Rushbrook. It is reproduced here with the extremely kind permission of the present owner.

In the months following the arrival of the English embassy, Lord Kensington and his colleagues wrangled with their French counterparts over the size of Henrietta Maria's dowry and the composition of her household. The talks went on so long that, thirteen months after they had arrived, Kensington and Jermyn heard that James I had died, and Henrietta Maria's prospective husband had become King Charles I.

Henrietta Maria's active mind was full of excitement and apprehension. She had been brought up with a single purpose, to become a King's consort. Everything she had heard about Charles was positive, especially his looks and his courtly charm.

Yet he was heir to a Protestant throne and the majority of his people were heretics. How could she expect to fare in the cold, barbarous Kingdom of England? Every night, whilst the English party gorged their way through mountains of roast boars and suckling pigs, the inquisitive Princess made tentative efforts to learn more about her future husband and home.

It was a difficult task. She had no talent for language, and she pronounced the smattering of English words she did know so badly that most of the English party could barely understand her, and their French was so terrible that she could not comprehend their replies. Lord Kensington, who could speak French, had the inscrutability of a true diplomat, and would not even show her the locket containing Charles's likeness, which she knew he had in his chamber.

But there was one exception: the very tall, handsome young man with a polished manner, and such wonderfully broad shoulders.

Henry Jermyn, who had wasted no time improving his French, could understand her very well even if she talked animatedly about her hopes and dreams for the future. Better still, Jermyn could reply without faltering too much.

As they talked, they became friends, and Jermyn fell completely under her spell.

There is a painting, attributed to John Hoskins, which shows Henrietta Maria with her hair curled in dense ringlets around her temples, except for one lock which had been allowed to grow so long it tumbled down, tied loosely by a pink satin ribbon, over the silky white skin of her shoulder.

Jermyn could hardly have failed to notice these appealing details in real life. He can hardly have felt anything other than delight at the prospect that, when he returned to England, this beautiful princess would be going with him. He had always been groomed to become a courtier, but so far being at court had been an end in itself. Now, the same prospect was charged with an emotional frisson that may have seemed almost overwhelming.

On Monday, 23 May 1625, the young princess Henrietta Maria of France finally set off for England to marry the new king, Charles I. A great retinue left Paris with her, including her new household of maids and ladies, nurses and priests. The English ambassadors went too, with their attending gentlemen, including young Henry Jermyn, all their servants and a colossal baggage train worthy of the army of Alexander the Great himself.

Exactly a month after their departure, they came up the steep hill to the forbidding stone edifice of Dover Castle, where the young King was waiting to meet them. Charles approached his new wife. Both were nervous, and after an awkward embrace, he stepped back and she burst into tears. Early that evening, Henrietta Maria entered the dank Great Hall of St Augustine's Abbey in Canterbury, to be married as the darkness gathered outside.

Even as she repeated her vows, she may have spared a glance

and a nervous smile for her tall friend standing solemnly with the rest of the congregation in the nave, his handsome face lit up by the flickering candlelight. Did Jermyn struggle with pangs of jealousy that night, as Charles left the banquet table to pay his first visit to his new bride's bed in the Abbey gatehouse?

The next day the great procession of English and French courtiers and servants marched out of the North Gate of Canterbury, its bright pageantry doing its best to rival the swathes of wild roses and poppies festooning the roadsides.

At Gravesend they embarked in a fleet of richly decorated barges, the royal barge itself towed by a vessel propelled by twelve strong rowers, with a flotilla of subsidiary barges carrying musicians and trumpeters. And in the evening, while soft June rain pattered on the barges' awnings, they arrived in London. Charles, Henrietta Maria – and Jermyn too – had arrived home.

One of the many questions Henrietta Maria no doubt wanted answering – and which Jermyn very probably tried to explain to her – was how and why George Villiers, Duke of Buckingham, exercised such power at Charles's court.

The truth was that, shaken by James I's death, Charles clung childishly to his late father's favourite for advice and counsel. The power-hungry Buckingham, certainly not ready to relinquish his pre-eminence at court, was delighted to bestow both advice and counsel in lavish proportions.

But Buckingham knew that keeping a monopoly of Charles's affections would not be as straightforward as it had been with the distinctly bisexual James. Buckingham now had an adversary of his own making in the form of the spirited girl who sat enthroned at Charles's side. Was he to lose his hard-won influence to a mere female? Unwittingly, Henrietta Maria had walked straight into the web of a particularly spiteful and devious enemy.

Once Charles and Henrietta Maria were married, Buckingham lost no opportunity to whisper in the King's ear about Henrietta Maria's faults. He pointed out how damaging it was for the country that she would not attend the state opening of Parliament or the Coronation, because she was a Catholic, and the ceremonies included Protestant services.

She preferred her own exotic clothes to the more modest English fashions. Her French household were treating the English courtiers with contempt. Her priests were arousing popular suspicion that Charles himself would become a Catholic. She was not bothering to learn English.

Under Buckingham's careful nurturing, Charles's animosity towards Henrietta Maria started to grow. At his favourite's suggestion, the King decreed that, to make her sound more English, she should be called Queen Mary. He told her to adopt an English hairstyle. He forced Henrietta Maria to accept Buckingham's sister and other female relatives as members of her retinue that, until then, had been exclusively French. She saw them as the spies they really were, and her resistance helped widen the divide, just as Buckingham had hoped.

The effect of all this on Charles and Henrietta Maria's sex life was devastating. Whilst contemporary records are not quite detailed enough to tell what happened when Charles did visit the Queen in her bedchamber, we know that they were spending increasing amounts of time apart, and having furious rows when they met. Small wonder no sign had appeared as yet of an heir to the throne.

The nadir came in June 1626. Abruptly ushering Henrietta Maria's French attendants out of her chamber, Charles told his wife that her retinue was to be sent home. First outraged and then terrified, she fell to her knees, weeping and begging the King to reconsider. Yet even as Henrietta Maria cried, she heard her faithful friends being ushered into carriages in the courtyard below. Flinging herself at the window, the near-hysterical Queen smashed several panes of glass to cry out to them, but all she could do was sob into her damaged hands while the carriages commenced their miserable journey back to France.

After the wails of her departing entourage had faded away, Jermyn was one of the few people – perhaps the only one – with fluent French, whom Henrietta Maria could trust to listen sympathetically to her troubles. Here was a man who, as the poet Cowley wrote, appeared to have 'a soul composed of the eagle and the dove', and perhaps that is really how she saw him as well – a hero, protecting her from the world, whose inner self was, for her, as soft and gentle as one of the white doves of Aphrodite, the goddess of love. Of that, we can but speculate, but it is certainly no surprise that, when her new and much reduced English household was appointed, Jermyn did his utmost to persuade Charles and Buckingham to include him in it. And Charles agreed. From then on Jermyn had the happy obligation of attending Henrietta Maria every day as Gentleman Usher of her Privy Chamber.

But despite Jermyn's presence, Henrietta Maria grew unhappier. She strove to be a good Queen, yet Charles now treated her with open contempt. Buckingham had the temerity to remind her how Charles's great-great uncle Henry VIII used to deal with unsatisfactory wives. Henrietta Maria was never to enjoy happiness nor power while the Duke remained dominant.

Jermyn, too, had no reason to love Buckingham. He had seen how unfairly Buckingham had treated poor Lord Bristol for the failure of the Madrid embassy. Buckingham had also lashed out at Jermyn's kinsman, Francis Bacon, charging him with bribery and stripping him of his office of Lord Keeper of the Great Seal. Yet, up to now, Jermyn and Henrietta Maria can only have toyed with dreams of how Buckingham might lose his power.

Then, in 1627, the Duke excelled himself. He persuaded Charles to declare war on France.

Buckingham's pretext for doing so was the continued persecution by the Catholic Louis XIII of the minority of his subjects who were Protestants or, as they were known colloquially, 'Huguenots'. Many Huguenots had gathered for safety in the town of La Rochelle on the Atlantic coast, where they were now being besieged by the French King's forces.

Imagining himself as the hero of the Protestant cause, Buckingham set sail in June 1627 with a fleet of English ships carrying arms and soldiers to help the La Rochelle Huguenots. In the crowded streets, mobs of Londoners, those distant, flea-bitten descendants of the sons of Troy, or so they believed, screamed out their hatred of the French Catholics. At court, men drank hearty toasts to the downfall of Papist King Louis.

Henrietta Maria herself withdrew to the peaceful Northamptonshire spa-town of Wellingborough. She made the plausible excuse that she needed to drink the spa's mineral waters, that bubbled up from the local springs, for the sake of her health and fertility. With her went her entire household, and of course that included Jermyn.

In August, Henrietta Maria chose Jermyn to travel to Paris to deliver personal messages to the Queen's family, especially to her brother Louis XIII, who was ill.

There may, however, have been much more to it than that. We know from reports written by the Venetian ambassador in Paris that, having delivered his supposedly personal messages to the King, Jermyn was rapidly referred on to Louis's First Minister, Cardinal Richelieu, who 'saw him gladly'.

Jermyn was ushered into parts of the Louvre he would never have seen before, past rooms where clerks transcribed royal proclamations and dark anti-chambers where spies and informers waited for their appointments with spy-masters, until he was brought into a sumptuously furnished office.

Kneeling, the fledgling diplomat Henry Jermyn kissed the ring of the most powerful, most infamous man in the whole of Europe, Cardinal Richelieu.

With his long patrician nose, grey goatee beard and penetrating eyes, Richelieu cut an elegant figure in the flowing scarlet robes of a Catholic Cardinal.

The elegantly devious Cardinal Richelieu

Richelieu was another man of the same calibre as Olivares and Buckingham. Having risen to his exalted position as the favourite of Henrietta Maria's mother Marie de Medici, the Cardinal was now virtual ruler of France on behalf of Louis XIII.

Richelieu may simply have probed Jermyn for any secret overtures of peace from Charles I, and been disappointed to find that he carried none. However, with Buckingham at war with Richelieu's France and thus the avowed enemy of Henrietta Maria, it seems possible that Jermyn's mission to Paris was not a purely social one. He may, perhaps, have proposed some scheme, contrived between himself and Henrietta Maria back in Wellingborough, aimed at engaging the Cardinal's help in engineering the Duke's downfall. We know that, soon afterwards, Buckingham's secret agent, Walter Montagu, was arrested whilst travelling through France. Was this due to a tip-off from Jermyn and Henrietta Maria?

More certainly, we know from the Venetian Ambassador's reports that, at this time, Richelieu formed clear plans to strike out, not randomly at England, but specifically at Buckingham. The Cardinal threatened making an alliance with the Dutch and the Spanish against England, hoping, specifically, to frighten Charles into backing out of Buckingham's war and thus, effectively, into dropping his favourite.

Failing that, the Cardinal would send a great fleet to England, not to invade but merely, as the Venetian ambassador wrote a few weeks later, 'to set Buckingham's party by the ears'.

Perhaps not surprisingly, however, evidence is lacking to make a direct link between Richelieu's sudden intention to strike out at Buckingham, and Jermyn's visit to Paris. It is likely, however, that Jermyn's journey to Paris marks the start of the life-long involvement of himself and Henrietta Maria in international politics.

In the end Richelieu's fleet proved unnecessary, for Jermyn and Henrietta Maria turned out not to be the only people with grudges against Buckingham. An army officer called John Felton had developed a passionate hatred of the Duke, who had blocked him from receiving a promotion.

On the morning of Saturday, 23 August 1628, Buckingham was swaggering in his usual ebullient fashion through a crowd of officers and local dignitaries at the Greyhound Inn, Portsmouth. The atmosphere was relaxed, as he threw a few suave little quips out to his fawning audience. Nobody noticed Felton pushing his way through the crowd.

Suddenly, a knife flashed as Felton lunged at Buckingham, stabbing deeply into the Duke's chest. The blow sent Buckingham staggering backwards, his hand groping desperately for the hilt of his rapier. But before he could draw it out of its scabbard he had collapsed, blood pulsing through his bejewelled silk doublet, and within minutes he was dead.

IV

TWO DISPUTED CASES OF PATERNITY
1628 – 1635

... an odd kind of lover. He comes
Into my lady's chamber at all hours;
Yet thinks it strange that people wonder at
His privilege. Well, opportunity
Is a dangerous thing; it would soon spoil me.
D'Avenant, *The Platonic Lovers* (1637)

Like most European courtiers, Jermyn and his colleagues were kept constantly on the move. Daily life involved following the King and Queen on a never-ending progress from palace to palace including Windsor Castle in Berkshire, Hampton Court in Middlesex and Theobalds in Hertfordshire.

The Queen's own household sometimes made its own journeys between her dower palaces, which stretched like a gilded daisy-chain from the crumbling Plantagenet palace of Woodstock in Oxfordshire down the Thames to Oatlands near Weybridge and continued on to Wimbledon; Sheen; Nonsuch; Somerset House in London and finally fragrant Greenwich.

The court also made journeys further a-field, taking Jermyn and his colleagues to stay with noblemen in the shires or to bet vast wagers on horse races at Newmarket in Cambridgeshire, fifteen miles west of Rushbrook. But Whitehall and St James's were the main royal residences and it was above their gilded towers that the golden lions of England on Charles's royal standard were most often to be seen writhing and snapping in the breeze.

Coming down King Street from Charing Cross – in modern terms, walking south down Whitehall from Trafalgar Square, though it was mostly countryside then – the first thing you saw of Whitehall Palace were the battlemented towers of the imposing Gothic gatehouse, which had been designed by the German painter Hans Holbein. To the young Jermyn, it must always have seemed as immensely impressive as Henry VIII had intended it to be. After he had seen the Classical splendours of Madrid and Paris, maybe it seemed less so: less monumental, more of a Medieval fantasy than an imperial portal. And such thoughts may have passed through Henrietta Maria's mind too, as she approached the Holbein Gate for the first time: unless she was filled with a dark foreboding of the future, and saw it as the prison gate that was about to close on her girlish life.

Beyond the Holbein Gate, Whitehall's skyline was a forest of vaulted and arched roofs; battlements; black and white chequered towers topped with pointed domes; spires decorated with brightly painted heraldic beasts and countless smoking chimney pots. A fantastic, picturesque jumble maybe, but far removed from the striking elegance of the Louvre.

Through the gate lay a world with which Henrietta Maria would eventually become extremely familiar, but which may at first have seemed an incomprehensible labyrinth of strange edifices, full of unknown faces, each chattering in that incomprehensible, haughty language of the English.

To the north of the gate lay a complex mostly devoted to courtiers' lodgings, known as the Cock Pit. It was dominated by the great, enclosed tennis court Henry VIII had built to entertain himself and his restless hangers-on. This was not the modern game of Lawn Tennis, which was only invented in the late nineteenth century, but Real or Royal Tennis, which is still played today by a coterie of enthusiasts. Jermyn and his friends

worked up vigorous sweats playing long volleys, the ball
bouncing off the roof with a resounding crash and down onto
the opponent's side of the central net. Points were scored by
hitting the ball through windows behind each player or through
the gallery windows that ran down the north side of the court.
Games became heated. Once, a dispute over the complex rules
as to where the ball had landed led Jermyn into a furious
argument, followed by a stiff royal reprimand.

Beyond an outdoor tennis court and before the high walls of St
James's Park stood the great octagonal Cock Pit itself. While the
courtiers loitered round the pillared gallery placing bets, trained
cockerels tore at each other with special iron spurs fastened to
their feet.

On the south side of King Street, isolated from the traffic of
carts and hawkers by a high wall, lay the Privy Garden. Here,
Jermyn and his friends used to mooch about its grid of gravel
pathways, lined with low box hedges. The square flowerbeds
were full of blossoms, from the first snowdrops at the end of
January until the last Michaelmas daisies faded away in
November. During the summer months a blazing succession of
gaudy wallflowers and roses, tulips and poppies threw a haze of
sweetly scented pollen into the air. Here, perhaps, where the
damask roses and heady jasmine twined round secluded arbours,
and she could temporarily hide away from the prying, censorious
eyes of the English ladies, Henrietta Maria might have felt more
at ease.

Ranged around the garden to the south and east were the
main buildings of Whitehall Palace, a labyrinthine collection of
halls and houses; kitchens and chapels; passages and courtyards.
South of these the Thames lapped against the Privy Steps, where
barges constantly collected and delivered courtiers, and

sometimes the King and Queen themselves.

In the centre of the southern range of the palace were Charles' apartments, separated from the Privy Steps by a small garden. On the other side were the smaller apartments assigned to Henrietta Maria, overlooking the garden and the river. Beyond the curtains, heavy velvet in winter and light cotton, patterned with flowers in the summer, her rooms were hung with portraits of her own family, which gave her constant pangs of sorrow as they reminded her of France.

It was a pleasant enough walk from Whitehall across St James's Park to St James's Palace. Dominating the palace were the crenelated towers of its gatehouse, which guarded the approach up Pall Mall from the cluster of houses around the Charing Cross.

The palace of St James's had been built a century earlier by Henry VIII, whose initials, along with the ill-omened ones of Anne Boleyn, still ornamented the gatehouse. Henry had built his palace around a series of quadrangles, all made from simple Tudor brick, with flat lead roofs edged with ornamental battlements.

The chambers of St James's Palace were hung with bright tapestries and filled with richly ornamented furniture and art treasures, many of which had been collected by Charles's deceased brother Prince Henry. One of the most special rooms was Henrietta Maria's chapel, later replaced by one specially designed by Inigo Jones.

Here, at least, Henrietta Maria could feel close to her home, and to her roots. Every morning, her Capuchin priests intoned the Catholic Mass amidst clouds of incense, at the very heart of Anglican England.

Charles and Henrietta Maria's apartments were close to each other on the south side of the palace, with views over the ornamental gardens to the deer grazing in St James's Park. Looking out of their respective windows, the King and Queen could see the roofs and chimneys of Whitehall dwarfed by the great Gothic spires of Westminster Abbey.

St James's Palace today, largely unchanged from Jermyn's time.

From the start of his reign Charles I had been intent on reforming the rather dissolute, disorganised court he had inherited from his father. Strict rules, many based on Elizabethan precedents and consciously copying those Charles had witnessed being practiced in Madrid, were established to regulate every aspect of court life, even down to what people wore and how they behaved.

Access to Charles and his wife became severely restricted and surrounded by immense layers of meticulously observed protocol. Those few subjects, the noblemen and specially sworn-in gentlemen, who were allowed to enter the King's Privy Chamber – the entrance to the monarch's personal rooms –

were forbidden to lounge around playing cards or even chess. Access to the royal bedchamber was restricted even further: only princes, gentlemen of the bedchamber and necessary servants such as his barbers and doctors were granted ingress. Equivalent rules – over which of course Henrietta Maria had no say – prescribed the Queen's own life and surroundings. The aim was both to promote order based around the royal couple, and to emphasise the King's position as the epicentre of the court and thus of the realm.

Rules that served to isolate the King and Queen from the outside world could also foster an extraordinary degree of intimacy between them and the immediate circle that surrounded them.

On evenings when Charles decided to sleep in his wife's bed, whether at Whitehall or St James's, he would make his way along the corridors that joined the two sets of apartments. If it was autumn or winter a page would walk in front of him holding a taper to light the way.

There is a story, admittedly recorded sometime after the event, that one evening, as dusk had descended and the corridors grew murky, Jermyn's cousin Tom Killigrew was performing the task of lighting the King's way. They went quietly, their feet scarcely making a sound over the rush-strewn corridor floor. Entering the Queen's bedchamber, Tom had a terrible shock.

Henrietta Maria was sitting on her bed, her slight body almost completely hidden by the tall, broad-shouldered body of Tom's cousin, Jermyn. Later to become a successful playwright, Tom now acted quickly and resourcefully.

He dropped the taper and then made a terrible fuss, jumping down onto his hands and knees in the doorway, scrabbling about to clear away the wax, apologising profusely and loudly to the King, who stood bemused in the corridor. By the time Tom had finished his performance and stood back for the King to look in, the Queen had composed herself and Jermyn had vanished.

There are several other stories of similar incidents. In one, the Marquess of Hamilton walked into a room at Somerset House and caught Jermyn and Henrietta Maria cuddling. Another story relates that Charles suspected his wife was becoming too familiar with Jermyn, but was unable to confirm his suspicions. An unnamed earl, hoping to earn the King's favour, offered to lead the King to the Queen's chamber at a time when he thought they could catch the two together.

Sneaking down the corridor they burst in. Jermyn and the Queen were indeed alone together, but on that occasion they were doing nothing more scandalous than talking. The King left red-faced, wondering if he had been wrong to doubt his beautiful wife's virtue.

Henrietta Maria was destined, in some quarters at any rate, to become an iconic figure, the piously Catholic widow of an heroic martyr-king. Like any icon, many accounts of her have become single-dimensional. They often quote a report that 'as to faith, or sin of the flesh, she is never tempted', and 'no one is admitted to her bedrooms except ladies, with whom she sometimes retires, and employs herself on light, but innocent matters'.

That seems to clear matters up until one realises these lines were written by a Papal agent, reporting what he had been told by the Queen's own Catholic confessor – the very last people from whom one might possibly expect an unbiased, or even truthful, view.

These views of Henrietta Maria as a faultless icon deny the possibility that, as a lonely girl in a foreign country, with a husband who trusted his male favourite far more than her, she might have felt any affection for anyone else.

We simply do not know whether Jermyn and Henrietta Maria had a sexual relationship: but if they did, we should not perhaps be too surprised, or think too badly of them as a result.

In autumn 1628, three and a half years after her arrival in England, Henrietta Maria discovered that she was pregnant. Throughout the winter and spring she nursed her swelling womb until, on 13 May 1629, one of the court mastiffs jumped up and knocked her, causing her to go into premature labour. She gave birth to a tiny son, Charles James Stuart, Duke of Cornwall and Rothesay.

He was named after not one, but two Kings, but who his real father was is open to question. The new heir to the throne of England and Scotland must have been conceived about the time when Buckingham was murdered, when Charles and Henrietta Maria's relationship was at its nadir, yet when the court was rife with rumours that she and Jermyn were having an affair. Can we even say with any conviction that, at this stage, Charles would even have cared very much who the baby's biological father was, so long as his impossible, highly-strung wife fulfilled her purpose of producing an heir to the throne?

Whoever he was, Jermyn or Stuart, the prince's little life was over barely after it had started. By the evening of the same day he had expired. He was buried in Westminster Abbey as 'Charles, Prince of Wales'.

That July, Jermyn escorted poor Henrietta Maria down through the Wealden forests to the spa town of Tunbridge, where she obediently drank the foul-tasting medicinal waters. Afterwards, they travelled north-west, through the bright summer countryside to Oatlands Palace, overlooking the meadows of the Wey near Weybridge. Here Charles I joined them.

A few months later she discovered she was pregnant again. For her confinement she chose the homely surroundings of St James's Palace where, on Saturday, 29 May 1630, another son was born. The child was Charles's heir apparent, the Prince of Wales and future King Charles II.

The new prince's appearance was extremely unusual. His skin was much darker than anyone expected. Henrietta Maria herself wrote (in French) 'he is so dark that I am ashamed of him'. His ever-so-slightly dark complexion stayed with him for life, earning him the nickname 'the black boy'.

The Prince of Wales's looks were probably inherited from his mother's Medici ancestors, but in this aspect he was unique amongst Henrietta Maria's children: all her subsequent offspring were fair skinned, just like Charles I.

It was not only the Prince's complexion that set him apart from his family. 'His size and fatness supply the want of beauty', Henrietta Maria wrote. Later, when the Prince was four months old, she added 'he is so fat and so tall, that he is taken for a year old'.

Slingesby Bethel, who served on Cromwell's Committee of Safety during the Interregnum, even claimed to have seen letters from Henrietta Maria to Jermyn confirming that Charles II *and* his younger brother, the future James II, were Jermyn's sons.

As Prince Charles grew, his stature remained exceptional. By the time he was fully grown he measured six feet two inches, significantly taller than average men of his time.

Had the Prince ever stood as a fully-grown man next to his father and grandfather he would have dwarfed them both: he towered even more over Henrietta Maria, who remained extremely short and slight all her life. He differed from them too in his sheer physical build. His broad shoulders and square jaw might have come from the Danish ancestors of his paternal grandmother.

Henry Jermyn as a young courtier by Van Dyck (left). The portrait on the right shows Charles II as a young man of similar age.

But the Prince's build and looks gave him more than a passing similarity to tall, broad-shouldered Jermyn. Comparison of the few surviving pictures of Jermyn with those of Charles II at similar ages does nothing to dispel the idea, but more intriguing are the references that emerge from contemporary sources, even the domestic state papers themselves, that belie an ocean of speculation. That 'the King was a bastard and his mother was Jermyn's whore' and 'all the royal children were Jermyn's bastards' were not uncommon assertions amongst those who were ill-disposed to the Stuart dynasty.

Had Charles I and Henrietta Maria remained as distant and antagonistic as they had been while Buckingham was alive, history may well have ascribed the paternity of Charles II to Jermyn without much hesitation. But Buckingham's assassination muddied the waters considerably, by removing the main obstacle to Henrietta Maria and Charles's friendship. Even by the time of Charles II's birth, the royal couple's growing closeness had all the appearance of true affection. Thereafter, observers concur that the royal couple fell deeply in love.

It was of course fortunate for Henrietta Maria that she could begin to enjoy, rather than dread, the King's increasingly frequent visits to her bed. Whatever she might have felt about Jermyn, she knew that her divinely-approved course of action was to sleep with and produce children by the King. Regardless of the truth about his paternity, Prince Charles's remarkable appearance, and the knowledge of what was being whispered all around St James's Palace, may have alarmed Henrietta Maria into trying, at least, to switch off her feelings for Jermyn, and to start attempting to love her husband in earnest. Or was it Jermyn who backed off, equally terrified by the genuinely awful consequences, for both of them, and even for his country, if they were ever found out?

It must, in any event, have been an emotionally turbulent time for Jermyn, listening to cannons booming over Westminster to herald the birth of the heir to the throne, yet knowing how many wagging tongues were busy asserting that the infant Prince of Wales was his own son.

Henrietta Maria's newly awakened sexual interest in her husband did not lessen the closeness of her friendship with Jermyn. 'But we can still be friends', is what people in similar situations might say nowadays. Jermyn and Henrietta Maria were many degrees removed from ordinary, modern people, but they may have entertained similar hopes in this one matter.

In most cases, couples who have spent their hitherto unrequited passion in an illicit fling, that ends of its own accord, tend, inevitably and almost always healthily, to drift apart. But when an affair ends because it must, and not because both or even just one party really wants it to, then at least one party is likely to be genuinely, emotionally bruised. And that suffering is far worse when circumstances make physical separation impossible.

The Queen and Jermyn were both prisoners of the court, and he worked for her as well. Leading independent lives was impossible. In any case, despite six years as Charles's wife, and despite Jermyn's best efforts to teach her, Henrietta Maria's English was still far from fluent, so she remained emotionally isolated from most of the courtiers around her. Whatever Jermyn and Henrietta Maria had, or hadn't been up to, they had very little choice but to continue as best they could, together, as friends.

While Henrietta Maria started to grow into her new life as Charles I's lover, twenty-five-year-old Jermyn made a valiant attempt to focus his mind elsewhere. Through his connection with the Queen, his own position at court became steadily stronger. He had already sat in two Parliaments, representing Bodmin (1625-1626) and Liverpool (1628-1629). This sounds important but, like many others at the time, these two Parliamentary seats comprised electors who generally voted as directed by their patrons. These patrons were Sir Robert Killigrew and Sir Humphrey May respectively, both relations of Jermyn's. For someone like Jermyn, sitting in Parliament was no more than a trifling extension of his busy life at court, except insofar as it gained him prestige, and influence, and the chance to become the sort of man whom lesser ones might want to bribe in return for favours.

His interest in money was not as venal as it sounds, or as his later detractors were to claim. Life at court, especially looking 'the part', not to mention the constant gambling that was an inherent part of court life, was extremely expensive, and one small salary from the Privy Purse was nowhere near sufficient to cover it. Through Henrietta Maria's influence, Jermyn had been granted the sinecure job of Joint Surveyor of the Petty Customs, a job entailing no work, but a fine income, that provided more funds to flow through his ever-hungry purse.

Through his job of Gentleman Usher of the Privy Chamber, Jermyn controlled who had access to his royal mistress and therefore played a key role in her household and, by extension, in the whole court. This too could be played to its advantage. His high standing with the Queen almost certainly contributed to his uncle, the seasoned diplomat Sir Robert Killigrew, becoming her Vice-Chamberlain. Jermyn's father Sir Thomas became her Master of the Game, responsible for the deer and other animals that were hunted on her estates. Jermyn's quiet elder brother Thomas added to the growing number of Jermyns employed at court by becoming Master of the Horse to the baby Prince of Wales.

These advances were far too little, however, to satisfy the politically ambitious young Jermyn. He had seen the gargantuan influence Buckingham had enjoyed wielding in England and which Richelieu possessed in France and Olivares in Spain. Now, he wanted nothing less for himself.

Henrietta Maria craved power too. Born the daughter of a great monarch, she wanted to share decision-making with her husband, whether it concerned what happened at court or the direction Britain took in internal and foreign policy. As we have seen, she and Jermyn may already have tried a little politicking in 1627, scheming to be rid of Buckingham. As they grew older, their desire to have a say at court and in the country could only increase.

The place in which Jermyn sought power, Charles I's court,

occupies an unusual position in English history. In recent years, the English Parliament had often been grudging and slow in allowing taxes to be raised, and often only did so if the King agreed to their own conditions. Fed up with this, and convinced that Members of Parliament were more concerned with their own self-interests than the common good, Charles had dissolved Parliament in March 1629 and began his eleven-year-long period of personal rule. From then on, the royal court, and more particularly the Privy Council within it, became by default the chief organ through which the King ruled.

'The Board', as it was also known, usually sat in the Council chamber facing the King's bedchamber at Whitehall, though when Charles travelled to other palaces, his counsellors dutifully trotted along after him. The Privy Council usually comprised about forty men, mainly office-holders and landed aristocrats, although only a core of its members was usually summoned to attend meetings.

The King, however, attended religiously and attentively. Although the council always deferred to the King's will, he was usually happy to follow its advice, sometimes even when it pronounced a unanimous opinion contrary to his own.

Implementing the Board's decisions fell mainly to the two secretaries of state, Sir John Coke, and Lord Dorchester, who was succeeded on his death in 1632 by Sir Francis Windebank. Coke and Windebank were astonishingly efficient administrators and neither seem to have held ambitions to wield genuine power in their own right. Usually they were more than happy to follow the King's wishes.

In his heyday, Buckingham, like Richelieu and Olivares, had held two unofficial and subtly different roles, those of *privado*, on whose whispered advice the King acted most, and First Minister. Whilst the term 'First' or 'Prime Minister' had not yet come into official use in England, the concept of a 'prime' minister', to whom the King delegated the majority of the day-to-day running of the realm, had.

Since Buckingham's death, the mantle of this unofficial role had fallen on the shoulders of Charles's Lord Treasurer, Richard Weston, Lord Portland, a pretentious man who once paid a large sum for a forged pedigree connecting him to royalty. But though Charles esteemed him for his quiet financial efficiency, Portland lacked the verve and relentless ambition – and, apparently, the ability to build up a power base by creating a patronage network similar to Buckingham's – to be a true royal favourite or *privado*.

Yet because power now lay, literally, in the King's house, other people at court, without any ministerial position, though often with some ceremonial position, had the opportunity to exercise a degree of power simply through their privileged access to the King's ear, and the role of *privado* was up for grabs.

In September 1628, Jermyn's mentor Lord Kensington succeeded Buckingham, albeit briefly, as the King's Master of the Horse, a position that guaranteed close access to Charles, especially during the large amount of time he spent hunting. Kensington seems to have had real ambition to succeed Buckingham as First Minister and royal favourite or *privado*. His attempts to secure Buckingham's old position of Lord Admiral for himself, however, failed. In the final analysis, Charles simply did not hold him in sufficiently high regard.

Kensington was replaced as Master of the Horse by the Marquess of Hamilton, another very influential member of the King's court, who carried the peculiar distinction of being next in line to the Scottish throne after the Stuart family. He vied with Kensington for the highest, unofficial honour, but he never quite convinced the King of his indispensability either.

Kensington, meanwhile, remained prominent, using his own

friendship and influence with Henrietta Maria to attempt a come-back, in 1636, by gaining office of Groom of the Stool. The job entailed responsibility for the King's chamber pot, a position that sounds quite revolting to modern ears, but one that guaranteed an equally very un-modern degree of intimacy with the sovereign, and thus offering considerable opportunities for any aspiring favourite.

Ultimately, however, both Kensington and Hamilton were wasting their time, for Charles never replaced Buckingham with another male favourite. As early as the end of 1628, however, the amount of affection he was directing towards Henrietta Maria led one courtier to anticipate that he 'had so wholly made over his affections to his wife that he dare say that they are out of danger of any other favourite'. But that courtier was wrong: the King did have a *privado*: it was none other than Henrietta Maria herself.

Yet, as a woman, and Queen, she could not possibly become First Minister. And thus, below the gilded ceilings of Whitehall, a new rivalry emerged.

Whilst Portland lacked his predecessor's outright hostility to Henrietta Maria, he was keen, none-the-less, to continue Buckingham's anti-French, pro-Spanish policies. That was enough to earn him both Henrietta Maria and Jermyn's animosity. And, in any case, a royal court big enough to accommodate one Buckingham was not sufficiently large to accommodate both Portland, and Henrietta Maria – not to mention her ambitious Gentleman of the Bedchamber, Henry Jermyn.

Early one morning at the end of March 1633, Lord Portland and his family heard a horse's hooves clattering outside their door, and a voice shouting up for Portland's son Jerome Weston.

Opening the window, they were astonished to see Jermyn in his flamboyant silk suit, his ruddy hair tousled by the gallop. The angry young man demanded to see Jerome, who came to the window. Jermyn then demanded that he should come with him to Spring Gardens, the pleasure gardens between Charing Cross and St James's Palace, to fight a duel with Lord Kensington over the Queen's honour.

The man Jermyn and his friends really wanted to remove from power was Lord Portland, but the opportunity to lash out at him through his son was too good to miss.

The 'Queen's quarrel', as the affair became known, had started when both Jermyn and Jerome were sent, independently of one another, to Paris. Jermyn's stated aim was to congratulate Henrietta Maria's sister-in-law, Queen Anne, on surviving a near-fatal coach crash.

The real purpose of his visit was more likely connected to Henrietta Maria's mother, Marie de' Medici. In 1631, Marie had clashed violently (again) with Louis XIII, but Richelieu had outsmarted her, and she was packed off to exile in Brussels. Henrietta Maria wanted her mother to come to London, but the thrifty Portland prevented this by persuading Charles that such a visit would cost the treasury too much money.

Instead, Henrietta Maria wanted Richelieu to allow Marie to return to Paris. Or, better still, she dreamed of removing both the Cardinal and Portland together. A plot was launched amongst Richelieu's enemies in France to replace the devious Cardinal with the dashing Marquess de Châteauneuf. Henrietta Maria was keen to offer her tacit support for this plot, and it is likely that Jermyn's visit to Paris was connected to these machinations.

Lord Portland's son Jerome had also been sent to Paris, but in his case the mission was for the King. Realising some skulduggery was afoot, Jerome started intercepting letters written between suspected plotters – postal espionage was rife in those days – and quite by chance found a letter from Lord Kensington to the gallant Châteauneuf. Tucked within it was another, written by none other than Henrietta Maria herself. Delighted with his discovery, Jerome had hurried back to London to present the unopened correspondence to his father and the King.

To Lord Kensington and Jermyn, this interception was a direct affront to Henrietta Maria's honour – and a fabulous excuse to lash out at the Portland family. When Jermyn delivered Kensington's challenge to Jerome, however, Lord Portland refused to allow his son to respond. Challenging people to duels was one of the dissolute activities Charles had proscribed in his strictly ordered court, so Portland sent a messenger to the King – who had feared something like this might happen in any case – who promptly placed both Kensington and Jermyn under arrest.

Kensington apologised immediately. But on this occasion Jermyn's usual suave courtliness was overtaken by his passionate loyalty to Henrietta Maria. When summoned to answer for his actions before the Privy Council, his behaviour was described as 'petulant and fleering'.

Jermyn was probably dressed at the time as he normally did, only perhaps with even more care, in his finest black satin coat, with the sleeves slashed debonairly to reveal his crisp white shirt underneath: his breeches, also of costly black satin, disappeared into an enormous pair of white buck-skin boots. Sweeping off his black hat, which was richly plumed with ostrich feathers, he stood in front of the long Council table like an arrogant magpie. He argued that the Queen's honour amply justified his actions. How dare the Privy Council suggest otherwise!

For two months Jermyn remained under house-arrest while his friends and family begged him to apologise for having delivered Kensington's challenge. Eventually, bored and no doubt very anxious to be reunited with Henrietta Maria, he gave in and said sorry. He was released at the beginning of May 1633.

Charles stoutly resisted the efforts of Jermyn and the Queen to topple Portland, who continued as Charles I's 'First Minister' until 1635, when he died. In the interim, however, a far more pressing problem arose for Henrietta Maria and Jermyn. The cause this time was not politics, but sex.

Whilst Henrietta Maria was now enjoying married life with Charles, and seeing her power and influence growing at court, Jermyn had been trying to fill his life with work, politics, and intrigue. But his emotional life was in ruins. Small wonder he had behaved so hot-headedly in the Queen's Quarrel. Finally, having perhaps deliberately avoided other women as a token of his true devotion to the now unattainable Henrietta Maria, he gave way to the temptation of distracting and consoling himself with one of the Queen's Maids of Honour.

There is no record of whether Eleanor Villiers, the niece of the late and largely unlamented Duke of Buckingham, was pretty or plain. If the majority of her family were anything to go by, however, she was probably very attractive. She certainly liked sex and, if Jermyn's later account of their affair is true, her desire for physical satisfaction far overrode any consideration of what the consequences might be.

Perhaps it was in her arms that Jermyn could try his best to forget the more exalted royal lovemaking going on in the Queen's bedchamber. But according to Jermyn, 'there never passed one word between us touching marriage'.

After a while they split up. Perhaps it was Eleanor's lust that led her into other men's beds. Or maybe she left Jermyn when she realised that she could only possess his body but never his heart. After a very brief fling with Lord Newport, who was no more interested in her emotionally than Jermyn had been, she suddenly fell in love with her first-cousin, Lord Feilding. That the two started sleeping together was well known because someone caught them in the act and spread the news around Whitehall. But Eleanor did not seem to care. As Jermyn wrote later, 'she hath herself confessed to me she loved my Lord Feilding more than any man living'.

Just as Jermyn emerged from his house arrest in May 1633, however, disaster befell them both. Eleanor discovered she was pregnant and her condition was too far advanced to enable her to convince Feilding that the child was his.

Scandalised, her cousin distanced himself from her. Forced to choose between her two former lovers, either of whom could theoretically have caused her pregnancy, Eleanor opted for Jermyn.

Jermyn was appalled. He had no interest in marrying a woman he did not love and accepting paternity of a child that could have been Newport's or even, for all he really knew, someone else's. But far more than that, even though marrying Henrietta Maria was out of the question, it seems that he could not bear the idea of making marriage vows to anyone else.

In her 2011 novel about the relationship of Jermyn and Henrietta Maria, *Cavalier Queen*, Fiona Mountain allows her fictional Jermyn to express what the real one may really have thought, in a speech she imagined him making to the Queen: 'I liked Eleanor well enough. There are plenty of other pretty girls I like well enough. But I will not settle for someone I can live with, when I have found someone I cannot live without. I am willing to remain a bachelor all my life, so that I may devote myself to your service.' These are made-up lines, but it is possible that they encapsulate Jermyn's true feelings on the matter very well indeed.

To the great delight of the gossips and the mortification of the Villiers clan, Jermyn announced publicly that he would not marry Eleanor.

When Eleanor's aunt, the widowed Duchess of Buckingham, offered Jermyn the colossal sum of £8,000 as a dowry, he must have hesitated. But then he sent back a haughty refusal. On Tuesday, 4 June 1633, incensed at this affront to his family's honour, Eleanor's brother Lord Grandison challenged Jermyn to a duel.

As before, news of the duel reached Charles well in advance of the event. A duel combined with sex outside marriage was precisely the sort of thing Charles feared would wreck the highly charged moral atmosphere of his court. In fact, it was one of the very few sex scandals that emerged in the entire course of his personal rule. In another, that led to the trial of Lord Castlehaven for sodomy and rape, Charles was so prudish as to forbid women to attend the proceedings on the grounds that they would 'ever after [be]... reputed to have forfeited their modesty'. Now, thoroughly weary of Jermyn's disruptive behaviour, he sent him, Grandison and, for good measure, Eleanor herself, to the Tower of London.

In Jermyn's time, the Tower was both a functioning fortress and a royal residence. On the southern side, a stone wharf lined with cannons faced the Thames, broken at the centre by the Traitors' Gate.

On the other three sides a deep ditch separated the outer walls from the rough pastures of East Smith Field and Tower Hill, on which stood the well-worn posts of a much-used scaffold. Within the Tower's outer walls, piles of cannon balls lay stacked up ready for use in the event of foreign invasion or civil uprising. In the powder house lay, stacked barrel-upon-barrel, the nation's invaluable store of gunpowder.

Clustered around the Norman keep, known as the White Tower, was a range of Medieval buildings including the King's lodgings and the Jewel House where the Crown Jewels sparkled in their secluded splendour. Strolling in the King's Privy Garden or entertaining his aristocratic drinking partners in his suite of rooms, Jermyn's life there would certainly not have been uncomfortable or perhaps even very dull. But knowing that Henrietta Maria knew all about his affair, yet not being able to see her and explain himself, must have been torture for the young man.

Guided by his father, Jermyn wrote Charles an eloquent and reasoned account of his relationship with Eleanor, that he hoped would secure his release. But the Villiers family were not prepared to let Jermyn to escape so easily. By refusing marriage, Jermyn was doing more than disgracing Eleanor: he was tarnishing the illustrious name of Villiers and the memory of the great Duke of Buckingham.

As the summer passed and Eleanor's pregnancy advanced, the Villiers family's protests to the sympathetic Charles grew more strident. He was far from unsympathetic.

Besides his natural affection for his late mentor's family and his hopes of raising the court's moral standards, Charles may have had other reasons for being harsh on Jermyn.

The fact that he had never caught Jermyn with his wife did not mean that he may never have suspected their intimacy. This, surely, was a good chance for the pallid King to gain some measure of revenge, or even to be rid of Jermyn for good. Therefore in September Charles sent Jermyn an abrupt ultimatum: marry Eleanor or be exiled.

But there was no real choice for Jermyn. Aside from any consideration of his feelings for Henrietta Maria, Jermyn could not marry a woman he had publicly disowned: the scandal of that really would have wrecked his chances of advancing further at court. His only real choice was to assert his innocence by accepting exile. With immense sorrow and trepidation he climbed aboard the French merchant ship that was to carry him to France. Jermyn was leaving behind his country, his career and the woman he loved. He had no idea what the future would bring.

Screaming in pain and frustration, Eleanor went into labour. Jermyn's father Sir Thomas, clearly feeling guilty by association, sent a midwife to assist with the birth. Throughout, Eleanor never ceased to swear 'with deep oaths' that the child was Jermyn's.

Without hope of a husband or of regaining her position at court, Eleanor became a spinster aunt living quietly with her Villiers relatives. She died in 1685 and was buried with her relatives in Westminster Abbey. Her daughter, also called Eleanor, married a Jamaican sugar planter called Philip Dakins. When she died in London in 1694, Eleanor Dakins left a small legacy to one of Jermyn's nieces, whom she at least asserted was 'my cousin'. Despite all Jermyn's denials, it seems that Eleanor Villiers had never changed her story that he was her daughter's father.

Even before Charles's ultimatum had reached Jermyn, it had been softened by Henrietta Maria's influence. Although Jermyn was sent into exile, he had not been dismissed from the Queen's household.

Jermyn's ship had scarcely unfurled its sails before Henrietta

Maria commenced the long process of persuading Charles to allow her favourite to come back. Had Buckingham still lived, she could never have succeeded. But now she and Charles were lovers as well as husband and wife. Ultimately, she hoped, the King would refuse her nothing.

The first part of Jermyn's exile – about which very little, sadly, is recorded – was spent in Paris, where he benefitted, no doubt, from his already friendly relationship with the French court.

As a first step towards his rehabilitation, Jermyn was allowed to leave Paris for Jersey. Since 1631, Jermyn's father had been Jersey's absentee governor. To the suggestion that Jermyn should now become the resident Lieutenant Governor, however, the island's Dean, Jean Bandinel, responded brusquely. The islanders had suffered enough abuses from Whitehall, he protested, without having a young philanderer like Jermyn foisted on them. When Jermyn stepped ashore there in 1634, therefore, it was merely as a private individual, though while he was there he was put in charge of destroying the island's tobacco crop, a step taken to promote the tobacco-based economy of the new colonies in America.

From the ramparts of Elizabeth Castle, Jermyn could look out across the narrow stretch of sea which separated the island from the coast of Normandy, but for all the hunts and balls to which the Governor's son was doubtless invited, Jersey was a wretched place for a high-spirited and ambitious young courtier.

Once she had worn her husband down sufficiently, Henrietta Maria sent Jermyn a letter telling him to write to the King to apologise profusely for his behaviour and beg delivery from his languishing condition. Jermyn did so and, probably rather against his better judgement, Charles relented.

After two years' exile the Queen's favourite sailed back up the

Thames to return to the court, the home of everything he considered worth having or doing, and especially, of course, of Henrietta Maria herself. Little did he suspect, however, the extraordinary, imaginary journey on which he was about to embark.

V

SIR WILLIAM D'AVENANT'S DREAM OF
MADAGASCAR
1635 – 1637

Some climb, and search the Rocks, till each have found
A Saphire, Ruby, and a Diamond:
That which the Sultan's glistering Bride doth wear,
To these would but a Glow-worm's eye appear:
Sir William D'Avenant, 'Madagascar' (1637)

Soon after Jermyn returned from exile, his old friend from the
Madrid embassy, Endymion Porter, introduced him to a man
who was to have a profound impact on the way Jermyn viewed
himself and his world, and indeed on the way we now view him.

The man's name was William D'Avenant, poet and
playwright. A year younger than Jermyn, and the son of an
Oxfordshire innkeeper, D'Avenant liked to boast when drunk
that his real father was William Shakespeare himself. His chubby
cheeks, bulbous eyes and long chin may not on their own have
been particularly unattractive, had he not also suffered from the
pox. Contracted, as he readily admitted, whilst being 'valiant in
a strange bed', syphilis had eaten away the bridge of his nose,
leaving the lower part sticking out like a spaniel's snout.

Yet through D'Avenant's ugly façade shone an exceptional
intelligence capable of appreciating and communicating ideas of
astonishing beauty. This gift, coupled with his witty tongue, had
attracted the curiosity of Jermyn's kinsman and possible mentor,
Francis Bacon, who had instilled in D'Avenant a love of Natural
Science – the new philosophy of learning about the world

through direct observation and experimentation. This became a dominant thread in D'Avenant's work. He also became inspired by Bacon's idea that, by understanding the world, man might one day be able to control it.

It was a noble vision worthy of a century that would see the invention of clocks and compasses, thermometers and microscopes. In 1610, by using the newly invented telescope to observe the moons of Jupiter, Galileo had proved the planets revolved around the sun. Isaac Newton, born in 1642, would later discover gravity. Robert Boyle, whose brother married Jermyn's first cousin Elizabeth Killigrew, would suggest that matter was composed of atoms and show how sound moved through air.

To such men, science was not an end in itself. It might be a means to enable mankind to overcome disease, famine, war and old age. But having done so, they hoped that science would elevate human souls towards God.

Another method of elevating souls, and of promoting a more general appreciation of science, was poetry. In the preface to his epic poem *Gondibert*, which set out and recommended Bacon's scientific goals, D'Avenant described his dream of a new nobility of spirit that would permeate society. He hoped that, as the seventeenth century progressed, western Europe and especially Britain, would rival and eventually surpass the achievements of Classical Greece and Rome.

For a Golden Age to come about, and for such nobility of spirit to permeate society effectively, D'Avenant had first to inspire its future leaders. And in that context it is fascinating that, out of all the courtiers laughing and joking in the chambers of Whitehall and St James's, the man on whom he chose to focus most of his efforts was Jermyn.

Superficially, Jermyn seemed like just another jovial drinker, a loud, arrogant fop who laughed at bawdy jokes and whose bright sword flashed up at the first hint of a brawl. But D'Avenant, like Cowley, after him, seems to have been astute enough to recognise a greater depth to Jermyn's soul – or at least, perhaps, the potential for one – and also saw Jermyn's potential to gain a status in England equal to that of Richelieu in France.

Through his poetry, D'Avenant tried to instil noble sentiments in Jermyn's mind. In his poem 'To Henry Jarmin' (in those days there was no concept of standardized spelling) D'Avenant listed the categories of men who stultified progress and kept Europe wallowing in the Middle Ages. He listed statesmen, seeking power because they were 'too haughty to obey'; proud scholars who concealed the world's simple truths behind Byzantine complexity and impenetrable terminology, and soldiers who fought only for their own glory. Addressing him as 'Arigo', the nickname Jermyn had acquired on his boyhood embassy to Spain, D'Avenant told him that these were stereotypes to avoid:

> This not implies, to be more proud than they,
> But bravely to be proud a better way;
> And thus (Arigo) I may safely climb,
> Raised with the boast, not laden with the crime;
> Those with their glorious Vices taken be,
> But I (most righteously) am proud of thee.

In his poem 'When Colonel Goring was believed to be slain', D'Avenant tried to make Jermyn think about the Golden Age by actually taking him there. A false report reached St James's that the young courtier George Goring had been killed fighting the Spanish at the siege of Breda. D'Avenant's poem describes an invented voyage in which Jermyn and Endymion Porter go in search of Elysium for Goring's soul.

While the spray falls on their faces, they stand in the prow of their ship, gazing ahead and singing alternate verses about their brave quest. Guided not by the compass but by Homer, the poet who had first sung of lofty Troy back at the very dawn of Classical Greece, Jermyn and his companions expect to find Goring happily living on the shores of Elysium, rejoicing in the company of brave Achilles, the greatest of the Greek heroes who fought at Troy, and the Greek philosopher Epicurus, and those magnificent generals, Alexander the Great and Hannibal. Bold and optimistic, Jermyn and Endymion Porter do not mourn but rather praise their dead friend as the crested waves bear them ever forward. But ultimately they realise that, if once they step ashore on Elysium, they will never be able to return alive. Turning their ship back for home, they console themselves that the poet's words can still take them where their physical bodies cannot travel.

Elysium was the stuff of Greek imagination. It existed outside the material world, as an ideal, a metaphor. So, finally and most spectacularly, D'Avenant created another poem, to take Jermyn on another imaginary voyage, but this time to establish a new, enlightened society on a real island on the other side of the world – a real Elysium, on which thoughts both imaginary and practical could find a foot-hold: Madagascar.

On Tuesday, 23 February 1636, soon after his return from Jersey, Jermyn appeared in a masquerade at the Middle Temple entitled *The Triumphs of the Prince D'Amour*. Masquerades were entertainments involving sumptuous scenery and costumes, music, dances and poetry. Although sometimes thought of as having been a distraction from the real world, masquerades filled an essential role in Charles's stilted, etiquette-bound court.

By their means, the King attempted to instill his political ideology into his higher-ranking subjects.

In a scene in this particular performance, the centre of the stage was occupied by a lawyer dressed as the flamboyantly dressed Prince d'Amour, flanked by two teenage boys, Charles Louis and Rupert. These were the Palatine princes, the two elder sons of Charles's sister Queen Elizabeth of Bohemia, she whose husband Frederick had been driven out of the Palatine by the Hapsburgs 16 years earlier. They had come from their home-in-exile at The Hague in the Dutch Netherlands on behalf of their mother, who wanted Charles to give them money and soldiers to recapture the Palatine. He would not, but the princes, especially Rupert, would soon play a significant part in a war that was much closer to hand.

They were not the only court luminaries on stage. On this occasion Henrietta Maria herself danced beside Jermyn and his friends, including Kensington and Goring. As ever, the costumes were splendid and bright with many classical and mythical allusions, whilst moving scenery added depth and excitement to their frolics.

During the 1620s, the architect Inigo Jones had designed and produced the court masques, with librettos provided by the playwright Ben Jonson. As the years passed, however, this pair of artists grew to absolutely loathe each other, so in the 1630s Jones started to work with other playwrights, finally forming a lasting collaboration with D'Avenant. While Jermyn and his companions danced on the stage of the Middle Temple, it was D'Avenant's libretto, not Jonson's, which was sung by the solemn baritones and cheerful sopranos.

In the weeks following the masque, Rupert and his brother spent a good deal of their time with Jermyn, Endymion Porter and D'Avenant. They hunted together in St James's Park, played cards, dice, chess and tennis in St James's Palace and practised shooting muskets in the rough meadows beyond the palace walls. As they laughed and joked, Endymion Porter amused them by showing off his treasures, including 'turtle shells... dragons' blood and diverse sorts of other gums' that had just been brought to London from the fabulous island of Madagascar.

But what was Madagascar? Millions of years ago, in a phase of geological time that was completely inconceivable to Jermyn and his contemporaries, who all concurred that the world was only some five and a half thousand years old, there had existed a great continent in the southern hemisphere, later known as Lemuria. As the world's plates shifted, Lemuria sank below what is now the Indian Ocean. As it buckled and shattered, fire and brimstone spewed up through the boiling waters to form great volcanoes, and the volcanoes in turn became Madagascar.

Twice the size of Britain, the island lies along the eastern coast of Africa. The natives called the highest peak of the Ankàratra mountains Tsi-àfa-jàvona – 'that which the mists cannot climb'. Below it rolls a vast plain, 5,000 feet above sea level, whose edges run down through the lemur-infested jungles to coral inlets, dunes and lagoons. In Jermyn's day, it was inhabited by a mixed population of Polynesian and African settlers, along with some long-standing Arab colonists.

At this time several English merchants became obsessed with the idea of establishing a colony there. 'Madagascar', one wrote later,

> may well be compared to the Land of Canaan that
> flows with milk and honey. Rivers of sweet waters
> and fragrant fountains flow out of the valleys and

the mountains; a land of wheat and barley, of vine
yards and fig trees and pomegranates; a land wherein
thou shalt eat without scarcity; neither shalt lack
anything therein; a land whose stones are iron and
out of whose mountains thou may dig brass.

Such enthusiastic and imaginative visions fired the fertile
imagination of Porter, and he transmitted his excitement to his
friends. Soon the headstrong Rupert could talk of nothing else
but the riches of Madagascar. Forgetting about the lost Palatine,
Rupert enthused Jermyn with schemes to sail to Madagascar
with their gallant companions and become masters of its riches.

Rupert's mother Queen Elizabeth of Bohemia was horrified,
complaining bitterly about the 'romance some would put into
Rupert's head of conquering Madagascar where Porter they say
is to be his squire when he shall Don Quixote-like conquer that
famous island.... I did not like it... besides', she added, sagely, 'I
thought if Madagascar were a place either worth the taking or
possible to be kept, the Portuguese by this time would have had
it'.

The astute Queen was right. As Porter told the wide-eyed
Palatine princes, Portuguese colonists had been lured to
Madagascar with tales of its great natural wealth, eager to rip
the silver from the virgin soil and strip the precious spices from
its great rain forests. They stayed there a few years until the war-
like ruling tribe, the Sàkalàva, speared their missionaries to
death.

A few years later, an attempt at colonisation by the Dutch
was similarly eradicated. But Rupert, Jermyn and Endymion
Porter had no doubt they would succeed where lily-livered
foreigners had failed.

For over a year they tried to raise ships and capital from the

East India Company, but all the time the Queen of Bohemia maintained her pressure on Charles to forbid the dangerous journey. Eventually she succeeded and, like a naughty schoolboy, Rupert went trailing home to The Hague.

The great voyage to Madagascar never took place. But the Madagascar which enticed Jermyn and Rupert with its promise of untold wealth was only loosely connected to reality. In the sixteenth century, a mix-up of map coordinates led to the belief that Mogadishu in Somaliland was located on the island which was, up to then, called San-Lorenzo. The island of San-Lorenzo consequently became known as Mogodoza, which was then corrupted into Madagascar. As far as anyone in Western Europe was concerned, therefore, the account that Marco Polo had written about Mogodishu was an accurate description of the *island* of 'Madagascar'. The Venetian explorer's account was in fact more highly coloured than anyone else's. According to Polo, Madagascar was even home to the last of the *rukhs*, mythical birds so enormous in size that they could carry off live elephants in their dreadful talons, and then kill them by dropping them down from great heights.

It was to this island of misplaced location and magical fantasy that D'Avenant decided to take his friends in his poem, 'Madagascar'. Dedicated to Rupert, it was published as the centre-piece of a volume of poems dedicated to Jermyn and Endymion Porter.

In 'Madagascar', D'Avenant let Rupert's much sought-after ships put out to sea at last, a strong wind billowing in their white sails as they ploughed south through the surging waves of the Atlantic. Aboard the flagship stood Jermyn, Endymion Porter and Rupert, the latter brandishing Charles I's trident as a symbol both of his role as admiral and of Britain's desire to dominate the oceans. From high up in the sky, the poet watched as they rounded the Cape of Good Hope and sailed up the east coast of Africa to the great island of Madagascar.

The sight of the great galleons lowering their anchors drew gasps of awe from the Madagascans assembled on the shore. A 'long-lost scattered parcel of mankind', D'Avenant called them, while also making the point that they still retained a savage innocence. The Madagascans were instinctively drawn to the royalty of Rupert's straight nose, his deep brown eyes and his lustrous curly brown hair that spilled down onto his broad shoulders. They acknowledged him unquestioningly as their over-lord. Prince Rupert had become Charles's viceroy in Madagascar. But in this poem, which was entirely a product of D'Avenant's imagination, their peaceful enjoyment of the island was not destined to last.

Heralded by their martial drums, the Spanish arrived, sent thence by their greedy king who, in his madness, had even laid claim to the sun. D'Avenant, who loathed war, made the Spanish propose an alternative to a pitched battle. Two champions alone from each side would fight and settle the ownership of the island. Rupert was quick to choose his –

> ... both I spy
> March to the List; whilst either's cheerful look
> Foretold glad hopes of what they undertook

The champions were of course the flame-headed Jermyn and Porter.

> You may esteem them Lovers by their hair;
> The colour warns no Lady to despair;
> And Nature seemed to prove their stature such,
> As took not scantly from her, nor too much;

> So tall, we can't misname their stature length
> Nor think't less made for comeliness than strength.

The combat began. Rapiers flashed under the African sun as two pairs of champions duelled, parrying and thrusting up and down the beach. For a while the two pairs seemed locked in an even contest. Both armies gaped in wonder at the skill being displayed before their eyes. But Jermyn and Endymion Porter had the upper hand:

> Each did disguise the fury of his heart,
> By safe and temperate exercise of Art:
> Seemed to invite those thrusts they most decline,
> Receive, and then return in one true line:
> As if all Archimedes' science were
> In duel both expressed, and bettered there...

Soon, the bodies of the two Spaniards lay twitching, their ruby blood seeping out onto the white sand. The contest was won, but the dishonourable Spaniards reneged on their agreement. Their war cries filled the air as they surged forward, rapiers and pistols at the ready. But even as they charged, Rupert's brow began to darken. With god-like fury worthy of his uncle Charles (D'Avenant was stretching the point here) he descended on the foe. Those Spaniards who were not hacked to pieces fled back to their galleons and were never seen again.

In D'Avenant's imagination the island brimmed with riches. In the fantasy world of the poem, Jermyn and his friends started digging down into the rich soil and almost immediately their eyes were delighted by the glitter of gold. When they dived below the warm waters of the Indian Ocean they found trees of rainbow-coloured coral

... where Mermaids lie,
Sighing beneath those precious boughs, and die
For absence of their scaly lovers lost
In midnight storms, about the Indian coast...

In the shallow waters they found centuries-old oysters, their shells gaping open, inviting the English adventurers to gather up their pearls. The only problem was that the pearls were so heavy only the strongest divers could carry them to the surface!

D'Avenant went on to imagine Jermyn and his companions climbing on the rocks above the beach, crying out with delight as they found sapphires, rubies and diamonds.

There was more. Black ambergris, a cholesterol-based substance formed in the intestines of sperm whales and highly prized as a fixative for perfumes, was washed ashore in such profusion that the stupid sailors were found using it as shoe polish. Hastening into the woods, Jermyn and his companions delighted in tasting and smelling the rich profusion of exotic fruits. Then, the natives led them to a grove where silk worms spun their threads so quickly they made Persian silk worms seem clumsy and lazy in comparison.

Under Rupert's rule, D'Avenant's make-believe Madagascar prospered. The natives accepted his government unquestioning-ly, and lived happily under it. Jermyn and Porter watched ships from India and China arriving to trade, so that all the wealth of the East soon poured through Madagascar. In the poem, the Golden Age had begun again.

In the real world, 150 settlers, inspired by such visionary writings as D'Avenant's, set sail for Madagascar in October 1644. They made it there safely, and established a colony south of Tuléar. The depth of St Augustine's Bay allowed their galleons to anchor close to the shore and the jungles provided a rich harvest of food.

Yet they had reckoned without the low-lying swamps and deltas that fed into the bay. Countless diseases, unimagined by D'Avenant, lurked there, waiting eagerly for just such a group of hapless Europeans. Within months, most of the colonists were inhabitants of nothing more than their own graves.

A further attempt at colonisation was made in 1649-50, on the island of Assada to the northwest of the mainland, but here a disagreement with the local king led to the deaths of most of the settlers. France finally established a lasting presence in Madagascar, but Jermyn still hoped that one day an English flag would flutter permanently over the island of his dreams.

When Jermyn heard in 1655 that a fleet of colonists under Admiral Penn was sailing south down the French coast, he wrote wistfully from Paris that 'they may be for Madagascar; their victualing makes it possible they are for some remote and hot part'.

Jermyn was very much a man of action, not a philosopher. D'Avenant's dreams of Madagascar probably amused and entertained him, but that was all. D'Avenant knew this, of course. Through his poetry, therefore, D'Avenant hoped to elevate Jermyn's mind so as to make him a beneficial force in the practical world of English politics. He also sought to inspire Jermyn by encouraging him to learn about another more practical art-form: classical architecture.

In Jermyn's time, Britain was still liberally scattered with Roman remains. Francis Bacon's home, St Albans just north of London, was littered with Roman ruins, and indeed London's Roman walls were still a conspicuous part of its topography, albeit misattributed in popular imagination to the British King Lud. Travelling in Spain, where the drier climate favoured their preservation, Jermyn probably saw more and better examples of Roman temples, amphitheatres and aqueducts.

It was in Madrid, too, and later in Paris, that Jermyn saw many examples of a new trend sweeping across Europe, a style called classical architecture. This sought to create new palaces, churches, bridges and even gardens according to the rediscovered principles of Roman architecture. Just as the Romans had copied the older, Greek principles of building to arrogate a monumental grandeur to their cities, so too had the educated Italians and Spaniards of the sixteenth century re-learned what the Romans had done, so as to confer an air of nobility on their own towns and palaces.

Marie de Medici had taught her little daughter Henrietta Maria to appreciate classical design, too, and it may have been she who explained its principles to Jermyn.

One of the ways Henrietta Maria tried to feel more at home in England was by commissioning new classical buildings. She was lucky in this respect to have inherited the services of England's only skilled classical practitioner from Charles's mother Anne of Denmark: Inigo Jones.

Born in 1573, Jones, the son of a London cloth-worker, developed an early enthusiasm for architecture and was fortunate in finding a patron in the Earl of Pembroke. Pembroke paid for him to visit Italy, where well-preserved Roman remains were two-a-penny. Fascinated, Jones studied each classical ruin and every new building built in the classical style and read every treatise on the subject he could find. He learned how to calculate the exact weight a Corinthian column could support and how to create buildings with perfectly harmonious proportions.

Besides several substantial commissions from Anne of Denmark and then from Henrietta Maria, Jones undertook private work on other buildings that Jermyn could see under construction around him in London. Jones's new squares at Covent Garden and Lincoln's Inn Fields had a direct influence on Jermyn's later decision to build a classical square at St James's.

The house Jones designed for Jermyn's progressive cousin Sir Peter Killigrew in Blackfriars, not far from St Paul's Cathedral, had simple geometric proportions and clean-cut use of brick and stone, both precursors of the design Jermyn used later for St James's. But it was Jones's almost continuous employment by Henrietta Maria over the next two decades that was to bring Jermyn into really close contact with classical architecture.

The project which affected Jermyn and Henrietta Maria most was the development of Greenwich. Behind the ramshackle Tudor palace at Greenwich, that fronted the Thames, Inigo Jones had already started work on a small classical lodge for Anne of Denmark. Under Henrietta Maria's patronage, he redesigned and enlarged it to create the Queen's House, her 'House of Delights'. By 1635, Henrietta Maria and Jermyn could gaze proudly at its gleaming white walls, perfectly straight with crisp, clear corners and elegant proportions.

Four years later the marble interior, complete with Ionic columns and ceilings painted in contemporary Baroque style, was finished. The first Italian-style villa to be built in Britain since Roman times, the Queen's House glowed like a great Mediterranean pearl amongst the jumble of red bricks and jutting timbers of Old England. Utterly *avant garde*, it attracted many admiring glances, but still more disapproving grumbles. Bluff Englishmen muttered that it was a foreign house built by Papists. Henrietta Maria and Jermyn loved it.

Had it been left to Henrietta Maria alone, Jermyn might never have done any more than simply admire classical architecture. But it was surely D'Avenant who encouraged Jermyn to think about it for himself, and listen attentively when Inigo Jones expostulated the profound philosophy that underlay his work. Between them, they made Jermyn want to grasp hold of the world around him and change it for the better.

This heady period of courtly education saw the genesis of a very grand design indeed. London was believed to have been founded as a new embodiment of Troy, the paradigm of ancient cities, and then rebuilt by Lud and inhabited by the Romans, but it was now in a very sorry state. What if it were rebuilt, in the new classical style, not as another Troy, but as a new Rome? What glories could Britain attain, if its beating heart was a city worthy of Augustus? Nothing could be done, as yet, about the sprawling mass of the City, but to the north of St James's lay meadows, the Bailiwick of St James's. Save for a couple of houses in the lane running north from the palace (later named St James's Street), the land was completely undeveloped. Better still, they were part of the dowry that had been conferred on Henrietta Maria when she married the King.

In 1640, Jermyn and Henrietta Maria organised a survey of this land, their minds teeming with plans and visions of what it could become. But alas, events conspired, not to destroy their plans altogether, but certainly to delay them for many years to come.

In March 1636, Jermyn celebrated his thirty-first birthday. With Eleanor Villiers and her toddler daughter safely excluded from court, Jermyn was free to devote his days entirely to his beloved Henrietta Maria. Whether dancing with her in a masque or leading her by the hand through palace gardens, his duty as her Gentleman Usher conferred on him the exquisite obligation to be in her presence from morning to night.

However much Henrietta Maria may have fallen in love with Charles I, and developed a successful sexual relationship with him, it seemed that nothing could dislodge Jermyn from the very core of her psyche. Even while Jermyn was in exile, Henrietta Maria had sought a philosophical framework to justify their unconventional relationship and, on a wider level, the relationships between herself and her attendant ladies, and the host of attractive yet (theoretically, at least) inaccessible young men who strutted about the court.

She found what she wanted in the writings of Honoré D'Urfé, Castiglione and of her own great-grandmother Margueritte of Navarre, all of whom advocated the idea of courtly love. For a gallant young man to adore a lady chastely was to make her *précieuse*. Far from being unfaithful to her husband, it was acceptable for such a *précieuse* lady to respond to such loving advances – provided it remained entirely non-sexual. It sounded perfect.

Indeed, because such love was purely spiritual, it was thought to be a form of religious devotion, pleasing to God. Arguing that the courtly lover 'covets but honest matters, and therefore may the woman grant him them all without blame', Castiglione argued that it was acceptable for married ladies to hold hands with their gallant admirers. For such couples to exchange kisses was praise-worthy as an act of 'knitting together both of body and soul'.

Far from concealing her now completely chaste love for Jermyn, therefore, Henrietta Maria made it fashionable. Soon the already heady atmosphere of Whitehall and St James's was thick with the coos and sighs of courtly lovers.

As an important step towards popularising courtly love, the Queen had commissioned D'Avenant to make it the subject of a masque. *The Temple of Love* was performed on Shrove Tuesday, 1634. The following year, D'Avenant developed the same theme in a play, *The Platonic Lovers*, which he dedicated boldly to Jermyn himself.

In his play, D'Avenant disguised Jermyn and Henrietta Maria thinly as the main protagonists, Theander (a Greek name meaning 'god-man') and Eurithea ('broad-goddess'). When Theander enters Eurithea's chamber late at night, she asks him,

> Where have you been so long?
> Alas, wherefore do I ask, since I
> So lately found you in my dream?
>
> This happiness is too great to last!
> Envy or fate must lessen it, or we
> Remove 'mongst the eternal lovers, and
> Provide our habitation near the stars!

Of course, Platonic Lovers must necessarily remain childless. This was certainly to be Jermyn's fate with regard to legitimate offspring: that he may have been the true father of Eleanor Villiers' daughter, and perhaps of one or more of Henrietta Maria's children too, remains an open question which the prudent D'Avenant avoided. Drawing on essays written by the childless Francis Bacon, D'Avenant justified childlessness in a speech delivered by Jermyn's character to another pair of platonic lovers – beautiful lines, just as appropriate for childless couples today as ever they were in the seventeenth century:

> .... you two may live,
> And love, become your own best arguments,
> And so contract all virtue, and all praise;

Be ever beauteous, fresh and young, at least
In your belief... and then you may
Beget reflections in each other's eyes;
So you increase not children but yourselves,
A better, and more guiltless progeny;
Those immortal creatures cannot sin.

When Theander is interrupted with the question 'But who shall make men, sir? Shall the world cease?', he replies

I know not how th'are made, but if such deeds
Be requisite, to fill up armies, villages,
And city shops; that killing, labour, and
That cousining still may last, Phylomont,
I'd rather nature should expect such coarse
And homely drudgeries from others than
From me.

These were beautiful sentiments. But whilst the words are D'Avenant's, they are not what he really believed. The father of a large brood of children, the poet seems to have been genuinely concerned for Jermyn's future as 'a sad platonical servant'. Eurithea's pragmatic maid prophesies (perfectly correctly) that Theander's name, if he continued '...ignorant o' th' use of marriage thus, must perish with Himself. I believe those babies he and Eurithea do beget by gazing in each other's eyes, can inherit nothing. As for Plato's love-laws', she adds scornfully, 'they may entail Lands on ghosts and shadows'.

Indeed, D'Avenant had his doubts as well whether red-blooded Jermyn would survive this new regime of non-physical courtly love. Eurithea describes Theander as

... an odd kind of lover. He comes
Into my lady's chamber at all hours;
Yet thinks it strange that people wonder at
His privilege. Well, opportunity
Is a dangerous thing; it would soon spoil me.

D'Avenant certainly did not think that Jermyn and Henrietta Maria's love had always been Platonic. At the end of the play, the narrator rather daringly addresses the audience,

Since not these two long hours amongst you all,
I cannot find one will prove Platonical.

The play was first performed at Blackfriars in 1635. To whom could these lines have been addressed other than Jermyn and Henrietta Maria themselves?

Through his time spent by Henrietta Maria's side in the Stuart court, Jermyn was heavily influenced by ideas about improving the world, especially through architecture. Yet it would be over two decades before Jermyn could translate any ideas of his own into action. For while he and the Queen laughed – or blushed – at D'Avenant's words at the end of *The Platonic Lovers*, they little suspected the extraordinary degree to which the mettle of their relationship was about to be tested by the traumatic times that lay ahead.

VI

'SPEAK WITH MR JERMYN ABOUT IT'
1637 – 1640

How wicked am I now? no Man can grow
More wicked, till he swears I am not so;
Since Wealth, which doth authorise Men to err,
Since Hope (that is the lawfull'st Flatterer)
Were never mine one hour, yet I am loath
To have less pride than Men possessed of both;

......

And thus (Arigo) I may safely climb,
Raised with the boast, not loaden with the crime;
Those with their glorious Vices taken be,
But I (most right'ously) am proud of thee.
Sir William D'Avenant, 'To Henry Jermyn' (1637) –
as in his other poems, Jermyn is referred to
by his Spanish nickname, 'Arigo'

Jermyn's coat of arms depicted a crescent moon between two stars. Since his triumphant return from exile, both these stars were firmly in the ascendant in the gilded firmament of Charles I's court that, while Parliament remained dissolved, was the epicentre of power in Stuart Britain.

His close relationship with the King's *privado*, Henrietta Maria, had done wonders for his family's fortunes. In 1638 Jermyn's pipe-smoking father Sir Thomas Jermyn was appointed Comptroller of the Royal Household, a post that entailed checking the accounts of the clerks responsible for buying provisions for the royal household. Shortly afterwards

Sir Thomas was promoted to be the King's Vice-Chamberlain. Jermyn's quiet elder brother Thomas, meanwhile, became a Gentleman of the King's Privy Chamber, a less important role which involved just about anything from keeping the monarch company to helping him get dressed in the morning.

Financially, Jermyn was not doing too badly. He had collected a succession of sinecure jobs and grants of land providing a huge income of over £4,000 per annum – the equivalent of some £2 million in today's money. Such comparisons are always fraught with difficulty due to the very different nature of economic life in Jermyn's day, but broadly speaking this figure (and the consequent jealously it inspired) is similar to the salaries now being earned by highly-paid international businessmen.

Later, Jermyn's enemies accused him of being 'full of soup and gold': of having an excessive love of worldly goods and luxury. He certainly made sure he had a great deal of both, and obviously enjoyed money, good food and drink and all the other trappings of the high life in the Stuart era. Yet there is no particular evidence that Jermyn's love of luxury was abnormal in the context of the court, where sumptuous clothes and ostentatious behaviour were *de rigeur*. To put things in context, when Jermyn compared his income to those of the great aristocrats of Charles's court, who derived incomes from their own great swathes of Britain, he still remained comparatively rather poor.

Perhaps what really inspired his enemies' animosity was not so much his money, or his power, as the apparent ease with which he had risen high enough to gain them. But then, anyone who is extremely good at a difficult task has the ability to make what they do look effortless.

An important step in Jermyn's continued rise took place on

Monday, 2 September 1639, when he was promoted to become Master of the Horse (or Equerry) to Henrietta Maria.

Technically, Jermyn had to walk by the Queen's horse when she rode in state, or went hunting. In practice, a Master of the Horse was expected to serve his master or mistress in the most confidential and intimate matters. In skilled hands, it allowed the holder of the office to wield much of the power and influence vested in their master or mistress. Olivares, after all, had been Philip IV of Spain's Master of the Horse, and Buckingham had held the same office under James I and Charles I. Why, Robert Dudley, Master of the Horse to Elizabeth I, had played his cards so well he almost married her!

Jermyn, of course, was only Master of the Horse not to a crowned monarch, but to a queen consort, but these were unusual times. Charles I, with his pallid complexion and baleful eyes, ruled England and Scotland. But especially after Lord Portland went to his grave in 1635, the King's vivacious *privado*, Henrietta Maria, could perhaps be said to have ruled him.

Courtiers and even government ministers who desired anything from a small favour to a major change in policy learned quickly that the person they really needed to convince was the Queen. Once she believed something needed doing, Henrietta Maria could usually persuade Charles to order it. But etiquette prevented courtiers from crowding up to the Queen clamouring for favours.

The shrewdest amongst them soon learned that the best way of engaging Henrietta Maria's interest in something was to share a relaxed flagon of wine or a vigorous game of tennis with her charismatic Equerry, Henry Jermyn. Once he had agreed something needed to be done, he could easily talk to the Queen about it, and she, with equal ease, might then persuade the King.

By the start of 1640, we hear that Jermyn was arranging for Sir Harry Vane to replace Sir John Coke in no less a position than Secretary of State, one of the most powerful, official posts in the realm. An observer wrote that Jermyn 'had engaged her [the Queen] by all the ways of his own supplications, and by the humble mediation of his friends', and that Henrietta Maria had become so determined to see it happen that those who opposed it 'will break up on a rock if they persist to espouse the business any longer'.

Jermyn had spent a decade imitating Cardinal Richelieu's ability to ingratiate himself with and influence the people around him. Ministers and aristocrats of the stature of the Earl of Leicester, Charles's ambassador in Paris, and even the great Marquess of Hamilton, royal commissioner in Scotland and next in line to the throne after the Stuarts themselves, were soon exerting themselves to cultivate the strapping young man who, only a few years earlier, had been a disgraced prisoner in the Tower of London.

Indeed Hamilton was so keen to gain Jermyn's good graces that he gave him free reign in disposing of all the positions and offices that were in his patronage.

What heady greatness seemed to stretch out ahead of him! Yet even as Jermyn's influence mushroomed, the very world in which he had been bred to flourish was falling under a sinister shadow.

At the root of the terrible social convulsions ahead lay a massive crisis of confidence, that in many ways we are still trying to work through to this day. Throughout the Middle Ages, the Catholic Church had held a virtual monopoly on what people were supposed to think about the great questions that trouble humanity – where we come from; how to conduct ourselves towards each other; what will happen after we die.

Charles I as he wished to be seen – an all-conquering, divinely-ordained sovereign.

The answers the Church provided were dazzlingly complex, and ultimately so unsatisfactory, that in the early sixteenth century a wave of protestants, led by Martin Luther, had finally rebelled, breaking away from the Catholic Church and establishing their own Protestant sects. But, for all its faults, the Medieval Catholic system had at least been consistent. The majority, who had no real desire to think for themselves, had no reason ever to have to.

Protestantism offered freedom of thought, but it opened a Pandora's Box of questions. If one thing, such as who was in charge of your church, could be questioned, then what about the rest? Did the sun go around the earth, or was it really, as Galileo had suggested, the other way around? Must we really love our loathsome neighbours?

Even the age-old myth that we came from Trojans, who came – by the indefatigable logic of the Medieval church – from Noah, who came from Adam and Eve, had started to seem less certain than before. But if that myth was not true, then it opened up a vertiginous problem: if we did not come from them, then from whom? Francis Bacon's Natural Science had already set out on its tentative course that, just over two centuries after the English Civil War, would lead to Charles Darwin's *Origin of Species* – and it was to be two centuries of very angst-ridden soul-searching indeed.

Closer to hand was the question of religious observance itself. In 1537, the questioning of Catholic authority led to Henry VIII's Protestant Reformation, that replaced the Pope with the King as head of the Church, 'Defender of the Faith', within his own dominions. But like all revolutionaries who question their leaders' authority, and then overthrow them, the English monarchs set themselves up for the inevitable follow-on question: if we didn't have to obey that leader, why must we obey you?

To defend their position, the English monarchs offered the only real argument they could – the very same one used by the Popes – that it was God's will. It was by Divine Right that the monarch held the office of Defender of the Faith. It was a belief to which Charles, like his father, clung with more tenacity than a barnacle to a rock. And in Charles's mind, the argument that secured his position as both King and Defender of the Faith also conferred on him a great obligation: to provide one, unified church to enfold and protect all his subjects.

As to the nature of that church, the devil lurked, as ever, in the particulars. Had Charles been like Henry VIII's son Edward VI, his church would have tended towards the lower, grittier, Calvinistic end of the Protestant spectrum, with spartan churches, unadorned ministers and plain-speaking sermons, leaving the congregation's souls naked under the all-seeing eye of God.

As fate would have it, though, Charles happened to favour a more Baroque establishment, not Roman Catholic, but not too far removed from it either. He, and not the Pope, was the Head of the Church, but below him, like the Pope, he liked his frocked archbishops and bishops and all the tiers of clergy, whose jobs it was to perform elaborate ceremonies that mediated benevolently between the people and the Almighty.

Charles's preference was far from universally popular in England, where many hankered for the more austere, Calvinistic type of Protestantism. This was the type of Protestantism that had taken hold in Scotland, fired in the mid-sixteenth century by the Calvinistic fervour of John Knox. Here, the emphasis lay on democratic assemblies representing the local church ministers and elders. God dealt personally with all, rather than delegating his grace down through a long chain of church officials.

Over the ensuing decades, the Church of Scotland vacillated over the question of whether they should administer themselves purely through assemblies of ministers and elders, or whether to retain the old Catholic office of bishops. In 1610, James VI and I had increased the power of the bishops, but their status remained considerably less than that of their English counterparts.

Then, in 1637, came the single, great error of judgement. Rather than allow the two national churches to continue to operate separately, Charles I, misguided terribly by his English Archbishop of Canterbury, William Laud, decided that the Scots must start following the English system, and he issued a new *Book of Common Prayer* for Scotland, that must be used in all services.

On Sunday, 23 July 1637, the Bishop of Edinburgh conducted a service in his cathedral. In accordance with the newly-revised rites, he turned his back on the congregation, just as priests had done before the Reformation. God loved his people, but instead of his grace flowing directly down to each of them individually, it was now being channelled symbolically through the Bishop.

Behind him, the Bishop heard a clamour of protest, and a stool hurtled past his mitred head and smashed against the altar.

Within days the protests at Edinburgh Cathedral had become the focus of a much wider frustration. When James VI of Scotland had inherited the English throne in 1603, his people thought they would rule Britain. But off King James had ridden to London, with his sons in his train. Now, Charles had spent so much time amongst the English that he might as well have been one, for all the care he took of them.

Members of the nobility, gentry and clergy and burgesses of the towns met together to form a council called the Tables, aimed at asserting the traditional liberties and laws of Scotland and its national church. In February 1638 the members of the Tables, in open defiance of the King's authority, signed their names to the Scottish National Covenant. From now on, the church would be Presbyterian, administered solely by local meetings of ministers and elders, the presbyteries, and General Assemblies of their representatives. That autumn, the General Assembly took the final step on the Scots' collision course with royal authority by formally sweeping away the bishops altogether.

These developments suited the French First Minister Cardinal Richelieu very well. It was the elegantly devious Cardinal's policy to keep his neighbours, including Charles, as weak as possible. His secret agents in Scotland promised the rebels French support if they continued to refuse to use the King's *Book of Common Prayer*.

So there it was. Charles I had what he saw as a simple desire to impose a blessed unity across the entire realm. Now the English were dusting off their muskets and the Scots were burnishing up their claymores.

For a supremely confident young man like Jermyn, with his sights set on ever-higher offices within the inner circle of the court, these developments probably did not seem nearly so ominous as they do to us now. As far as he was concerned, these disobedient subjects of the King simply needed teaching a lesson, after which they would return to full obedience to the Crown. That Charles would succeed was beyond question.

Richelieu had no doubt of this either, but, simply to prolong the English king's struggle, he threw in a new and extraordinary obstacle for him to overcome. Since she had been exiled to Holland, Henrietta Maria's mother Marie de Medici had been longing to come to London. So now, the Cardinal's agents encouraged her to set off.

Just as a tiny hole in one of the dykes that protect Holland from the sea can suddenly burst into a jet of water, that breaks down the whole barrier and allows a colossal weight of water to overwhelm the polders beyond, so did the formidable matriarch rise from her bed and embark on a course of action that nobody could prevent.

Having the old dowager and her vast retinue of outlandishly dressed servants to stay for an indefinite period was the last thing Charles wanted, when every penny he had was needed for the impending war. But worse than the expense was Marie herself – Italian Catholic by birth; intimate friend of the Pope and ex-regent of virulently Papist France. He might just as well have invited the Pope to St James's and started burning his Protestant subjects all by himself.

On Thursday, 13 September 1638, Jermyn rode over London Bridge with a retinue of servants and bodyguards. At the Sussex town of Rye, which in those days had a wide river navigable by large ships, Jermyn boarded a specially chartered frigate. As the royal standard streamed from the mast-top, his ship carved a furrow of white foam through the green-grey waters of the English Channel. From Dieppe, he rode hard down the highway to Paris. Flanked by both English ambassadors, he swept into the royal audience chamber at the Louvre and bowed low before Louis XIII and Queen Anne.

In his most eloquent French, Jermyn presented Charles and Henrietta Maria's congratulations on the birth of Louis' new son and heir, also called Louis – the future Louis XIV. As before, Jermyn's presentation of compliments was intended only as a cover for his secret mission. In a private audience, he begged Louis and Richelieu to withdraw their support for the Scots rebels and to allow Marie to return to Paris, thereby diverting her from her descent on London.

Jermyn had learned a lot since he had first entered the Louvre, as a mere attendant of Lord Kensington's, back in 1624. In the years that had followed he had been back thrice. On each occasion he had studied the protocol and personalities of the French court with ever increasing keenness. He was already amongst the Englishman most adept at negotiating with the French.

But for all that, he had no hope of succeeding this time. Neither Louis nor his First Minister would so much as acknowledge that they were having anything to do with the Scots. And all Jermyn achieved regarding Marie was a nebulous promise to reconsider the terms of her exile, which of course they did not act upon.

So, despite Jermyn's efforts, Marie crossed the Channel and bore down on St James's Palace.

'How shall I recognise her?' asked one courtier.

'She brings with her six coaches, seventy horses and a hundred and sixty in her train', retorted another dryly, so the task of spotting her should not be too difficult.

As predicted, the presence of Marie and her priests in St James's Palace made Anglicans and Puritans alike tremble with indignation. It reminded them of the Catholic Masses being said there daily in Henrietta Maria's private chapel. It seemed as if the entire royal court had been infested with Papists.

In February 1639, desperate to see an end to the rumbling complaints and the vast cost of the visit, Charles and Henrietta Maria sent Jermyn back across the storm-tossed Channel to try again. But if Jermyn had any real hope that Louis and Richelieu might have changed their minds, he was disappointed. Back home amongst the sumptuous tapestries of St James's, he explained awkwardly to Marie that her son would never allow her to go back to France.

Jermyn's next task was to report to Charles. To do so he was faced with a long ride north to York, where the King was now assembling an army to subdue the Scots, whom Jermyn described contemptuously as 'such beggarly snakes [who] dare put out their horns'.

Having delivered his report, Jermyn hurried back to join Henrietta Maria in London. But at the end of May messengers brought them worrying news from the north. The Scots had responded to Charles's threat by raising their own army to defend the Covenant, with the Earl of Argyll at its head.

A cold, scheming man, Argyll had acquired his family estates before his father's death and repaid his good fortune by keeping the old earl in poverty. Having treated his own father thus he seems to have had no compunction about defying the King himself. Indeed, far from attacking Scotland, Charles was now being forced to defend England from invasion.

Riding north again in June, Jermyn found the King's army braving the brisk North Sea breezes at Dunse Low near the border town of Berwick-on-Tweed. Facing them across the dunes were Argyll's army of pike- and musket-wielding Covenanters. The fight for Madagascar had only been a piece of poetic fiction: now Jermyn braced himself for his first, real-life battle.

Before the first shots were fired, however, the pallid King's courage crumbled. A messenger rode out from Charles's camp to tell Argyll that Scotland could keep its Presbyterian Covenant. The two armies withdrew and Jermyn galloped uneasily back to join Henrietta Maria at St James's. He was painfully aware, as he wrote later, that affairs in Scotland 'are not so settled as was to be wished'.

By now Jermyn and the Queen were under no delusions about how fundamentally ill-equipped Charles was for dealing with crises. When tact and diplomacy were required, the King could be intractably stubborn. When firm leadership was called for, he dithered or backed down. Help was clearly needed. Both they and Archbishop Laud cajoled Charles into summoning Thomas Wentworth, soon to become Earl of Strafford, from Ireland to Whitehall, to become his special advisor on military affairs.

Tall and thickset like Jermyn, 'Black Tom' had gained his nickname from his dark hair, and because of the heavy-handed approach he took to anyone who crossed his path. As Lord Deputy of Ireland, Strafford had stamped out piracy, inflicted severe punishment on corrupt English officials in Dublin and used corrupt juries to make the whole of Connaught into Crown property. When the Queen had asked him to give various posts in Ireland to favourites of hers, he had refused. Jermyn and Henrietta Maria may not have liked Strafford much, but they couldn't help admire his dogged single-mindedness and superlative military skill. These were exactly what Charles needed to restore his dwindling authority in Scotland.

Charles's troubles, however, were now spreading south of the border. Since 1629, he had ruled England without summoning Parliament. But under the terms of Magna Carta he could not raise financial subsidies without Parliament's consent.

Only a tax called Ship Money was exempt from this rule. But when Charles tried levying it in 1636 and again in 1639, there were widespread protests and rioters in London smashed shop windows. In April 1640 he summoned what would later be called the Short Parliament, hoping – indeed, expecting – thus to rally the nation behind him, and to obtain a substantial financial subsidy to pay for troops to help him restore his authority in Scotland.

This was the first Parliament to be called for eleven years. Its members were likely to include a considerable body of landed gentry and merchants with a considerable back-catalogue of grievances to air. Therefore, as many courtiers as possible used their influence with – and power over – the small number of people who were actually entitled to vote, to have themselves elected. By such means, Jermyn was elected to a seat with which he had no discernible family or property connection – Corfe Castle in Dorset.

Not all the Parliamentary seats, however, could be occupied by men as loyal to the Crown as Jermyn. And none were more disaffected with Charles's period of personal rule than John Pym.

A former Exchequer clerk, Pym had represented his native Taunton in the Parliaments of the 1620s, during which he had been a leading voice against the Duke of Buckingham. Pym was one of the growing body of men who disliked the increasingly Catholic tendency within the Church of England and court. He believed it was Parliament's duty to restore the balance.

During the Short Parliament, this plump man with his pudding-bowl haircut, 'spoke much, and appeared to be the most leading man, for besides the exact knowledge of the forms and orders of that Council, which few men had, he had a very comely and grave way of expressing himself, with great volubility of words... and had observed the errors and mistakes in government, and knew well how to make them appear greater than they were'.

Under Pym's emerging leadership, the majority of members, Anglican gentlemen from the shires, demanded that Charles must address their complaints before any discussion could be had of money. To them, war with the Presbyterian Scots smacked of a Catholic conspiracy, nurtured in the Queen's court. Instead of voting the King more money for the war, they decided to issue a petition opposing further fighting.

Charles's furious response to this was to dissolve Parliament after a mere three weeks – hence its name 'the Short Parliament'. Greatly encouraged by this display of English disunity, Argyll's Covenanting army – that very force raised in Scotland to defend their national church from the perceived Catholic tendency of Charles's court – came storming south.

They rampaged through Northumberland, seizing Newcastle and then marauded on through County Durham. Scrabbling together money from personal loans – for Parliament had not voted him a farthing – Charles raised a new army and hurried north.

In his absence, the King delegated the task of running the government to Henrietta Maria. At last, the gender-barrier had been breached: the *privado* had entered its chrysalis, and emerged in the new, butterfly colours of First Minister.

But Henrietta Maria was heavily pregnant, so behind her wings, the new, true *privado* emerged. By this sudden, entirely unforeseen combination of circumstances, Jermyn felt his influence soar. Appointed to the lucrative position of Keeper of Greenwich Park, and with rumours flying that he might become both a viscount and Treasurer of the Royal Household, Jermyn was still far from the English equivalent of the all-powerful French First Minister, Cardinal Richelieu. But he was certainly hurtling in that direction – so long, that is, as the King's authority was enforced.

As the summer heat raised the stenches and tempers of London, men on every street corner spoke boldly of Parliament's heroic stand against royal despotism. Unwilling to blame the King directly, they swore that his Papist wife and mother-in-law were turning him against his own people. Marie de Medici was not (for once) being over-dramatic when she complained she could not sleep for fear of the mob. In mid-summer, therefore, the royal barges slipped quietly away from the Privy Stairs at Whitehall to carry Henrietta Maria and Jermyn away from this tumult to the peace of Oatlands Palace, near Weybridge in Surrey.

The great rambling complex of Oatlands Palace was built around a succession of large courtyards fronted by gabled Tudor buildings. Above these loomed a great hexagonal tower. From this vantage point, Jermyn and Henrietta Maria could see the beautiful views over gardens and vineyards to the village of Weybridge and the meadows of the River Wey. Beyond these to the north ran the wide sweep of the Thames valley, whilst to the south they could see the blue outline of the North Downs.

The most magnificent building at Oatlands was a house for silkworms, which had been designed by Inigo Jones. Behind its classical exterior the worms munched their way through the leaves of mulberry trees, before spinning their cocoons of silken thread, that the weavers of Bethnal Green, in London's East End, would later transform into sheets of shimmering fabric.

Sitting in the shade in the Privy Garden at Oatlands, Henrietta Maria and Jermyn rested, eating sweetmeats and smelling the scent of the roses and lilies. On Wednesday, 8 July 1641, she went into labour and gave birth to a baby boy. She named him Henry, apparently honouring her father, and perhaps Henry VIII as well. But it is not hard to guess that the real Henry on her mind was the one who stood devotedly by her bedside, ready to shield her with his arms from the oncoming storm.

Despite all Strafford's fiery counsels, Charles's second encounter with the Scots culminated with him granting yet more concessions and also promising to summon the English Parliament again. It met in November 1640, and later became known by the ominous name of 'the Long Parliament'.

Attempts by the court to ensure that men who would support the King were elected were generally unsuccessful. 'Safe' seats were in such short supply that Jermyn resigned his own seat of Corfe in favour of Secretary of State Sir Francis Windebank, so that the elderly and highly-skilled statesman could be present to fight the King's corner in the Commons.

But even Windebank's arguments could do little to deflect John Pym's offensive. The rotund statesman was now the unquestioned leader of the majority of the Members, who believed in upholding Parliamentary authority against the court.

These were extraordinary times. The Scottish army had openly threatened to march on London if Charles dissolved Parliament, nor would it retreat until Parliament had voted the King money to pay it off. By the same token the King could not dismiss Parliament until it had voted him the money he also needed to pay his own forces in the north and maintain his authority.

He could, therefore, do nought but grant his assent to whatever Parliament wanted. The machinery of the King's personal rule – the Privy Council advising him, the secretaries of state implementing his decisions and the prerogative courts through which royal will was enforced in the country – was in disarray.

Secretary of State Coke, who had played a vital role in implementing royal decisions since 1625, had retired at the start of 1640. His replacement, Sir Harry Vane, a nominee of Jermyn's and still ostensibly a loyal courtier, was starting to show alarming Parliamentarian sympathies. Worse, Parliament – or more particularly Pym – now attacked the leading ministers who had made Charles's personal rule work. Poor Windebank, fiercely loyal to the King, was accused of conspiring with Jesuits and found himself impeached, that is, accused of disloyalty to his country, and faced with trial and, probably, execution. Impeached too was Lord Keeper Finch, who owed his recent appointment directly to Henrietta Maria's influence.

Both Windebank and Finch had the sense to flee abroad before they could be brought to trial. Lesser ministers were 'caged', as the term was, on all manner of charges. Archbishop Laud and Strafford fared worse than any. Parliament flung them both into the Tower on charges of High Treason.

Standing indignantly at the Bar of the House of Lords, Strafford was accused of having conspired to bring his army over from Ireland to oppose Parliament. By putting Strafford on trial, Parliament was in effect directing a martial challenge at the power of the King himself. Charles and Henrietta Maria insisted on attending each day of the trial, returning home exhausted every evening.

After supper they would lock themselves away with Jermyn to discuss what strategies might possibly save both their friend and indeed the Royal Prerogative itself.

During these extraordinary months of the Long Parliament, the dignified, protocol-ridden court continued, ostensibly as before. But behind its serene façade the long-established balances of power were in turmoil. It was within this maelstrom, in which Pym picked off long-established ministers one by one, that Jermyn emerged, somewhat by default, as one of the King's most prominent – if not *the* most prominent – henchmen at court. One observer described Jermyn as a man 'looked upon by the whole court, and everything approved being done by him', while the remaining ministers found that, if they needed anything done, the best solution was to 'speak with Mr Jermyn about it'.

There were, it must be admitted, other prominent men left. There was Bishop Juxon, the Lord Treasurer; Lord Cottington, a prominent and flamboyant member of the Privy Council, and of course Lord Hamilton, the King's Equerry and principal advisor on Scottish affairs. Yet Juxon had no interest in politicking and Cottington had only the year before contemplated retirement. Only Hamilton could be spoken of in the same breath as Jermyn.

For all the rumours of grandiose promotions, Jermyn was still merely the Queen's untitled Gentleman of the Horse. Yet, to all practical purposes, according to the contemporary accounts of courtiers trying to make sense of a world plunged into confusion, it was through Jermyn, more than through any of the remaining government ministers, that the King was perceived to be exercising his remaining power.

How Jermyn reacted to this advance in fortune is suggested by a contemporary observer, Sir John Temple, who commented, 'he does with great dexterity bring all his pieces together'.

In other words, far from being daunted by his new unofficial status, Jermyn embraced it with gusto. Much as he may have dreamed about gaining such power, it would be absurd to say he had planned it. Far from it – most of his actions during this period were really reactions to the extraordinary external forces he encountered. But we can be sure the King's henchman looked forward to a healthy promotion once the crisis was over.

Now that Jermyn had become so influential, it was down to him to end the crisis. To accomplish this, he was handed a number of opportunities. One of the more ambitious projects had been hatched by Marie de Medici herself.

During Marie's exile in Holland, she had become friendly with Frederick Henry, Prince of Orange. Since the expulsion of the Spanish, Holland had been ruled by an assembly called the States General, and they employed the Princes of Orange as hereditary military leaders, known as *Stadtholders*.

Frederick Henry therefore commanded a powerful army and navy but lacked – and hankered after – the status of a sovereign ruler. Marie's plan, then, was to marry Frederick Henry's fifteen-year-old son William to Henrietta Maria's pretty ten-year-old daughter Mary. The Prince's family would come a step closer to royalty and the needy Charles would gain a son-in-law with powerful military forces at his disposal.

While Strafford's trial was in full process, therefore, Jermyn participated in secret talks at Whitehall with the Prince of

Orange's two envoys, Sommelsdijk and Heenvliet, to agree on a suitable marriage settlement.

Quiet conversations in the gardens of Whitehall and the corridors of St James's had provided Jermyn with an insight into the attitudes and motivations of a whole swathe of courtiers and members of Parliament. Acting closely with Lord Hamilton, he planned a new government incorporating staunch supporters of the King. Shrewdly, they decided to include and effectively buy-off the leading Parliamentarians, including Pym himself, whom Jermyn nominated for the exalted post of Chancellor of the Exchequer – not a bad progression for a man who had started off as an Exchequer clerk.

Whilst the conflict between King and Parliament that led to the Civil War is often thought of as a class struggle between the King and nobility on one hand, and the people on the other, the truth was far more complex. Many staunch supporters of the King, after all, sat in the Commons, whilst when the conflict escalated many titled aristocrats sided against the Crown.

Whilst many of 'the people' would be stabbed or shot fighting on both sides in the ensuing conflict, that nebulous mass of souls below the level of the landed gentry had very little voice in the proceedings. In reality, the Civil War was never a class war: it was a conflict waged by one half of the privileged elite against the other, both claiming to have the King's and country's best interests at heart, but all naturally angling for the best deal they could get for themselves.

In nominating Pym and his colleagues for governmental positions, Jermyn showed how firmly he believed that the pursuit of power through royal favour was the chief motivating factor of his contemporaries. In the case of the seven men who accepted, including the overtly Parliamentarian Oliver St John, who became Solicitor General, Jermyn was right.

Jermyn probably experienced some consternation when some of the others, led by Pym, refused. Either their principles really were superior to their pursuit of power, or they felt greater benefit would come to them by continuing their opposition. Either way, the plan to buy them all off was largely a failure, and Jermyn's name was added to Pym's mental list of royal officials who needed to be purged.

It is unclear whether, during this period, either Charles or Henrietta contemplated giving Jermyn an official post in the government, particularly by making him a Secretary of State. If they did, he side-stepped the position, recommending instead an older man and lawyer, Edward Nicholas.

Perhaps he did so simply because he thought Nicholas would be better at it. But more likely, he turned the job down because he already had plans hidden up his black satin sleeve. Plans that would be much easier to bring to fruition if his role in the royal power-structure remained ambiguous. They were plans that, if discovered and prevented, would bring far less harm to Charles if Jermyn's connection to the Crown remained undefined.

These were the plans on which Jermyn was about to gamble his entire future.

The 'Ark of Union', a metaphor for the State, is guided to safety by Cromwell, Fairfax and their chums. Meanwhile, the Royalists flounder in the sea, and Jermyn supports Henrietta Maria in a rather suggestive manner that reflects the widespread belief that they were lovers. (Credit: Fotomas Index)

VII

'DO SOMETHING EXTRAORDINARY'
1641

What sound is that! Whose concord makes a jar?
'Tis noise in peace, though harmony in war:
The drum; whose doubtful music doth delight
The willing ear, and the unwilling fright.
Had wet Arion chosen to lament
His grief at Sea on such an Instrument,
Perhaps the martial music might incite
The Sword-fish, Thrasher, and the Whale to fight...
Sir William D'Avenant, 'Madagascar' (1637)

At the start of 1641 Jermyn's East Anglian cousin, the poet Sir John Suckling, wrote to him, urging him to advise the King to 'do something extraordinary'. But it was Jermyn more than Charles who took this advice to heart.

Jermyn, Charles and Henrietta Maria had already discussed bringing Strafford's army of Irish Protestants over to England to subdue Parliament and repulse the Scots. They had decided against this because the wild behaviour and bad discipline of the Irish soldiers were likely to create more antagonism between Charles and his people than there was already.

Now that Strafford was on trial, the opportunity to use that army was passed anyway. But vastly outnumbering the Protestants in Ireland were the Catholics. Jermyn was now approached by the flamboyant Catholic peer, Lord Cottington, who asked to be appointed to the vacant Lord Lieutenancy of Ireland. Once in office, he would raise the King such an army of loyal Catholic Irishmen as had never been seen before. For several months Jermyn waited, assessing the feasibility of the plan, before rejecting Cottington's offer. If the English would find a force of Irish Protestants tramping across their fields hard to stomach, just imagine the uproar if the army were brandishing Papist crucifixes!

If no armies from Ireland could be used, then they must rely on their own people. In the north, the army that Charles had raised to guard against the Scots was still armed. Many of its officers were fiercely loyal to the King, as Jermyn knew very well.

Sir John Suckling was extremely keen on war. It was not so much the possibility of fighting, as the opportunity it might afford him to wear glamorous uniforms, that really attracted the poet to the idea. At some point in the early spring – it is impossible to say exactly when – he, Jermyn and D'Avenant resolved to 'do something extraordinary' indeed. They would bring the northern army down to intimidate Parliament, capture the Tower of London and free Strafford.

The idea met with the Queen's enthusiastic approval. Probably through her persuasion, Charles himself agreed to the plan, but with the caveat that George Goring should be involved and become Lieutenant General of the army. Three years younger than Jermyn, Goring was both a courtier and a seasoned warrior, who was held in high esteem by many of the officers, and trusted deeply by the King and Queen.

This whole plot seems to have existed as no more than an idea, however, until a young officer called Captain James Chudleigh came riding into London on Sunday, 21 March. He had come from the northern army and carried in his pocket a petition from his fellow officers, protesting at Parliament's failure to allow the King any money to pay them.

Whether by accident or some design – one suspects the latter – the first person he encountered was D'Avenant, who told him his petition 'was a matter of greater consequence that he imagined'. Quickly, D'Avenant brought him to Jermyn and Suckling.

Strafford's trial was still progressing, and Jermyn knew that the officers' discontent could be manipulated to make the projected Army Plot a reality. He was quick to assure Chudleigh that 'the Parliament was so in love with the Scots that the army was not likely to be paid…' but that 'the King would pawn jewels rather then leave the army unpaid…'. While Jermyn had the petition copied for the Queen to see, Suckling sounded Chudleigh out about the King's desire to appoint Goring as Lieutenant General.

Jermyn was not alone in thinking up ways to use the army to good effect. It appears that, early in March, another plot had been hatched by Harry Percy, the spirited younger brother of the Earl of Northumberland, and Prince Charles's Master of the Horse. Percy's cabal of co-conspirators, all officers in the army, comprised Harry Wilmot, the son of an Irish nobleman and commissary-general of horse in the army; Daniel O'Neill, a gentleman of the King's bedchamber; Jack Ashburnham, the ruddy-faced son of a Sussex squire; Sir Hugh Pollard, a seasoned soldier and politician and – perhaps significantly – Jermyn's first-cousin Jack Berkeley.

Their plan was nowhere near so bold as Jermyn's, though. They thought it would be enough if the army merely declared its open support for the King in the face of Parliamentary opposition.

When Percy revealed his plan to the King, Charles agreed to it but 'desired Goring and Jermyn should be taken into the plot'. This was presumably because he already knew of Jermyn's plot, and thought it best to combine the two separate efforts into one. It is impossible to say for sure whether he did so in order to temper Jermyn's ambitious scheme with Percy's milder one, or to bring Percy round to Jermyn's bolder way of thinking. The evidence of the Tower Plot, described below, suggests the latter.

Until this point, Goring, although much discussed, had not actually been recruited. Jermyn's opportunity to do so came on Sunday, 28 March when, as his coach passed the end of St Martin's Lane near Charing Cross, he saw Goring's coach. Goring described later how Jermyn sent his footman to ask him to meet him at Suckling's house and how, once there, Jermyn invited him to the Queen's drawing chamber that evening.

Goring appeared in the Queen's rooms as invited. Jermyn was about to take him into the Queen's bedchamber when Charles himself appeared, looking agitated – the trial of Strafford was still in full flow – and whispered that they should meet the following day. On Monday 29th, then, the three men, Jermyn, Goring and the King, met again, and the King asked Goring enigmatically to help 'set my army into a good posture'. To this, Goring agreed.

It was now Jermyn's job to bring all his pieces together. That same evening, he took Goring to Percy's chambers in Whitehall. Here, in the presence of Percy, Wilmot, Ashburnham, Pollard, Berkeley and a new conspirator, Captain Neville, Goring was sworn to secrecy and admitted to their plot. Jermyn then revealed to the stunned circle of men his more ambitious plot of bringing the army south and capturing the Tower. Most were uneasy about the plans. 'We disliked them', Pollard later asserted, 'because Sir John Suckling and they were in it.... we did not very much like the men, for Suckling, Jermyn and D'Avenant were in it'. But that was Pollard's view with hindsight. At the time he fell in behind Jermyn's lead, just like the rest of them.

After the meeting, Percy and Jermyn reported back to Charles. Having previously, if nervously, supported Jermyn's scheme, the King now called it 'vain and foolish, and he would think of them no more'. Had he really lost his nerve, or was he speaking simply of the scheme to bring the army down, and not of the Tower Plot?

What happened next, however, confirms that Charles had his doubts. The Lord General of the Army, Lord Northumberland, had malaria and needed replacing. His brother, Harry Percy favoured the moderate Lord Kensington, but Jermyn and Goring wanted to see the much more hard-line Lord Newcastle take charge. In this case, Jermyn did not have his way, for on Friday, 9 April, the King chose Kensington and, by implication, a more passive role for the armed forces than storming down to London.

Charles may have made this decision through cowardice. He may, however, have had a more realistic view than Jermyn's of the unconditional support he could expect from the whole army. Indeed, it later transpired that some of the officers had been decidedly unenthusiastic about the prospect of having Goring as their Lieutenant General.

The result of the decision was a surprising one. Goring, though trusted by King and Queen alike, told Lord Newport about the plot. This was the same Lord Newport whose brief liaison with Eleanor Villiers had become public knowledge due to Jermyn's refusal to marry her in 1633. As a result of this Newport bore Jermyn a bitter grudge and it is no surprise, therefore, to find that it was he who repeated everything Goring had told him to Pym himself.

Goring may have been disloyal. He may have betrayed the plot in a fit of pique when he realised he might not become Lieutenant General after all. He may even, as Professor Russell has argued, have done so at the King's connivance. Charles may have hoped that the fact that he *could* bring the army south if he so chose might be enough to intimidate Parliament into obedience. It is true that, during these months, Jermyn and Suckling spread stories that the French would send armed help for the King. These stories were quite without foundation, and were presumably spread for the same purpose of trying to cow Parliament. If scaring Parliament was the plan, however, it was a foolish one – and if the King did indeed instruct Goring to leak details of the plot for this purpose, then he had made a deliberate decision to betray Jermyn. But all that is mere speculation.

Initially, Pym said nothing to Parliament about the plot, but he did take immediate steps to conclude Strafford's trial before the army could start marching south.

Ever the expert on Parliamentary proceedings, Pym sprang to his feet in the Commons on Wednesday, 21 April, and proposed that the House should pass an act of attainder. This was a seldom-used Parliamentary device, whereby they could declare Strafford guilty without having to finish the trial. Only 59 members, including Jermyn's brother Thomas and Endymion Porter, voted against the motion that declared Strafford guilty. In the streets of London the mob howled for the immediate execution of 'Black Tom' Strafford.

Like Pym, Jermyn knew he had to act quickly.

Five tense days later, a small fleet of Dutch ships glided up the Thames and weighed anchor by the Tower. Aboard was young Prince William of Orange, nervously anticipating his nuptials with Princess Mary. More importantly from Jermyn's point of view was the Prince's bodyguard of four hundred heavily armed Dutch soldiers. Although the Army Plot seems to have been abandoned after Kensington's appointment as Lord General on 9 April, the Tower Plot was still definitely active.

At Suckling's behest, one of Strafford's Irish officers had started recruiting Londoners as soldiers on the pretence of sending them to serve under the King of Portugal. The real aim, though, was to use this new mini-army of one hundred men to overpower the guards that Parliament had set about the Tower, and let in the Dutch bodyguards. Once the Tower, and the nation's precious supply of gunpowder was in royal hands, Parliament would be, literally, powerless.

The Royalists decided to act on May Day. The day dawned bright and clear and soon the temperature began to rise. Dressed in his most ostentatious uniform, Suckling sent his recruits marching up to the Tower, where they asked to be admitted. The Lieutenant of the Tower, however, was not fooled by their story – that they had come on the King's order simply to guard the Tower and its munitions against possible general disturbance. The gates of the citadel remained shut and Suckling's men had no choice but to withdraw.

The next day the Royal Family and the remnants of their subdued court assembled at the King's Chapel at Whitehall for the wedding of William and Mary. Despite the ominous dread of civil unrest that pervaded the proceedings, the adults made an effort to feast and toast the child bride and groom, and nothing untoward happened.

On 3 May, the House of Lords asked Kensington, Hamilton and Essex to ask the King to disband Suckling's soldiers. Charles refused. The Lords sent another, larger deputation demanding the discharge of the recruits. Meanwhile, independent of the King, they appointed none other than Jermyn's adversary Lord Newport to take command of the Tower.

On Thursday, 4 May, the blow fell. Whilst the House of Lords argued over whether or not to execute Strafford, Pym heaved himself onto his feet in the Commons. In his loud voice he revealed how close the Tower Plot had come to succeeding. Then he revealed everything Goring had told Newport about Jermyn's Army Plot. The Commons listened to him in shocked silence.

Parliament knew they had been provoking the King and his court, and had heard rumours of reprisals. But it was quite another thing to hear evidence of an actual plot to use armed force against them. They immediately voted for Strafford's execution. They also sent a messenger to Whitehall asking Charles – they could not order him, for he was the King – to detain every member of the Queen's household for questioning in connection with the plot.

We can well imagine the pale King trembling with anxiety. Henrietta Maria flushing with indignation, expostulating in French and English at the appalling impertinence of the English Parliament, who presumed to tell their divinely-anointed sovereign what to do: *her* father would never have stood for it! Jermyn giving in to his frustrated anger, incredulous that someone – presumably he did not know whom – could have betrayed his plot to Pym.

Then the sickening realisation swept over all of them that, like Strafford, Jermyn would be arrested, tried and condemned to death for High Treason.

Unlike Strafford, who, as a peer of the realm, would 'enjoy' the privilege of a quick – or quickish – death by being beheaded, Jermyn was a commoner. He would be strung up at the gibbet on Tower Hill and left to dangle while the noose tightened round his neck.

When he was almost dead from strangulation, the rope would

be cut, allowing his body to crash down to the ground. Revived by the shock, Jermyn would watch as the executioner's knife plunged into his belly, ripping away the tender flesh. The executioner would then thrust his hands into the wound to wrench out handfuls of Jermyn's intestines, bowels, stomach and liver and throw them down to tremble in the blood flooding out of Jermyn's convulsing body. While Jermyn was still semi-conscious, the executioner would take up his axe and one by one chop off his groaning victim's legs and arms. Only at that point would the pain and blood-loss allow Jermyn to abandon consciousness and seek relief in death.

There was nothing Charles could do to protect Jermyn from this dreadful fate, so long as he remained in England. While the Queen's anger turned to despairing grief, Charles scratched his signature on a special warrant allowing Jermyn to travel to France. Without time even to change out of his fine black satin suit and white calfskin boots, Jermyn stuffed money and jewels into his pockets. Kissing the hands of Charles and Henrietta Maria, he hurried down the Privy Stairs and clambered into a boat that carried him swiftly across the Thames to Lambeth.

If he paused then and looked back, what did he see? Through his tears at his separation from his beloved Henrietta Maria, Jermyn he would have seen Whitehall and behind it the high gate towers of St James's, the palaces around which his whole life had revolved. Places where, until that very afternoon, he had been pre-eminently powerful. Where Henrietta Maria would now be sobbing alone, without him to protect her.

His feelings were probably of impotent rage against Parliament and everything it stood for; of profound disbelief that such a thing could happen. And a desperate, even childlike hope that, somehow, everything would be made right.

By the time dusk was falling over St James's, Jermyn was

already galloping down the road to Portsmouth. There, he presented himself, exhausted, to the new governor – Goring. Jermyn had no idea that all this was Goring's fault. His friend, now feeling guilty for what he had done, decided to make amends by helping Jermyn to escape. Jermyn toyed briefly with the idea of staying in Portsmouth and sending dispatches to Paris, begging for reinforcements, but dismissed the idea almost at once.

On Friday, 7 May 1641, as Parliamentarian soldiers galloped into the town brandishing orders for his arrest, Jermyn's ship heaved anchor. The vessel's sails billowed in the gentle breeze as it glided serenely out of Portsmouth harbour. As the setting sun turned the English Channel into a dazzling sea of gold, Jermyn's ship bore him away toward a new and uncertain future in France.

VIII

COLONEL LORD JERMYN
1641 – 1643

At Aldbourne with sad eyes they view our Horse;
The valiant Jermyn stops their hasty course...
What was an Host to him? he charged it through;
With unfeared noise the bullets round him flew.
Though causeless was their hate in peace before,
He showed in war none could deserve it more.
Cowley, *The Civil War* part 3 (1643)

Many years later, Jermyn is reported to have said of Henrietta Maria 'that the fortunes of the most exalted & those that appear the most fixed are subject to the greatest changes'.

It was now that this change began in earnest. 'I have fallen into unimaginable miseries of every kind...', the tearful Queen confided to her sister Christine of Savoy. 'The people who are faithful to our service [are] sent away and indeed pursued for their lives, because they have tried to serve the King'.

She had been planning to leave London, for Portsmouth at least, for several weeks. In her distress at Jermyn's departure she resolved to go – perhaps even to follow Jermyn to Paris. Alarmed, her priest, Fr Philip, begged her not to. If you go now, he told her bluntly, you will convince the world that you are Jermyn's mistress.

Disconsolate, she set off instead for Oatlands, with Jermyn's father puffing his pipe anxiously by her side. Terrified of the consequences if he refused, Charles signed Strafford's death warrant.

The Earl of Strafford was taken to Tower Hill on Wednesday, 12 May. Archbishop Laud stretched his hand out through his own prison bars to give him a final blessing, before fainting. Bravely facing a mob of over 100,000 people, Strafford placed his head on the block, and down fell the executioner's axe on 'Black Tom's' neck.

Prince William of Orange and Marie de Medici both took ship from London. Marie died the following year, virtually destitute, at the Brussels home of her friend the painter Peter-Paul Rubens.

A few months later Jermyn was tried *in absentia*. As his friends and family feared, he was indeed sentenced to death for High Treason. More immediately, and also as a direct result of his Army Plot, Parliament passed an act preventing itself from ever being dissolved. It seemed that the whole world Jermyn had known had fallen to pieces.

After he stepped ashore at Dieppe, Jermyn found a crest-fallen Sir John Suckling waiting for him, with news of their fellow Army Plot conspirators. Young Harry Percy had been wounded while escaping from England, and was lying in a fever at Calais. Poor D'Avenant had been caught and was standing trial in London.

Downhearted and angry, Jermyn rode down the dusty road to Rouen, where he met Walter Montagu. Following Henrietta Maria's example, Montagu had become a Catholic and was soon to become Abbot of Pontoise. The two men arrived together in Paris. Montagu was a favourite of Queen Anne, but despite this there was nothing he or Jermyn could say to persuade Cardinal Richelieu to help Charles.

While they kicked their heels in Paris, reliant on loans and the kindness of the French court for their sustenance, they were joined by Percy. Then one morning, to Jermyn's joy, D'Avenant came riding up. Pym was happy to execute soldiers and statesmen who crossed his path, but apparently executing poets risked turning them into martyrs, and this he would not do. It turned out, too, that the staunchly Republican poet Milton had intervened on his fellow writer's behalf. So D'Avenant had been allowed to go.

In the end, it was Suckling, that foppish soldier-scribbler, who was the least fortunate, but it was not Pym who killed him. His own servant, who merely intended to rob him, hid a razor in Suckling's boot. When Suckling pulled the boot on, he severed a vein in his foot and bled his way to an agonizing death.

In February 1642 Henrietta Maria boarded the *Lion* at Dover and braved the North Sea to take Princess Mary to join her new husband in The Hague. Mary had not gone straight there after her wedding because she was so young: now, however, she gave Henrietta Maria just the excuse she needed to slip away abroad.

The King had tried to arrest Pym and his colleagues, but they had been warned, and evaded them. Parliament was now stronger than ever. Charles now planned to go north, to join his army and declare war on Parliament. Hidden in Henrietta Maria's luggage were some of the Crown Jewels, which she intended to pawn for money to raise arms and men for the Royalist cause.

Jermyn's first reaction was to join her at The Hague. But when he reached the Dutch frontier, the surly border guards barred his way. The Dutch parliament, the States General, whose sympathies lay with Parliament, had refused permission for any of the Queen's 'poor traitors' to cross their borders.

While Jermyn languished in the Spanish-ruled province of Brabant, Henrietta Maria complained to Charles, 'I have nobody in the world in whom to trust for your service, and many things are at a standstill, for want of someone to serve me'.

Eventually, the Prince of Orange persuaded the States General to order the border guards to turn a blind eye to Jermyn and his friends. They travelled rapidly north under the immense canvas of the Dutch sky, through a flat landscape crisscrossed with ditches and dykes, each lined with rows of green willows and silver-leafed poplars.

On the night of Tuesday, 14 June 1642, while the Puritan burghers of The Hague snored peacefully, the Queen's coach clattered down the Staedt-Straat, the street leading to the gates of her temporary residence, the New Palace. Out into the moonlight stepped three cloaked figures: Percy, D'Avenant and Jermyn.

Taking the Queen's chaotic paperwork in hand, Jermyn set to work finalising the loans she had secured on the pawned Crown Jewels, buying ammunition and hiring ships and men.

On bright mornings, while the seagulls wheeled and cried overhead, Parliamentarian agents lurking about the bustling quays of the main Dutch seaport, Hellevoetsluis, were unnerved to see upwards of eighty Englishmen and volunteer French officers, especially Jermyn and the dashing Marquess of Vieuville, merrily toasting the first supply-ships departing for England.

Jermyn's influence on royal policy, which had been curtailed so dramatically in May 1641, was now re-established in a profound manner. Charles and Henrietta Maria communicated by a secret code, involving the substitution of letters by numbers. Henrietta Maria used to infuriate the King by misreading her code sheet and thus sending him unintelligible messages.

Once she painstakingly deciphered a letter from her husband

only to find that it contained a testy criticism of her mistakes. 'It is a great trouble to me', she ciphered back laboriously, 'to write the number of letters which I must write in cipher; for, since I have been in Holland, I have almost always pains in my eyes, and my sight is not so good as it was'.

She asked the King to allow Jermyn to cipher her letters for her, reminding him 'as to our affairs, he knows them already, for you know how you and I trust in him, and that we have always found him faithful'.

From then on, Jermyn ciphered Henrietta Maria's letters to the King and deciphered the returning correspondence too. He became thus uniquely and automatically privy to the most intimate correspondence between the separated King and Queen.

And because Jermyn was writing the Queen's letters for her, there was nothing she could not discuss with him. Jermyn's ideas could reach to the very heart of Henrietta Maria's decisions, making it impossible in most instances to determine where Henrietta Maria's ideas stopped and Jermyn's started. They were just as D'Avenant had characterised the perfect union of lovers in another of the poems in *Madagascar*,

> Live still, the pleasure of each other's sight;
> To each, a new made wonder, and delight;
> Though two, yet both so much one constant mind,
> That 'twill be art and mystery to find
> (Your thoughts and wishes being still the same)
> From which of either's loving heart they came.

That is exactly the problem faced by historians and biographers reading Henrietta Maria's letters from this period – and a problem deftly sidestepped by them all, for they generally ignore

Jermyn altogether. Yet in fact there is no problem at all. To try to make sense of Henrietta Maria's actions without Jermyn, or vice versa, is impossible. From now on, most of the time, Jermyn and Henrietta Maria would unite to present the world with a resilient, dynamic front.

On Friday, 22 August 1642, Charles I unfurled his standard at Nottingham. News reached Holland. The Civil War had begun.

On hearing the news of the outbreak of the Civil War, Jermyn and Henrietta Maria hired two hundred soldiers in the southern province of Zeeland and engaged eighteen ships to carry them and a large supply of ammunition to Portsmouth, where George Goring, who had decided after all to side with the Crown, was now being besieged by Parliamentarians.

Just as the Queen and Jermyn's ships were ready to sail, however, the local authorities impounded them. When Jermyn went to Zeeland himself to protest, the authorities took malicious pleasure in throwing the handsome Cavalier into prison. It was not until mid-September that the Prince of Orange managed to secure Jermyn's release and also to enable the ships to set sail for England.

Other vessels set out too to bolster the northern army, which was now commanded by the Earl of Newcastle. One vessel carrying the unfortunate D'Avenant was captured at Yarmouth. After that, the wind changed and the remainder of Henrietta Maria's fleet tossed uselessly at anchor at Hellevoetsluis.

It must have been an extraordinary feeling for Jermyn to stand on the low dunes at Hellevoetsluis, gazing out across the Haringvliet, one of the branching mouths of the mighty Rhine, as it poured into the North Sea near The Hague. In front of him swayed a forest of bobbing masts, whilst the air was full of the sounds of creaking timbers, the slapping of rope against mast, and the wind whistling through the furled sails. Five hundred and seventy eight years earlier Duke William had assembled his fleet of ships further down the coast in Normandy and sailed out to conquer England. Some two thousand years before that, they believed, Trojan Brutus had beached his black ships on Devon's shores, to rid fair Albion of giants. Now, Jermyn and Henrietta Maria were braced to embark on an enterprise that seemed to them no less audacious – to wrest their country from the grip of Parliament.

But it was not until January 1643 that Jermyn and the Queen, pacing frustratedly about their temporary home, the New Palace in The Hague, were finally told the wind had changed. On Thursday, 19 January, they hastened along the coast to Scheveningen, the fishing village that doubled up as The Hague's harbour. Here, they climbed aboard the *Princess Royal*, weighed anchor and set out across the rolling seas.

Together with eleven transport ships and Admiral Tromp's escort of Dutch warships they ploughed steadily northwest across the North Sea.

All went well until they drew near the English coast. Then the sky darkened and a gale started to tear at the ships' sails. At one point they could even see the Yorkshire coastline between the towering waves. Below the decks the noise of the sea hissing and crashing was almost drowned by the shrieks of the Queen's attendants, women and men alike.

Only Henrietta Maria and Jermyn remained calm. God had never allowed an English queen to drown, she told Jermyn cheerfully, and he was unlikely to start now. She was right. Their nine-day voyage ended when they were swept back into Scheveningen terrified and exhausted, their clothes caked in salt.

After two weeks the wind relented. Gathering together their

traumatised household they set out again. The weather was calmer now and, on Friday, 10 February, Henrietta Maria and Henry Jermyn stepped onto the stone quay of the Yorkshire fishing port of Bridlington.

Later that day, Lord Newcastle, commander of the King's northern army, rode into Bridlington. After a celebratory meal, they settled down to sleep in a house near the quayside.

At five in the morning Jermyn awoke to the sound of cannons booming out at sea and cannon balls crashing into the nearby houses. News of their arrival had reached the Parliamentarians. During the night, a squadron of Parliamentarian ships had sailed up to the harbour and had now opened fire.

Dragging Henrietta Maria out of bed, Jermyn ran with her down stairs and out of the front door. Suddenly, she gave a cry, turned round and dashed back upstairs. To the astonished Jermyn, she shouted that she could not leave her little lapdog Mitte behind in such dangerous circumstances. She emerged a minute later, the ugly little dog tucked safely under her arm.

They ran together through the dark night, crouched low to avoid the cannon balls that whistled past their heads. One servant collapsed when a bullet struck him. Jermyn and Henrietta Maria threw themselves into an icy ditch, gasping for breath, their hearts pounding in their ears.

There they hid until Admiral Tromp manoeuvred his ships around to return fire. If it was not for him, they might have been captured. But thanks to the Dutch cannons, the sails of the Parliamentarian ships disappeared at last into the dank fog of the January dawn.

Drying off their armaments and mustering their bedraggled household, Jermyn, Henrietta Maria and their officers rode three miles inland to Boynton Hall.

Here, they began recruiting soldiers. The local gentry, many of whom were Catholics, flocked to them with more men, arms and horses. When they marched to York, even more Yorkshiremen came to swell their ranks.

Taking command of the ancient city, that had once been the capital of Roman Britain, they sent their troops to help Lord Newcastle drive General Fairfax's Parliamentarian army out of the county. But before they were able to complete the task Charles, whose own army was under threat in Oxford, ordered them to come south.

On Tuesday, 23 May, the newly-promoted Colonel Henry Jermyn proudly unfurled the new flag of the Queen's Lifeguards. On its red field was a single gold fleur-de-lys, representing Henrietta Maria's native France, surmounted by the golden crown of the Queen of England. Some five thousand foot soldiers and fifty companies of cavalry and dragoons, led by a mixture of French and English officers, marched out of the southern gate of York.

Their horses and oxen strained to pull six cannons, two mortars and a hundred and fifty wagons of baggage and powder. Precious too were their supplies of matches that, in the days before flintlocks, were used to light the gunpowder that fired cannon and musket balls alike.

Their friend Will Crofts, whose family were Suffolk neighbours of the Jermyns, held his head up proudly as the regiment's new Lieutenant Colonel. But most excited of all was Henrietta Maria, the 'she-majesty generalissima', as she described herself proudly in a letter to Charles, 'over all'. She was not playing at being a general: the daughter of the great warrior-king of France, Henri IV, really was one. Gone were her gilded carriages. Now, she rode on horseback alongside Jermyn in wind and rain, eating her meals at a simple table within sight of her soldiers.

'Generalissima', sneered the Parliamentarian pamphleteers 'and next to herself, Harry'. But for all their enemies' scorn, their march south was a conspicuous success. The Parliamentarian garrison of Burton-on-Trent opened the town's gates to them, 'and at Nottingham', wrote the Queen, 'we had the experience that one of our troops had beaten six of theirs, and made them fly'.

On Sunday, 18 June, their brave flag fluttered over the town of Newark. They paused there to refurbish their supplies and recruit new soldiers.

This delay was a mistake, for it meant they did not reach Tamworth in time to stop it falling into Parliamentarian hands. But 'it is not a great matter', Henrietta Maria told Lord Newcastle, optimistically, for 'it will not prevent me from going on Wednesday to join the King. To-morrow, I will send you my cipher; it is Jermyn's fault that you have not had it', she added, 'for I had given it to him to copy'.

Just as the Royalists quickly earned the nickname 'Cavaliers' – from the French word for mounted warriors, so too did their adversaries acquire a sobriquet – 'Roundheads'. It is often thought this came from the rounded helmets they wore, but in fact the term was coined by Henrietta Maria herself. One day, watching Strafford's trial in Parliament, she had seen Pym's pudding-bowl haircut, and asked 'who is that round-headed man?'. The term was later expanded from Pym to encompass the soldiers who supported his cause.

Now, it was these very Roundheads, led by Lord Essex, whose superior numbers now threatened Jermyn and Henrietta Maria, as they hurried south-west towards Stratford-on-Avon, where they hoped to meet Prince Rupert.

The two Royalist forces rendezvoused at Stratford on Wednesday, 12 July. The excitable teenager who had shared his dreams of Madagascar with Jermyn was now a dashing Royalist general and already one of the Roundheads' deadliest enemies.

That night they sat down with Rupert to a triumphant dinner in the house where Shakespeare had lived and died, and were waited on by the playwright's granddaughter.

Two days later they entered Kineton Vale below Edgehill, their splendid banners fluttering under a broad blue July sky, and saw Charles riding towards them, flanked by crowds of courtiers including an effusive Endymion Porter.

Beyond them lay Oxford, a city that had remained staunchly loyal to the King. On Friday, 14 July, they rode triumphantly past the trenches and earthen ramparts that encircled the great city of learning, while the crowds threw their hats in the air with joy.

The first thing Henrietta Maria asked Charles when she reached Oxford was for Jermyn to be made a baron.

This was no mere act of empty gratitude. Being ennobled would entitle Jermyn to sit in the House of Lords. But, more pertinently, it would guarantee him a swift beheading, rather than a lengthy death by hanging, drawing and quartering, should Parliament ever capture him. It seems unlikely that Jermyn himself ever seriously contemplated such a fate – his dogged determination to win the war could brook no possibility of failure – but at least Henrietta Maria could feel that, for once, she had done something to protect him from the worst excesses of Parliamentarian vengeance.

On Friday, 8 September 1643, at the stamp of the King's seal on the letters patent, Colonel Henry Jermyn became Henry, Baron Jermyn of St Edmundsbury in the County of Suffolk. Four months later, Henrietta Maria made a more personal affirmation of his unique position of trust by making him her Lord Chamberlain, and thus placing him in complete overall control of her entire household.

Their arrival at Oxford with a fresh regiment was most timely. Their men, officers, arms and ammunition, all brought success-fully from Holland via Yorkshire, freed Charles from having to remain holed up behind the town's ramparts. During the remainder of the summer the King, and Rupert, marched through Somerset, capturing Bristol and laying siege to Gloucester. With Lord Essex's advance, however, the King was forced to withdraw and both sides started a desperate race back towards London – and it looked as if Essex might win.

As the Parliamentary forces neared Newbury, Lord Jermyn raised his standard once again and rode out of Oxford at the head of his regiment, intending to delay Essex, while the Royalist army caught up.

While Henrietta Maria fretted anxiously in the oak-panelled lodgings which she shared with Jermyn in Merton College, her new Lord Chamberlain marched his men along the winding lanes of Berkshire and down into Wiltshire. Essex reached Swindon on Sunday, 17 September and the next day Jermyn encountered a detachment of Roundheads on the stubble fields of Aldbourne Chase. At last, the heroic champion of Madagascar had real enemies to fight.

Instead of Endymion Porter and Rupert, however, Jermyn was flanked by the Marquess de Vieuville, the leading French officer who had accompanied them from Holland, and George Digby. The son of Lord Bristol, and Jermyn's old friend from the Madrid embassy, Digby was now a grown man, 'graceful and beautiful... of great eloquence and becomingness in his discourse, save that he sometimes seemed a little affected'. He had started his Parliamentary career siding with Pym, but had rapidly changed sides and was now an ardent Royalist.

Jermyn drew his rapier and gave the order to attack. With

musket balls whistling past their ears, the Cavaliers charged forward to engage Essex's infantry at close quarters.

Once, a Parliamentarian officer, anonymous behind the sinister iron grill of his helmet, fired his pistol point-blank at Digby. Urging his horse forward, Jermyn ran the officer through with his sword and, turning, must have been relieved to see Digby, his big elegant face flushed scarlet, alive and unhurt. Suddenly, there came cries from the rear. Essex's cavalry had made their way round behind them. The foot soldiers of the Queen's Regiment, fearful of being trampled to death, were fleeing.

Jermyn and his officers found themselves trapped, guns and pikes before them and cavalry to the rear. Conferring hastily, they agreed that it would be both honourable and probably somewhat safer to charge forward into the enemy's infantry than to try to retreat. Their colours flying – four of Jermyn's standard-bearers had not fled – they charged forward shouting their war-cry 'God for Queen Mary!', the English version of the name of their heroine, Henrietta Maria herself.

Leaning down from their saddles they slashed their rapiers at any Roundheads bold enough to stand in their way. It was a terrifying spectacle for both sides: a mass of darkly-clad Roundhead foot soldiers surrounding a small party of brightly-dressed Cavaliers, their swords dripping with blood as their chargers reared and pounded their way forward.

Within sight of clear ground Jermyn felt a searing pain in his arm as a bullet penetrated his sleeve. Despite this, he managed to keep his grip on the reigns. Another pistol bullet struck Vieuville, piercing straight through his gleaming breastplate. The marquess slumped over his horse's neck and fell to the ground, dead. Goaded by anger, Jermyn and the other remaining Royalists cut their way through the last ranks of the enemy and galloped away, bullets raining down around them.

So perilous was the danger and so brave the escape that even Jermyn's harshest of critics, the brilliant lawyer Edward Hyde, soon to become Charles I's Chancellor of the Exchequer, praised 'the excellent temper of his arms'. The poet Abraham Cowley was carried away by the excitement. What was a formidable army to Jermyn, he asked? 'He charged it through; with unfeared noise the bullets round him flew'. Unless the adrenaline-rush had overpowered Jermyn completely, he would have been terrified. But he had survived and brought his horse clattering back into the courtyard of Merton College.

Henrietta Maria tended to his wounded arm as best she and the academics of Oxford could. For days, Jermyn lay in bed, sweating and delirious. But at last the fever passed, and the wound healed without developing an infection, or the need for agonising amputation.

Meanwhile, after the skirmish at Aldbourne Chase, the armies had regrouped. Jermyn's men joined with the King and Rupert to meet Essex's Roundheads in the Battle of Newbury. Essex scored a significant victory, not by any means destroying the King's forces, but halting any hope of advancing on London that season.

Although he was later to write proudly of the courage of 'my troopes', Jermyn never fought again. His regiment, under another commander, was annihilated at the battle of Shelford House in 1645. Yet just because Jermyn never fought in another Civil War battle does not mean his part in the conflict was at an end.

In the history of the bitter struggle between King Charles I and Parliament, Jermyn's involvement had only just begun.

IX

'THE STRONGEST PILLAR IN THE LAND'
1644

Fair as unshaded light; or as the day
In its first birth, when all the year was May;
Sweet, as the altar's smoke, or as the new
Unfolded bud, swelled by the early dew;
Smooth, as the face of waters first appeared,
Ere tides began to strive, or winds were heard;
Kind, as the willing saints, but calmer far
Than in their sleeps forgiven hermits are:
You that are more than our discreter fear
Dares praise, with such dull art, what make you here?
Sir William D'Avenant, 'To the Queen…' 1637

In the winter the roads became so waterlogged that soldiers could sink up to their knees in mud. The harsh frosts bit through the thickest cloaks.

Because of this, armies rarely campaigned during the winter months.

As soon as the autumn fogs began to settle, the opposing armies ensconced themselves in their winter quarters. At the King's base at Oxford all the colleges and houses rang with the rousing songs of the Royalist officers and their wives, while the hovels of the poor were overcrowded with carousing infantrymen.

In Merton College near the River Thames, which Oxford's dons call the River Isis, the newly ennobled Lord Jermyn drank and sang with old friends and made new ones.

Amongst the latter was a young man called Abraham Cowley. The son of a London grocer, Cowley was destined to become just as popular a poet in his own time as D'Avenant, although neither would remain so well known in later centuries: their poetry was primarily for their own age, rather than for all time.

Cowley had already met Jermyn's cousin John Hervey of Ickworth. Through Hervey, he was now introduced to Jermyn himself. Cowley was immediately drawn to the imposingly-built Cavalier who had devoted his life to the service of the Queen of England.

There is a story that exists in several incarnations, set in various places, and concerning either the King or Prince Charles. One version places it in Oxford, at this time, and concerns the King, Jermyn and Cowley, and is as follows.

It so happened, one day, that Charles I followed a common aristocratic practise of the time, by trying to divine his future by pointing at random to a passage in Virgil's *Aeneid*, that stirring tale of how Aeneas had left the burning ruins of Troy, and journeyed across the Mediterranean to found a Trojan colony in Italy, from which would emerge the great city of Rome. Charles picked some lines that happened to be the lines spoken by Queen Dido of Carthage when, finding that Aeneas must abandon her in order to continue his divinely-ordained mission, she laid a terrible curse upon him. None of them could agree on a lyrical translation, so Jermyn sent it to Cowley, and this is what the poet wrote:

> By a bold people's stubborn arms oppressed,
> Forced to forsake the land he once possessed,
> Torn from his dearest son, let him in vain
> Seek help, and see his friends unjustly slain.

Let him to base unequal termes submit,
In hope to save his crown, yet loose both it
And life at once, untimely let him die...

Aeneas had been forced to forsake Troy, and saw many of his friends slain, but the rest of the curse did not fall on him. How ironic it was that Charles, who believed himself to be descended, via the Welsh ancestors of the Tudors, from Aeneas's great grandson Brutus, was to become the recipient of all these other outpourings of jilted Dido's venom.

Ever since Jermyn's attempt in 1641 to quell Parliament using the King's army in the north, Parliamentarian propaganda had identified Jermyn and, by association, Henrietta Maria, as being amongst the most enthusiastic promoters of the war. While in public they both voiced their support for a peace plan proposed by Kensington, their general policy was indeed to encourage the King to fight rather than compromise with his enemies. Their deep conviction was that the prerogative of power should lie with Charles alone. In any event, Parliament had declared Jermyn a traitor and had even impeached Henrietta Maria, *in absentia*, in May 1643. No room was left for compromise: the Royalists simply had to win.

Together with his new friend Cowley, Jermyn spent many hours at an Oxford scholar's writing desk in his temporary home overlooking the peaceful Fellows' Gardens at Merton, composing articles for the propaganda newsbook *Mercurius Aulicus*.

To be feared less than Parliament, he realised, was proving to be of no advantage to the King's cause. So when Rupert proposed that Royalist troops should exact the same sort of reprisals on civilians who had helped Parliamentarians as the enemy practised on those who helped Royalists, Jermyn supported him. Henceforth houses were burned, women raped and men beaten and robbed by Royalists as well as Roundheads. The war was a real one and Jermyn shared Rupert's iron resolve to win it at whatever price.

The political intrigue and the seventeenth century office politics which had riddled the peace-time court in London was nothing compared to the insecurities, jealousies and back-stabbing that seethed behind the ramparts of Oxford that winter. Lord Percy tried to persuade Charles to dismiss Jermyn from the Queen's household, arguing that, as the most instrumental figure in the Army Plot, his presence in Oxford cast the King in a bad light. As in the Eleanor Villiers scandal, Charles may have been tempted by this excuse to separate Henrietta Maria from her favourite, but a stern rebuke from his wife made him drop the idea.

'The fault is partly yours', she chided her husband, 'for if a person [like Percy] speaks to you boldly, you refuse nothing'.

A more serious challenge to Jermyn's position came from George Digby, the straight-nosed and slightly conceited son of the Earl of Bristol and one of Jermyn's companions on the embassy to Madrid, right back at the start of his career. Digby had chosen the Royalist side over the Parliamentarians, but at The Hague, his pompous behaviour towards the Prince of Orange had done nothing to help the cause, and had greatly diminished his standing in Henrietta Maria's eyes.

The ambitious young courtier was acutely jealous that the Queen rated Jermyn's diplomatic skills far higher than his own. Charles – perhaps deliberately – took precisely the opposite view, promoting Digby to the Privy Council and making him, not Jermyn, his second Secretary of State. From this new position of power, Digby felt confident enough not to conceal his personal contempt either for Jermyn or Jermyn's friend, Prince Rupert.

As soon as the winter frosts were over and enough green grass had begun to sprout up to feed horses on the move, Rupert marched away to relieve Newark from a Parliamentarian siege. Once the Prince had left, Digby did everything he could to undermine him, so Jermyn became the Prince's protector. When Digby talked Henrietta Maria into opposing Rupert's appointment as military President of Wales, Jermyn had to persuade her to change her mind.

Aware that Digby was deliberately starving Rupert of supplies and intelligence reports, Jermyn sent him both. The effort was enormous. 'This is of more trouble to me', Jermyn commented once, 'than it would be pain to me at parting of my flesh and bones'. But overall, he succeeded. 'I find Prince Rupert nor all the numbers in arithmetic have any efficacy, but are cyphers', a courtier commented wryly, 'without lord Jermyn'.

But mere concerns over troop movements and siege works took second place in the minds of some courtiers to more trivial concerns which added a somewhat surreal touch to life in Oxford. One of the oddest was a certain Mrs Frescheville's 'most violent ambition to have her husband created a Baron'.

Having been bombarded with evidence of the hen-pecked Mr Frescheville's right to two baronies, Charles delegated to Jermyn the somewhat daunting task of giving her a warrant for only one. As the parchment was snatched out of his hand, Jermyn started to explain the situation, but Mrs Frescheville's rage was unstoppable and she fell 'into intemperate expressions both of the King and Queen'. By all accounts, Jermyn retreated from this unexpected battlefield without daring to put up a fight.

* * *

Throughout the winter, Henrietta Maria and Jermyn lived together at Merton College, while Charles slept in his own, cold bed across the meads in Christ Church College. This does not mean that she was spending the nights with Jermyn – indeed, surrounded by ladies of the bedchamber, that would scarcely have been possible. Yet we cannot rule out the possibility that, increasingly irritated by her husband's failure to measure up to the decisive military genius of her late father, and increasingly dependent on Jermyn, with his soul composed of 'the eagle and the dove', Henrietta Maria was seeking solace – we do not know whether we can correctly add the word 'again' – in her Lord Chamberlain's arms.

In any event, Henrietta Maria became pregnant again. Now, as the March days lengthened, news reached them that Roundhead troops were closing in on Oxford.

The prospect of a siege unnerved Henrietta Maria considerably. Morbid visions of delivering her new baby straight into the waiting hands of a coarse Parliamentarian gaoler swarmed through her mind. Perhaps too, if the baby was actually Jermyn's, she did not want to give birth under Charles's nose. For either or both reasons, she told Jermyn she wanted to leave Oxford before the siege began.

'I was never more against anything in my life than this remove', Jermyn told Rupert. There was no telling what disasters would befall them on the open road. And just as serious, for Jermyn, was that his renewed absence from the court would allow Digby to gain more political ground at his expense.

But despite all his impassioned arguments, Henrietta Maria remained adamant. Her bones ached due to fever and her voice was weak from coughing, but she set off, with a detachment of

Jermyn's regiment as a bodyguard, on Wednesday, 17 April 1644. Her anxious husband went with her as far as Abingdon. There he stood and waved farewell as her little party started winding its way away through the Vale of the White Horse. He would never see her again.

Urgent business for Rupert detained Jermyn at Oxford another week. Then, he said his farewells, final ones, as it transpired, to the King and to his own father, now a sprightly seventy-three-years old, still puffing away at his clay pipe. And then he came galloping after Henrietta Maria, to be by her side once more.

In order to protect her from the jolting of a carriage, the Queen was carried in a litter, an enclosed coach carried on shafts slung between oxen. As this ungainly conveyance lurched along she coughed weakly and nursed her belly.

With her travelled a small collection of attendants, a select microcosm of her once enormous entourage of ladies, gentlemen, monkeys and dwarfs. In the litter with her was Jeffrey Hudson, a midget from Rutland, whom Buckingham had presented to her, probably as a veiled insult to her own relatively short stature, but whom she had come to love as a surrogate child. Her chief lady-in-waiting, the Duchess of Richmond, sat with the Queen, trying to comfort and amuse her. Jermyn and Will Crofts rode by the side of the litter, their careworn faces growing brown in the strong spring sun. Behind them marched their soldiers carrying pikes and muskets over their shoulders.

They passed through the Somerset fens, made bright by pied daisies, blue violets and golden swathes of buttercups. But rather than listen to the skylarks warbling overhead, their ears strained in case they heard the rumbling of Roundheads galloping after them. Passing Bridgewater they lumbered through the quiet Devon lanes until at last they reached the safety of Exeter and the welcoming smile of its governor, Jermyn's cousin Jack Berkeley.

Even as Henrietta Maria prepared herself for the ordeal of giving birth, news reached them that the army of their old Parliamentarian adversary Lord Essex was marching on the city.

Jermyn was sanguine that Exeter could withstand a siege of two months, 'there being provisions and ammunition amply for so long time'. He was far more concerned about Henrietta Maria, wracked with what is now thought to have been tuberculosis, 'ill at ease and full of fears' and still 'not brought abed'.

In the seventeenth century, the chances of an average woman dying in childbirth were almost seventy times higher than they are today. Henrietta Maria's debilitated condition made the odds greater still. She herself was convinced she would not survive. She even entrusted Jermyn with a last message to take back to the King.

On Sunday, 16 June 1644, she went into a long, dangerous labour, resulting in the birth of a healthy baby girl, Henrietta Anne. 'Anne' was chosen to flatter Anne, Queen Regent of France: 'Henrietta' could have been after Henrietta Maria herself, or her father or, again, it is not impossible that the Queen intended this female form of Henry to honour her friend and guardian, Henry Jermyn.

Perhaps, we may speculate, the name commemorated an even closer connection between Jermyn and the little princess – of father and daughter. It is impossible to say for sure. But the biological truth is not so important or relevant as the emotional truth that, throughout her life, the dominant father-figure in Henrietta Anne's life would always be, not Charles I, but Henry Jermyn.

Henrietta Maria survived, but only just. Temporarily unable to see through one eye, she had lost the feeling in one arm and could scarcely breathe, whilst her legs felt like ice. Jermyn insisted she must rest. But 'it was not possible', Jermyn told Digby, 'for her to overcome the apprehension she had of being shut up'. She decided she could only be safe in France and 'therefore exposes herself to more dangers than those she could have undergone in this city in respect of her health and the sea'.

Roundhead soldiers patrolled the countryside outside the city walls, forcing her party to split up and leave in small groups. It was impossible to take the baby princess with them, for her cries would have given them away in an instant. Feeling wretchedly powerless, they had no choice but to leave her behind, to be nursed by Lady Morton.

A mere three miles out of Exeter, Henrietta Maria's party heard Roundheads coming, and were forced to hide under a pile of rubbish, she trying desperately not to cough while the enemy soldiers poked about nearby. Only once they had gone away could she join Jermyn, little Jeffrey Hudson and the rest of her attendants, as arranged, in a hut on the Plymouth Road.

Their excruciatingly slow flight took them around the southern edge of Dartmoor, past Totnes, where they probably saw the very stone onto which Brutus was said to have stepped, when he first came ashore to fight the giants. Now, fleeing their own monsters, they hastened over the Tamar into Cornwall. A Parliamentarian propagandist described their journey, with Henrietta Maria in her litter and Jermyn

> riding by her, and upon every stop (as she made many) the courtier's officious hand appeared to support her weak body upon occasions of stirring or removing herself in the litter, and when she was pleased (contrary to the directions of her

physicians) to walk on foot, his arm (which she conceives as mighty as the strongest pillar of this land) warranted her health more than... the most skilled physicians.

Jermyn was even ready, wrote the propagandist, sarcastically, to throw his fine cloak down over any mud they encountered, a clear allusion to the story of the gallantry Sir Walter Raleigh was said to have shown to Elizabeth I.

The Royalist Francis Basset, who saw them passing through Launceston, told a truer story. 'Here is the woefullest spectacle my eyes yet ever looked on, the most worn and weakest pitiful creature in the world, the poor Queen shifting for an hour's life longer'.

A devious Jermyn scowls at the world from this unflattering anti-Royalist cartoon of him, printed during the Civil War.

At last they reached the tiny harbour-town of Falmouth and its granite manor house, Arwenack, the ancestral home of Jermyn's mother and of his Killigrew cousins. Henrietta Maria's nerves may have been soothed by their excited chatter, and she may have relaxed a little, gazing out with her one good eye through the narrow casement windows, across the brilliant blue waters of the Fal estuary. Meanwhile, Jermyn could ride up the hill to inspect the powerful Tudor fortress of Pendennis and to confer with its governor, his cousin Sir William Killigrew.

The stronghold seemed almost impregnable, yet nothing would induce Henrietta Maria to remain on British soil any longer. With the Killigrews' help, Jermyn engaged ships to take them to France. On Sunday, 14 July they boarded a man-of-war and set sail with an escort of ten Cornish merchantmen.

The escort was certainly necessary. Scarcely had they left the protective range of Pendennis' cannons than Parliamentarian sails appeared on the horizon. The prospect of capture was unbearable. The Queen ordered Captain Colster that, if it seemed certain they would be caught, he must light the gunpowder in the hold and blow them all to pieces.

Arwenack, Falmouth, home of Jermyn's mother's family, the Killigrews.

The chase continued right across the Channel until, within sight of Jersey, French ships appeared and the Parliamentarians turned away. But even then, safety was not ensured. As fast as their enemies' sails disappeared, black clouds sped across the sky and a gale blew up, scattering their own fleet and driving the

Queen's ship out towards the perilous Atlantic. Colster's men battled frantically with the sails, forcing the storm-tossed vessel ever closer to the Breton coast until at last they were nearly cast onto the rocks of a wild cove at Chastel near Brest.

Clinging to the sides of their ship's longboats, the Queen, Jermyn and their companions were rowed through the crashing surf. Their clothes saturated by the cold salt water, they scrabbled about trying to steady themselves on the murderous rocks. And then, just as safety finally seemed assured, they saw the dark shapes of peasants running down into the cove, brandishing hoes and scythes. Jermyn and Crofts could not use their pistols because the powder was drenched. Instead they dragged their rapiers out of their damp scabbards and Colster brandished his cutlass.

At their feet, the two-foot high Jeffrey Hudson brandished his own tiny sword, fiercely keen to protect the Queen by any means he could. Above the boom of the tide and the howling of the wind, Jermyn shouted out that he was the Lord Jermyn, Lord Chamberlain to the Queen of England.

The uncomprehending peasants shouted back in their guttural Breton that they would kill them for being pirates, and bore down on them. Jermyn shouted even louder, in his best French, trying to make the peasants understand that they were not pirates. Waving his rapier towards the Queen, who was floundering about in her long skirts in the surf, coughing violently and trying to catch hold of the lap-dog Mitte, Jermyn finally succeeded in explaining to the peasants that they were in the presence of none other than Henrietta Maria de Bourbon, daughter of King Henri IV of France.

After an uncomfortable night spent in the peasants' hovels, Henrietta Maria and her company set off slowly for Bourbon, where she intended to relax and, as was her wont, drink its bitter but supposedly medicinal spa-water. But Jermyn took a different route, galloping away alone to Paris. After a 375-mile ride across the parched fields of northern France he presented himself, dusty and exhausted, in the office of the new French First Minister, Cardinal Mazarin. Having secured formal permission for Henrietta Maria and her retinue to enter France, Jermyn then galloped back to be at her side again.

He found the Queen resting at the beautiful Château of Amboise overlooking the broad sweep of the Loire Valley. With its high white towers with slate-blue roofs, Amboise had been the beloved retirement-place of Leonardo da Vinci, only a century earlier. Now it served as a temporary haven for Jermyn and Henrietta Maria before they embarked in their stately barges to travel up the Loire, past Orléans and Nevers and into the very heart of France.

The bitter mineral waters of Bourbon soothed away the worst of Henrietta Maria's toothaches, migraines, agues and coughs. She never fully recovered her health and her cough was to plague her for the rest of life. But when they began their slow journey to Paris that autumn, they both felt refreshed.

Their arrival in Paris had the air of a triumphal march, the French royal family riding with them in their gilded carriages over the Pont Neuf while the crowds cheered the return of Henri IV's daughter. Jermyn's mind was already brimming with schemes to help Charles win the war. Some were in effect already. As they entered Paris, Jermyn and Henrietta Maria looked forward eagerly to being able to enter London again soon, riding at the head of an all-conquering invasion force.

X

'SOME SUCCOUR FOR ENGLAND'
1644 – 1645

But to this end your Highness must enter into a true knowledge of our affairs, and must begin to think on what in all appearance may bring us through; and to resolve yourself not to use only ordinary means, but to use all other whereof we may stand in need.

Jermyn to Frederick Henry, Prince of Orange, 6/16 August 1644

The French court that gave such a warm welcome to Henrietta Maria and her Lord Chamberlain was very different to the one Jermyn had known before the war.

On Sunday, 4 December 1642, while he and the Queen waited for the wind to change at Scheveningen before sailing to England, Cardinal Richelieu had died. Five months later Louis XIII followed him to the grave, leaving the widowed Queen Anne to become Regent of France on behalf of her little son Louis XIV. For her First Minister she had turned unhesitatingly to Richelieu's debonair Roman protégé Giulio Mazarini, Cardinal Mazarin.

Three years Jermyn's senior, the Roman-born Cardinal had a handsome, rounded face with expressive brown eyes and a moustache and beard clipped immaculately to form a 'T' shape across his pursed pink lips.

But appearance aside, Mazarin and Jermyn had a great deal in common. Both were consummately good at being courtiers. They had devoted their lives to serving queens and had won vast amounts of power and money as a consequence. Like Jermyn,

Mazarin's relationship with his royal mistress went far beyond mere servitude. The boy-King Louis XIV was born twenty-three years after Louis XIII and Anne's wedding. Few writers then or now have doubted that Cardinal Mazarin was the real father of the young King of France.

Jules, Cardinal Mazarin

At Jermyn's request Mazarin and Anne gave Henrietta Maria use of the old royal apartments in the Medieval heart of the Louvre. The Louvre is one of the buildings most closely associated with the French nation, yet while Jermyn and Henrietta Maria lived there a surprising amount of English political decisions were made under its roof.

With the French court now enjoying the newer Palais Royale over the road, the Louvre was no longer the sumptuous palace either Jermyn or Henrietta Maria remembered. Its rich tapestries and furniture now adorned the walls of the Palais Royale, leaving the Louvre's cold corridors echoing with the clatter of the royal printing press and the coarse laughter of the masons who were busy building, chiselling and hammering stones for a new gallery running north from the section where they lived.

From the streets nearby they could hear the catcalls and curses of the tradesmen. A fetid smell arose from the rubbish piled in the moat, masked only in high summer when it was surpassed by the stench of the Seine.

Gradually, though, it became home. Cowley, D'Avenant and Jermyn's cousin Jack Berkeley were amongst those who escaped from England to join them. Cowley became Jermyn's secretary, ciphering all his business letters – but he did not, as his biographer later claimed, cipher those of Henrietta Maria. That most secret of work remained Jermyn's exclusive preserve.

Better for their spirits than the Louvre was Henrietta Maria's childhood residence, Saint-Germain-en-Laye. Mazarin and Anne gave them use of apartments in the Château Neuf at Saint-Germain, and they spent as much time there as possible enjoying what Jermyn termed its 'country air'.

Set on a wooded escarpment the palace complex of Saint-Germain centred on a towering, octagonal Italianate castle called the Château Vieux, built almost a century earlier and occupied by Henrietta Maria's brother Gaston of Orléans. Nearby stood the Château Neuf, built two storeys high out of warm-coloured brick by Henrietta Maria's parents. Down the steep slope below tumbled the famous 'hanging gardens' – terrace upon terrace full of statues; fountains and frescos – right down to the meadows.

From the balustrade in front of the château, Jermyn and Henrietta Maria could gaze out over the Seine valley as it curved away southeast towards the chimney-tops of Paris, five miles distant. It was a beautiful view, but it was also one that served as a sharp reminder of something both Henrietta Maria and Jermyn felt with equal concern – how far they were becoming from the centre of things.

* * *

In his first audience with Mazarin, Jermyn begged successfully for his soup and gold, persuading the Cardinal to grant Henrietta Maria a pension. Out of this he tried to feed and clothe their household and the many Royalist exiles who flocked to join them. He also had to provide the constant flow of supplies that Charles's armies needed so desperately. Even supplementing the pension with loans raised on the Crown Jewels was not enough, so Jermyn turned to other means.

Jermyn's father Sir Thomas died in January 1645, harassed with fines levied by a vindictive Parliament, and smelling strongly of stale tobacco. Jermyn inherited his father's Governorship of Jersey and obtained royal licenses for ships to plunder any merchantmen from Parliamentarian London that happened to sail past.

By a special patent, Charles granted Henrietta Maria the monopoly on selling tin from Royalist Cornwall. A fleet of loyal merchant vessels, including Captain Colster's, ran to and fro across the Channel, landing tin in the French ports and returning with Jermyn's newly-purchased military supplies. A typical letter from Jermyn to Secretary of State Digby, who was with the King in England (Friday, 9 May 1645), tells Charles that the Flemish Captain Haesdonck

> is gone from Dunkirk three weeks since with four frigates, 6,040 muskets, 2,000 pair of pistols, 1,200 carbines, 150 swords, 400 shovels, 27,000 lbs of match and 50,000 lbs of brimstone. I hope he has arrived before now. His arms were all embarked before [Capt] Allen arrived there, so that I cannot assure you that Allen will be provided with that proportion which I sent you word would be sent to

the Marquess of Montrose. The Queen has sent 400 barrels of gunpowder to Dartmouth, of which 200 have arrived there, and the rest will presently. She could not get the merchants to undertake the transport of these powder barrels without enlarging her credit for them in case they should not be paid in England.

Such a complex task of juggling loans, creditors, merchants and sea captains would have been almost impossible even without the obstructions created by the Dutch States General and the English Parliamentarian navy, to say nothing of the weather. And, whenever things went wrong, Digby lost no opportunity of placing the blame on Jermyn.

Then in May 1645, and without any warning, Digby persuaded Charles to transfer the tin monopoly to Sir Edward Hyde, the head of the Prince of Wales's household in the West County.

The sudden loss of income expected from the next shipment of tin had a devastating effect on the Louvre's system of rolling debts. Jermyn had just obtained an advance of money from the French to enable him to send supplies to the glamorous Scottish royalist Montrose, secured on the Queen's French pension for the next four months.

He had expected to pay the loan back with profits of fifteen shillings per hundred-weight from the next tin shipment. Now that these profits were to go to Hyde, Jermyn had to use a gift of money (20,000 pistoles, worth *very* roughly £10m in modern terms) from the French court, which he had intended to use to pay for Dutch ships to sail England, to send further supplies to Montrose instead. He had also to raise a further personal loan from the Venetian merchant Cantarini to redeem one of the pawned Crown Jewels, before it was lost forever.

The winner in this inter-Royalist tussle, Sir Edward Hyde, was the son of a family of prosperous Wiltshire gentry.

A thickset man even when young, he had a prominent double chin, eyes more contemplative than penetrating, and long, fair hair. His brilliant mind brooked no idleness in the country, so he had trained as a lawyer at Oxford and the Middle Temple in London.

Hyde had rapidly become one the best lawyers in the profession, with a well-deserved reputation for fair-mindedness, coupled with a strong sense of loyalty to his friends. Becoming a Member of Parliament, he sided initially with Pym, attacking corrupt royal judges and helping to prepare the motion that sent the Earl of Strafford to the executioner's block.

But Hyde was also a staunch Anglican and, when it emerged that Parliament was not whole-hearted in its support of the Established Church, yet the King was, he changed sides adroitly. Rapidly promoted in 1643 to be Chancellor of the Exchequer – the head of the Royalist government's finances – Hyde was ever afterwards as implacable a Royalist as Jermyn, working indefatigably to serve first the King and then the young Prince of Wales, who was put into his care in 1645.

Hyde also had a sharp wit, but it was tempered, as Bishop Burnet complained, with 'too much levity'. Whilst he shared Jermyn's love of good food and drink, and eventually grew extremely rotund, he never openly consumed either excessively. Unlike Jermyn, Edward Hyde was never the jovial life and soul of the party.

Worse still, Hyde's relative abstinence from physical excess was not matched in his ability for self-praise, which allowed him to write of himself 'his integrity was ever without blemish, and believed to be above temptation'. This left him open to charges of pomposity yet, as Burnet continued, he 'would disparage the pretensions of others, not without much scorn, which created him many enemies'.

Hyde first encountered Jermyn in 1633, when the Villiers family called on him to help persuade the King to force Jermyn to marry the pregnant Eleanor. To a man of Hyde's high morals, Jermyn appeared to be nothing but a feckless bounder, and this was an impression of his rival that the lawyer never amended. That they were united only in their common loyalty to the Crown is amply demonstrated by the dispute over the tin trade.

'You will make an inconsiderable contemptible benefit to the Prince', Jermyn told Hyde angrily, 'whereas if [the tin patent] had remained in the Queen's hands she would have made a great one'. The battle-lines between the brilliant lawyer and the consummate courtier had been drawn.

When Charles said good-bye to Jermyn at Oxford he had, as Jermyn wrote, 'withal commanded [me] to make overture for some succour for England'. Besides becoming a base for his money-making activities, Jermyn's ornately furnished office at the Louvre also doubled as a make-shift English foreign ministry, from which he coordinated negotiations for help from the foreign powers, including France, Holland, Rome, Lorraine, Denmark, Sweden and even the Baltic duchy of Courland.

The first plan that Jermyn and Secretary of State Digby contrived together – for, despite their differences, they knew they must co-operate – was for a Triple Alliance between the Royalists, France and Holland, whereby Mazarin would allow the Irish and Scots regiments serving in the French army to be transported to England in ships loaned by the Prince of Orange.

In August 1644, Jermyn returned to Cardinal Mazarin's opulent chambers to ask for his participation in this international coalition against Parliament. Jermyn urged him to remember that, 'unless France did not presently think on some preparations, it would not be possible for the King's cause to get the desired fruit thereof at the end of this summer campaign'.

It was not that the French did not want to help Charles. Many French noblemen, including Henrietta Maria's brother the Duke of Orléans, made assurances to Jermyn and the Queen of their genuine eagerness to help them subdue the impertinent Parliamentarians. And nor did Anne and Mazarin wish any permanent harm to the Stuart dynasty. It appalled and frightened them that an anointed monarch, so closely connected to the French royal family, should be treated so insolently by his subjects.

Yet it seems that whenever Mazarin felt an urge to agree to Jermyn's requests, the spectre of Richelieu would hover before him, admonishing him, as he had done so often whilst still alive, to make France strong by keeping its neighbours weak. So Mazarin replied to Jermyn's requests for help by saying, 'we might think on it', adding

> ... it might happen that before this campaign [of France against the Spanish] ended, some occasion might offer itself to take this business again into consideration, and that the conjunctures might perhaps yield better expedients to bring it to a good conclusion than yet did appear.

Such language did not fool Jermyn for a minute, but what could he say? Everything depended on inducing Mazarin to take positive action.

'He dares not offend the Cardinal's dog', mocked an exiled Royalist who shared Hyde's hostility to Jermyn. But to Jermyn, no effort to please Mazarin was too great if it would gain French military assistance for the King. 'You must call him *my cousin*', Jermyn told Charles, 'and at the bottom [of letters], your *affectionate cousin*'. Yet, despite many such efforts of this sort, French assistance remained frustratingly unforthcoming.

Of all the rulers whom Jermyn contacted, Frederick Henry, Prince of Orange, was by far the most enthusiastic supporter of the royalist cause.

The Prince's chief motivation was his desire to elevate the House of Orange from mere *stadtholders* – military commanders – to monarchs in their own right. He had regarded the marriage of his son William to Charles and Henrietta Maria's daughter Mary as a valuable step in this direction – but only if the English king retained his power. Now, to encourage him further, Jermyn secretly suggested that Orange's daughter might become the wife of young Prince Charles. He omitted to mention in doing so, however, that he had also offered Prince Charles's hand to the Duke of Orléans' daughter, with the similar aim of strengthening Orléans' resolve to help the King. All Jermyn could do was hope neither found out until the greater end of ending the war had been achieved.

The Prince of Orange promised to help Jermyn by providing ships to transport the Scottish and Irish regiments to England. But it soon became clear that Mazarin would never release them from their servitude in the French army. So Jermyn was forced to seek an army elsewhere. He found one in the mercenary troops maintained by the Duke of Lorraine.

The Duke had been expelled from his French duchy in 1634 and had spent the intervening years marching about Europe, hiring out his army of professional soldiers to whoever needed them. When Jermyn asked Mazarin for the money to hire

Lorraine's army, he pointed out sagely that sending the Duke to
England was a good way of stopping him marching back into
France to reclaim his lost patrimony. For once, Mazarin agreed.

By January 1645, thanks to Jermyn's deft negotiations,
Lorraine had agreed in principle to embark for England with
10,000 well-drilled troops. But despite this success, Mazarin
dispensed the promised funds sparingly, grudgingly and late.
And to Jermyn's equal frustration, the Dutch Parliament, the
States General, raised constant obstructions to prevent the
Prince of Orange from lending Jermyn the ships. To rectify this,
Jermyn's agent in The Hague, the Puritan clergyman Stephen
Goffe, embarked on an ambitious program of bribing the
leading members of the States General.

As these frustrating negotiations dragged on, and no armies
actually sailed for England, Jermyn kept in constant touch with
the King. The news he heard from the Royalist camp was very
seldom encouraging. But in June 1645, a disaster took place that
would have made a lesser man than Jermyn give up altogether.

XI

THE 'GREAT HELL-CAT'
1645-6

'The torment of misfortunes which have overborne us of late and brought
us from so high into so desperate a condition is now so insupportable to
me in any thing as when I think of the Queen, unto whom… the sadness
of my heart will not permit me to write'.
Cardiff, 5 August 1645, George Digby to Jermyn

To Jermyn and Henrietta Maria, Saturday 14 June 1645 was just
another day in exile.

They were at home, as usual, in the Louvre Palace, Paris. That
spring, the thirty-five-year-old Queen had suffered several fits of
ague, a term used for sharp attacks of feverish chills. Although
recovered from these, Henrietta Maria was still frail.

Far more than her health, however, her worries focussed on
her family, not least little Henrietta Anne, whose first birthday
was due to fall in two days' time. After the Queen had been
forced to abandon her in Exeter, the little Princess had remained
in England: neither Henrietta Maria nor Jermyn had seen her
since.

Jermyn was now 40 and in very good health. Like his royal
mistress, however, he was exhausted by his on-going efforts to
help the Royalist cause, juggling bills and loans, seeking help
from foreign powers and monitoring the situation in England
and abroad through the by now formidable network he had built
up of correspondents, agents and spies.

Yet on that same day, 14 June, momentous events were
unfolding. Some 300 miles to the northwest, the morning mists

cleared over Naseby Ridge in Leicestershire to reveal what was, even by the standards of the Civil War, an anything but ordinary scene.

Drawn up in battle order were two great armies. On one side, the King's Royalists, including Charles's nephew Prince Rupert, were massed in their gorgeous finery, the gold-embroidered Royal Standard flashing in the first rays of the summer sun. Confronting the King's men was not the customary raggle-taggle turnout of assorted Roundheads. What faced Charles I that day at Naseby was the might of Parliament's New Model Army, commanded by Sir Thomas Fairfax.

Up to now, the armies of both sides had consisted mainly of landed proprietors leading men conscripted from towns and villages, part-time soldiers, many armed with no more than farm implements. The New Model Army, however, was entirely different. Raised and paid for by Parliament at a cost of some £45,000 a month – about £4 million pounds in modern money – its ranks had been drilled rigorously as professional soldiers.

The army included some ex-Royalists who had been pressed into its ranks, but most of the soldiers belonged to the Independent denomination, an English form of Presbyterianism that believed in a church without a hierarchy. For these psalm-singing Puritans, the Civil War was not just about reshuffling which aristocrats got to be closest to the King. It was a struggle on behalf of God and the English people against the forces of the Pope and the Devil.

Among the New Model Army's leading lights was Oliver Cromwell. Born in 1599 into a family of minor Huntingdonshire gentry, Cromwell was described in 1640: 'his linen was plain, not very clean: and I remember a speck or two of blood... his stature was of a good size, his sword stuck close to his side, his countenance swollen and reddish, his voice sharp and untuneable, and his eloquence full of fervour'.

Cromwell had been one of the Puritanically-inclined members of Parliament who had followed Pym's lead in Parliament. In December 1643, however, Pym died 'with great torment and agony, of a disease... which rendered him an object very loathsome'. His condition was probably bowel cancer.

In the vacuum created by the demagogue's absence, Cromwell was rapidly becoming one of Parliament's leading lights. But it was on the field of battle that Cromwell really excelled.

Being naturally good both at military strategy and commanding the respect of his men, Cromwell rose quickly to become a general. Royalists quickly learned to fear him. Jermyn's opinion of Cromwell was unequivocal. Referring to him in conversation once, Jermyn called the Parliamentarian general 'that great Hell-cat'.

'I can say this of Naseby,' Cromwell himself was later to state of the events of 14 June 1645, 'that when I saw the enemy draw up and march in gallant order towards us, and we a company of poor ignorant men, I could not but cry out to God in praises, in assurance of victory.'

Initially, Cromwell's confidence in God may have seemed misplaced. A brilliant cavalry charge by Prince Rupert smashed through the New Model Army's left flank. It seemed that Charles's Royalists were going to win both the day and maybe the entire war too.

But instead of rounding on the undefended Roundhead infantry, Rupert decided instead to plunder the undefended Parliamentarian baggage wagons. While the Prince made this foolish blunder, Cromwell himself led the New Model Army's right flank in a merciless onslaught on the Royalists' left flank.

At this critical juncture, Charles had a rare flush of courage, and decided to counterattack. But he was dissuaded from doing so by one of his attendants who physically turned the head of the King's horse away from the battle. The opportunity was lost and, by the time Rupert and his cavalry returned from their pointless plundering, the Royalist lines had been shattered. It was all Charles and his officers could do to escape the carnage, fleeing west to take refuge at Hereford.

The hopes of the King and his scattered attendants now turned even more desperately to Jermyn and Henrietta Maria at the Louvre.

Jermyn's negotiations with the Dutch were still being held up by the States General. But he had been working hard through correspondence, agents and spies to obtain armed assistance from Ireland.

The terrible troubles in Northern Ireland are not just a recent phenomenon, but date back centuries. When the English Civil War erupted, Ireland disintegrated into three main factions – Scottish Presbyterian settlers in the north; English Protestant settlers mainly around Dublin, and other English lords who, together with native Catholics led by their tribal chiefs, formed a confederacy at Kilkenny.

Through tortuous diplomacy, Jermyn persuaded the Kilkenny confederates to send an army to England to save Charles. This army, however, was hijacked by a Catholic extremist – a papal envoy, no less – who dispatched it instead on an orgy of killing non-Catholics in northern Ireland, resulting in tens of thousands of Presbyterian settlers being massacred.

It is a massive tribute to Jermyn's persistence that he still managed to acquire some Irish soldiers for the war. Led by his friend the Earl of Antrim, a small force of Catholic soldiers managed to cross the Irish Sea to Scotland, where they reinforced the army of Scottish Royalists led by the dashing Marquess of Montrose. Supplied with weapons and ammunition by Jermyn's privateers, the combined army of Scots and Irishmen was initially successful, driving back the Covenanting army and its leader the Presbyterian Earl of Argyll. On Friday, 15 August 1645, Montrose won what appeared to be a decisive victory at Kilsyth.

When news finally reached the Louvre, Henrietta Maria ordered *Te Deums* to be sung in church. But on the very day appointed for this, a messenger came galloping into the courtyard of the Louvre. On Friday, 12 September 1645, they were told, Argyll had decimated Montrose's army at the Battle of Philliphaugh.

It seemed like every time letters reached Jermyn and Henrietta Maria, they contained news of some fresh catastrophe. A month earlier, on Thursday, 14 August 1645, Sherborne Castle in Dorset fell to the Roundheads. More valuable to the victors than the castle was a portable cabinet containing Lord Digby's correspondence with Jermyn. In March 1646, while Lorraine's troops still lounged about uselessly on the Continent, waiting for ships to carry them to England, Parliament published extracts of this correspondence in Dutch.

Members of the Dutch States General read, goggle-eyed, how Jermyn and their own military leader the Prince of Orange had schemed 'for the insensible engaging [of] the Hollanders in the war.' For his part, the Prince of Orange read with astonishment how, although Jermyn had encouraged him to help by promising to make Prince Charles his son-in-law, Jermyn had made exactly the same promise, for exactly the same reason, to Henrietta Maria's brother, the Duke of Orléans.

The publication of Jermyn's letters reinforced the States

General's opposition to any further involvement with the Royalists. The prospect of ever having a Dutch fleet at his disposal dissolved before Jermyn's eyes. The likelihood of not being able to help Charles regain his throne threw Prince Frederick Henry into a deep depression. A broken man, he died the following year.

Ireland. France. Holland. Lorraine. One by one Jermyn's hopes for armed foreign intervention collapsed. And as each desperate day passed, Jermyn knew that the King remained in England, suffering defeat after defeat, the prospect of his regaining the throne growing ever more hopeless. Yet each day, he sat in his gilded office in the Louvre, surrounded by correspondence, ciphers and maps, sifting through reports from his spy network, desperately trying to find a way to save the day.

There was still one possible, if surprising, source of help: the Scottish Covenanters.

In 1644, the Earl of Argyll's Covenanting army had agreed to side against the King in return for Parliament imposing the Covenant in England, thus making Presbyterianism, not Anglicanism, the established church south, as well as north, of the border.

Even at that early stage, Jermyn had considered outbidding Parliament by trying to persuade Charles to reverse his religious policies and agree to religious toleration for all. By such a means, the Scots could keep their religion, and might also agree to support their King.

To make his audacious plan work, however, Jermyn had the unenviable task of persuading both Argyll and Charles to cooperate. To achieve this he gained the help of two men, Montereuil and Moray, to act as his representatives in Britain.

Jean de Montereuil was Mazarin's ambassador in England and

had access both to Charles and to Argyll's Presbyterian Commissioners in London.

Aware that the plan to destabilise Charles had now gone too far, but still unwilling to commit to sending troops to England, Mazarin was very keen to support Jermyn's plan. He readily allowed Jermyn to make full use of Montereuil's services as a spokesman.

Jermyn's other agent, Sir Robert Moray, is one of the most unusual and mysterious characters in the drama of the seventeenth century.

The son of a Scottish laird, Moray was a deeply spiritual man. He was one of the most prominent intellectual heirs of Francis Bacon, eagerly pursuing scientific experimentation wherever he could – an interest that later led to his becoming a founder member of the Royal Society.

As a young man, Moray served as a soldier in the French army. He later joined the Scots Covenanting army on its march south to Newcastle in May 1640, when his initiation into Freemasonry was recorded. Ever afterwards, Moray's signature was accompanied by a Masonic pentagram, coincidentally reminiscent of the two five-pointed stars on Jermyn's own coat of arms. In 1643, Moray's innate loyalty to the Crown overcame his desire to support the Covenant, and he joined Charles in Oxford, where he met Jermyn.

After this, Moray went to the Continent where he was captured and held to ransom by an unscrupulous nobleman until Mazarin, probably at Jermyn's behest, paid for his release.

Moray's role in Jermyn's negotiations was to do what Montereuil could not. Using his web of personal and Freemasonic contacts within the Royalist and Scottish camps, Moray could slip unnoticed between London and Oxford, furtively bringing about an agreement beneficial to Charles.

By March 1646, Jermyn's plan had started to work. Moray and Montereuil had persuaded Charles to make a declaration of limited religious toleration in Britain. Moray meanwhile tried to persuade the Scottish Commissioners to declare their support of Charles before all was lost.

In April, however, when the publication of Jermyn's captured correspondence caused the prospect of foreign help to melt away like winter snow under the spring sun, Montereuil made a fatal mistake.

Acting on a misunderstanding, the French ambassador told the King that the Scottish generals had promised Moray they would receive their King with honour. As the Roundheads closed in on beleaguered Oxford, Charles slipped away to arrive unannounced amongst the Covenanters at their camp near Newark on 5 May 1646.

It was now that Montereuil's mistake became gut-wrenchingly apparent. Nobody in the Scots' camp was expecting the King to appear. But far worse than the absence of a red carpet, it quickly transpired that the Scots had never agreed that a mere declaration of religious toleration would suffice to persuade them to fight for the King. They now demanded that Charles should swear to uphold the Presbyterian Covenant itself. The shocked Defender of the Faith refused absolutely. By the time the next post reached Jermyn and Henrietta Maria in Paris, Charles I was no better than a prisoner of the Scottish army.

After Charles had become the Scots' prisoner, the only effective Royalist army left in Britain was in the West Country, under the nominal leadership of the sixteen-year-old Charles, Prince of Wales,

The young Prince, like Jermyn at his age, had the advantage of being both charismatic and attractive. By now a strapping sixteen-year-old, he was fast approaching his full height of six feet two inches. His hair fell in lustrous curls over his starched white collar. Large eyebrows curled sensuously above the deep brown Medici eyes he had inherited from his mother.

Under the merciless onslaught of the Roundheads, even the young Prince's brave troops fell back through Devon and Cornwall until by August only Pendennis Castle remained. Early that month, Jermyn wrote to his cousin Sir Henry Killigrew,

> My Dear Cousin Harry,
> I have received your [letters], and truly do, with all the grief and respect that you can imagine to be in any body, look upon the sufferings and bravery in them; and do further assure you that the relief of so many excellent men, and preservation of so important a place, is taken into all the considerations... that can be in the Queen to contribute...
> I have only time to tell you, that I am confident those little stores that will give us, and you, time to stay and provide more, will be arrived with you; and I do not so encourage you vainly, but to let you know a truth that cannot fail... already some money is at the sea-side for this purpose, and more shall daily be sent... God of heaven keep you all, and give us, if he please, a meeting with you in England. I have no more to add. I am, most truly,
> Your most humble and faithful Servant,
> He[nry]. Jermyn

But Jermyn's supplies arrived too late. He never met Harry Killigrew again in England or indeed anywhere else. Starved of food and ammunition, Pendennis capitulated on Monday, 17

August 1646. Although its defenders were allowed to leave, Harry Killigrew died shortly afterwards of a wound received during the siege.

Even before this disaster fell, desperate efforts were being made to rescue as many of the royal children from England as possible. They were only partially successful. James, Duke of York, would remain a prisoner of Parliament until 1648, when two friends of Jermyn's Freemasonic contact, Sir Robert Moray, spirited him over the Channel, disguised as a girl.

His brother Prince Henry, Duke of Gloucester, the prince who had been born under Jermyn's watchful eyes at Oatlands in the troubled summer of 1640, remained under house arrest until Parliament finally let him join his mother in France in 1650.

Poor Princess Elizabeth, Henrietta Maria's second daughter, was a prisoner in the Isle of Wight, where she was destined to waste away in grief until consumption put a final end to her loneliness in 1650.

A happier fate lay in store for little Henrietta Anne, the baby born in 1644 in Exeter. Her guardian Lady Dalkeith disguised the baby as a boy and, evading the Roundheads' clutches, reached the Louvre in August 1646. From then on, the happy gurgles and squeals of the little princess made the corridors of the rambling palace seem much less empty.

Prince Charles and his household had escaped too, whisked away in fast ships across the bright sea to Jersey. Besides Cornet Castle on neighbouring Guernsey, Jersey was now the only piece of the King's domains left in Royalist hands, and was destined to remain so until its fall in 1651. Jermyn, who was its governor, had scraped together enough money to garrison and supply the island's stronghold, Elizabeth Castle. But he could still not be confident of the Prince's safety there. Dark fears of Parliamentarian warships surging across the Channel to capture

the Prince filled Jermyn and Henrietta Maria's minds, and they
wrote to him, urging him to come to Paris at once.

But this was not part of the plan of his chief counsellor, the
brilliant lawyer and statesman Sir Edward Hyde, Chancellor of
the Exchequer, the implacable enemy of Jermyn.

Jermyn and Henrietta Maria were, in fact, equally concerned
that Hyde had already turned the very impressionable Prince
Charles against them, and this added extra weight to their desire
to bring him to Paris. For his part, Hyde was anxious not to lose
– and to Jermyn, of all people – the political clout he exercised
through his custody of the Prince of Wales. Hyde's ingenious
response was that, if the Prince left Jersey, the remaining
Royalists would all lose heart and admit defeat.

Knowing this was Hyde's ruse, Jermyn and Henrietta Maria
repeated their orders. They also sent Hyde a letter that Charles I
had sent the Queen bidding her 'send mine and thine own
positive commands to him [Prince Charles] to come to thee...
[he] should be now with thee in France'. But stubborn Hyde
refused even these and subsequent orders.

In mid-June, 1646, Jermyn set out from Paris in his
customary black satin suit, with long-nosed George Digby, his
poets D'Avenant and Cowley, seventy-eight other Royalists and
countless servants and baggage wagons. At Courtainville in
Normandy they squeezed themselves into six ships and sailed
across the narrow strait to Jersey.

On Saturday, 20 June, the harbour below Elizabeth Castle
reverberated with cannon-fire and trumpet-blasts to salute the
arrival of Henry Jermyn, Governor of Jersey. Waiting to meet
him at the quayside was Chancellor Hyde, and by his side the
excited young Prince of Wales.

After lengthy arguments in the grand counsel chamber of
Elizabeth Castle, Hyde still refused to back down. In the end,

Jermyn and Digby simply marched the Prince onto their ship and left Hyde behind. Disconsolate at his loss, Hyde was genuinely concerned at what bad influences the profligate Jermyn and Catholic Henrietta Maria might have on the heir to the throne.

He passed his time growing cabbages, writing his history of the Civil War and spreading a story that Jermyn was planning to sell Jersey to France in return for a dukedom and £200,000 to line his own pockets – a story that seems without foundation. Jermyn may have loved his soup and gold, but he was not nearly as avaricious as Hyde believed him to be.

What is beyond doubt is that Jermyn had been right to overrule Hyde. That July, the King wrote to Henrietta Maria:

> tell Jermyn, from me, that I will make him know the eminent service he hath done me concerning Pr. Charles his coming to thee, as soon as it shall please God to enable me to reward honest men.

But for now, Charles I was in no position to reward anyone. The King of England was a prisoner of a Scottish army on English soil. And Jermyn and Henrietta Maria knew it was down to them to save him.

XII

'THE LOUVRE PRESBYTER'
1646 – 1649

*If he were ever affected with melancholy, it was in considering what
religion to be of, when that which he professed [Presbyterianism] was so
much discountenanced that he was almost weary of it; yet few men were so
often upon their knees, or so much desired to be thought a good Protestant
by all parties which professed that Faith, and could willingly comply with
all of them, and yet took time of the Roman Catholics to be better
informed.*

Sir Edward Hyde, Earl of Clarendon, on Jermyn

Young Prince Charles's dark complexion was inherited from his
mother, but his height and build were startlingly different from
both the King and Queen. Throughout his life, there were rumours
that Prince Charles was really the son of the equally tall, well-built
Lord Jermyn. What was beyond speculation was that, from 1646
onwards, Jermyn took on the fatherly role towards the Prince of
Wales that the imprisoned Charles I was now unable to fulfil.

From now on, it was Jermyn who administered Prince Charles's
finances and allowed him pocket money out of his French pension.
It was Jermyn who delicately tempered Henrietta Maria's instinct to
pamper and cosset her son and checked the adolescent lad's instinct
to rebel against her.

It was Jermyn, too, who appointed Prince Charles's tutors and
decided what they should teach him. He became the boy's friend
and tried to encourage and protect the Prince through the traumatic
years ahead. He became, in a very real sense, the boy's father.

* * *

When Charles I became a prisoner of the Scots army, Jermyn and the Queen ceased to be the King's chief diplomatic agency and started, through pure necessity, to become the de facto Royalist government. From now on, it was they who directed policy and attempted to communicate it to the imprisoned King, rather than vice-versa.

Charles did not complain. His only grouse with them was that they did not write enough with news of his family. 'Harry', the King wrote in May 1645, 'this is chiefly to chide you that I had no letters from you this last week... not to hear every day from you... is a cruel thing failing thereby of my expectation'.

As the Royalist cause foundered, an increasing number of Royalists came fleeing to Paris seeking sanctuary and support. Having grown used to managing their own small court in Paris, Jermyn and Henrietta Maria were now besieged by a host of Royalist exiles.

Jermyn's signature, showing his fluid style of handwriting

Used to enjoying incomes from landed property, very few of

the exiles had the slightest idea how to work for a living. They made constant demands on Henrietta Maria's coffers. Many resented Jermyn's control of the royal finances, moaning – not always without just cause – that 'Lord Jermyn kept an excellent table for those who courted him, and had a coach of his own, and all other accommodations incident to the most full fortunes'.

Finding all the money and power in the hands of Jermyn and his favourites made many Royalists writhe with jealousy. There are numerous accounts of arguments between Royalists who were unable to put their differences aside even in the face of dire adversity.

At Saint-Germain in October 1645, for example, Jermyn had a furious argument with two of the Royalists with whom he had hatched the Army Plot of 1641, Wilmot and Percy. They alleged – absurdly – that Jermyn's friend Prince Rupert had designs on the Crown. Rapiers flashed as they prepared to settle the argument with blood, jostling down the corridor until Henrietta Maria came running out of her chamber crying out for them to stop.

Exactly two years later, when Rupert came to blows with Secretary of State Digby over who was more responsible for the failure of the Royalist cause, Jermyn took the opportunity to express his own frustrations with the way he believed Digby had undermined his own efforts.

Rupert and the Secretary of State prepared to fight a duel early in the morning, at the Cross of Poissy in the autumnal forest of Saint-Germain, and Jermyn agreed readily to be the Prince's second. He waited anxiously, ready with bandages and brandy in case Rupert was injured, hoping, despite their erstwhile friendship, that it would be Digby who would lose. At the last minute, and to Jermyn's immense relief, the fight was averted by Prince Charles, who came galloping through the foggy dawn to stop them. But Jermyn and Digby's already damaged friendship was now far beyond repair.

Back in England in 1647, King Charles I was a prisoner of the Presbyterian Scots. Yet he was still their king, and to a man they swore to put him back on his throne if only he would take the Covenant, by swearing to uphold and protect Presbyterianism in Scotland, and to impose it in England as well.

When the pragmatic Jermyn and Cardinal Mazarin heard this, they both urged him to acquiesce. But Charles refused. He had lost so much that his principles were, literally, all he had left. Rather sanctimoniously, Charles replied that his coronation oath to uphold the Church of England was inviolable.

Jermyn sent D'Avenant to try to persuade the King to change his mind. Charles merely told the poet that 'Lord Jermyn knows nothing about religion!'. Jermyn then wrote the King a series of letters conjointly with John Colepeper the Chancellor of the Exchequer, and his Army Plot colleague, Jack Ashburnham. They tried every argument they could to make Charles back down, but without success. Clearly exasperated, they gave Charles a blunt ultimatum: be 'a king of Presbytery, or no king at all'.

Finally, the Scots grew so fed up with Charles's intransigence that, in one of the most bizarre twists of the Civil War, they sold him to Parliament for £400,000 and packed him off to London.

This coincided with a serious rift amongst Charles's English enemies. Parliament wanted to disband its large, costly army. But the soldiers did not want to lose their jobs, whilst the generals feared a collapse in law and order if the army was no longer there.

On Thursday, 3 June, a soldier called Cornet Joyce arrived at Holdenby House, where Parliament was keeping Charles, and took him into military custody. Cromwell seems to have been complicit in this, because now he had control of the most important pawn in the British power-struggle – the King. The army began a slow march on London, side-stepping any serious efforts to resolve its differences with Parliament. On Friday, 6 August, Oliver Cromwell and his fellow generals entered London. Parliament could say what it liked, but now, with the army behind him, Cromwell had become the effective master of England.

Jermyn and Henrietta Maria were quick to realise the new, if highly unpalatable, opportunity that this offered them. From Paris, they sent Jack Ashburnham and Jermyn's own cousin Sir John Berkeley with offers of almost unlimited wealth, lands and titles for Cromwell and his associates if they would only restore the King.

Like most of the gentry who had sided against the King, Cromwell was not a convinced anti-monarchist. He merely believed the King's powers should not be absolute. He was now in a severe dilemma, but what helped convince him to refuse was his concern that the soldiers, who were strongly Republican, might turn on him.

But as the option of Cromwellian help faded, the possibility of help from Scotland suddenly re-emerged.

In December, helped by Ashburnham and Berkeley, Charles escaped to the Isle of Wight. Here, he met representatives of the Scottish Covenanters. Worn down by his recent captivity, Charles was finally prepared to do what Jermyn had been urging for over a year.

At Carisbrooke Castle on Boxing Day, 1647, which was a Sunday, Charles signed 'The Engagement', agreeing to abandon the Church of England and establish Presbyterianism in England for at least three years.

Discovering what had happened, the Castle's governor arrested the King and sent a messenger to Cromwell. Desperate to save Charles, Jermyn ordered a ship to be sent from Jersey to whisk him away.

When it arrived, Charles tried to escape through a window, and nearly succeeded. But his foot got stuck, and he was apprehended. The 'great Hell-cat' Cromwell had the King in his claws once more. This time, he would not let Charles slip away.

Charles I was a prisoner again, but now Jermyn's long-projected alliance between the Royalists and Scots Presbyterians had become official Royalist policy. Jermyn now made it the centre-piece of an elaborate new plan to win the war.

Through his agents Stephen Goffe and Sir Robert Moray, he encouraged his connections in Scotland, especially his old friend from the pre-Civil War court, the Marquess of Hamilton, to overrule Lord Argyll and bring the Covenanting army south to fight the New Model Army. To give the army a potent figurehead, Jermyn proposed to send Prince Charles to Scotland.

The pro-Anglican Privy Counsellors in exile in France, especially Secretary of State Nicholas and Sir Edward Hyde, were appalled at the danger of the enterprise, at the prospect of their Prince of Wales becoming a Presbyterian – and of Jermyn having such supreme control of Royalist policy.

In May 1648, when Jermyn wanted the Privy Council to approve his plans in practise, he had to resort to Machiavellian methods, calling a meeting so abruptly that those whom he knew would not agree with him could not make it.

At this time, a small fleet of English navy ships mutinied and offered their allegiance to the Royalist cause. Jermyn raised a personal loan from Venetian merchants to pay the sailors' wages, took Prince Charles to Calais and put him aboard, ready to sail for Scotland when the time was right.

Through his quiet brother Thomas Jermyn, his suave old mentor Lord Kensington – he who had negotiated the marriage of Charles and Henrietta Maria – and many other friends in England, and benefiting greatly from his extensive communications network, Jermyn was an important link in the chain of high-ranking Royalists who co-ordinated a series of Royalist risings from Pembroke to Kent. Meanwhile, the great army of Scots Presbyterians began to lumber south.

In Paris, Jermyn and Henrietta Maria prayed for victory. But on Thursday, 17 August, Cromwell fought a savage battle against the Scots at Preston, Lancashire, and won. The risings were too small and too few in number to be effective, and were brutally crushed by Cromwell's troops. Amongst the prisoners taken were Lord Hamilton and Lord Kensington. They were taken to Tyburn and, kneeling side by side, their handsome, refined and infinitely noble heads were chopped off.

Prince Charles, thank goodness, was safe, for his little fleet had not sailed to Scotland, and now he was in Holland, wondering what to do next.

Another concern now raised itself, in the form of Cromwell's attack on Guernsey. Acting on his own initiative, Prince Rupert sailed there, secured it for the King, and then landed in Ireland. All eyes now turned to Ireland, as the next, best hope for the King.

Raising another personal loan, Jermyn sent the Marquess of Ormonde, the former Lord Lieutenant of Ireland, back to Ireland to make peace with the Confederation of Catholic lords at Kilkenny. Ormonde succeeded, writing triumphantly to Jermyn that Ireland was 'ours' at last and an army might now be sent to England to save the King. 'We must look upon your endeavours that are abroad', Ormonde added, 'to furnish us in the best proportion you are able, as well with money as with ammunition'.

This Jermyn started to do at once. But having worked tirelessly throughout the Civil War to help save the King, time had run out. Due in part to these very same Royalist efforts, Cromwell and his cronies had concluded that there could be no peace in England while Charles remained a focus for unrest. In December, the army, with Cromwell's subsequent approval, purged Parliament of all members likely not to acquiesce to their wishes.

On Monday, 1 January 1649, at the generals' behest, the Commons declared it treasonous for the King to levy war on his own Parliament and kingdom, and put their anointed sovereign on trial.

Charles I, King of England and Scotland, was tried in Westminster Hall. On Saturday, 27 January, he was found guilty of having made war on his own people in order to further his own ends.

Three days later, he left St James's Palace for the last time and walked across the frosty grass of St James's Park to the Banquetting House in Whitehall. The Banquetting House had been built by Inigo Jones for James I, thirty years before. Now, a hastily assembled scaffold loomed up against the building's elegant classical façade.

The King's last act was to make sure his hair was tucked under his cap, so as not to obstruct the single, deadly blow that cut off his head.

Cromwell was installed as President of the Council of State, the body that now assumed the sovereignty of the realm. For the first and only time in history, Britain was a republic: and Oliver Cromwell was its leader.

Jermyn had lost the struggle to save Charles I. But now he had a new mission to fulfil. It was one of extraordinary magnitude and audacity: to destroy Cromwell's fledgling republic and enthrone the young Prince Charles – the man who was so widely rumoured to be his own son – as Charles II, ruling monarch of England and Scotland.

XIII

'OUR OWN CONDITION IS LIKE TO BE VERY SAD'.
1649 – 1656

Jermyn in whom united doth remain,
All that kind Mothers wishes can contain;
In whom Wit, Judgment, Valour, Goodness join,
And all these through a comely Body shine,
A Soul composed of th' Eagle and the Dove;
Which all men must admire, and all men love.
Abraham Cowley, *The Civil War* (1643)

Even before Charles I's execution and the foundation of the first non-monarchical government in British history, Jermyn and Henrietta Maria's world was shaken by revolutionary events much nearer their own door.

For the last half a decade, resentment had been building up in all classes of French society against First Minister Cardinal Mazarin's on-going policy of centralising power under the Crown.

In the months leading up to Charles's execution in England, the autocratic Prince of Condé led an armed rebellion in France, aimed at forcing Queen Anne to dismiss Mazarin. The rebellion was termed 'the Fronde', from the French for 'sling', alluding to the way naughty boys only use their toy slings when the teacher's back is turned. Paris degenerated into anarchy and Anne fled with her court up to Saint-Germain. Henrietta Maria, Jermyn and their household in the Louvre found themselves blockaded inside the turbulent city.

'Our own condition is like[ly] to be very sad', Cowley wrote from the Louvre on Monday, 8 January 1649, 'the Queen being left here without one penny of money to buy her bread tomorrow. Yesterday my Lord [Jermyn] went to St Germain's with an intent to return this morning, but is not yet come back, neither have we heard from him'.

Soon after Cowley wrote this, Henrietta Maria wrapped herself in a servant's cloak and slipped out of the palace, holding her little daughter Henrietta Anne's hand. But the Parisian constables recognised her distinctive stoop as she hurried through the Tuileries Gardens and sent her home brusquely. Jermyn reached the Louvre soon afterwards too, tired and empty-handed, for Queen Anne had had no spare money to give him.

A month later, freezing cold and with their gold exhausted and their soup in terribly short supply, Jermyn and his friends were reduced to breaking up the remaining furniture in the Louvre to fuel the dwindling embers in the fireplaces.

News of Charles I's execution eventually filtered through to Jermyn, on Thursday, 8 February. To seventeenth-century Royalists like Jermyn, the act of beheading an anointed sovereign – *his* anointed sovereign – was unthinkable. On a purely personal level, though, and however dreadful he may have felt as a result, is it conceivable he was secretly pleased that now there was nobody who could come between himself and Henrietta Maria?

But if so, that satisfaction lay in the future. For the present he was faced with a terrible prospect: breaking the news to the Queen.

He started doing so while they ate their meagre breakfast. But once he had told her about Charles being led on foot to an execution block outside the Banqueting House, the look of blank dismay in her eyes made him falter.

Anything was preferable to telling her the truth. Instead he told her that the crowd had cried out in protest against the abominable act that was about to take place. By weight of numbers they had overpowered the soldiers, freed the King and carried him away to safety.

Henrietta Maria told him to send a messenger to Saint-Germain to see if Anne had heard any more news. Jermyn pretended to send the messenger, and then asked one of the household priests, Père Cyprian Gamache, to help him tell the Queen the truth.

After fretting through the dismal afternoon, they sat down to supper with the Queen. At first they talked about trivialities and the Queen started to cheer up. Then she complained of the messenger's failure to return. Gamache, to whom we owe the story of that dreadful day, describes what happened next:

> Lord Jermyn took this opportunity to suggest that the gentleman was so faithful and so expeditious in obeying her Majesty's commands on these occasions, that he would not have failed to come, had he any favourable intelligence. What then is the news? I see it is known to you, said the Queen.
>
> Lord Jermyn replied, that he did know something of it, and when pressed, after many evasions, to explain himself, and many ambiguous words to prepare her, little by little, to receive the fatal intelligence, at length he declared it to the Queen, who seemed not to have expected anything of the kind, [and] was so deeply struck, that instantly, entirely speechless, she remained voiceless and motionless, to all appearances a statue, without words and without tears. A great philosopher has said that

ordinary griefs allow the heart to sigh, and the lips
to murmur; but that extraordinary afflictions,
terrible and fatal, cast the soul into stupor, and by
locking up the senses, make the tongue mute, and
the eyes tearless.

To this pitiable state was the Queen reduced, and
to all our exhortations and arguments she was deaf
and insensible. We were obliged to cease talking, and
we remained by her in unbroken silence, some
weeping, some sighing, and all with sympathising
countenances, mourning over her extreme distress.
This sad scene lasted till night-fall, when the
Duchess of Vendôme, whom she greatly loved,
came to see her. Weeping, she took the hand of the
Queen, tenderly kissed it, and afterwards spoke so
successfully that she seemed to have recovered this
dislocated Princess from that loss of all her senses,
or rather, that great and sudden stupor, produced by
the surprising and lamentable intelligence of the
strange death of the King.

Dare we presume to wonder if it was her guilty knowledge of
earlier infidelities with Jermyn that made Henrietta Maria turn to
the Duchess, and not to him? Almost at once, at any rate, she left
the Louvre for the Carmelite convent in the rue Saint-Jacques,
where she remained for several weeks, crying into her black lace
veil, and praying fervently for her late husband's soul.

Then Henrietta Maria came home again, to be by Jermyn's side,
and the gossips started whispering. Madame de Motteville, who
visited the Queen that spring, thought that the presence of 'le
Favori' was making Henrietta Maria much happier than she ought

to have been. In the streets the rebel Frondeurs read malicious pamphlets comparing Anne's fondness for Mazarin with Jermyn and Henrietta Maria's 'shameful attachment' which, they asserted, had led to Charles I's downfall.

Before long, rumours arose of a private marriage contracted at the Louvre between the widowed queen and her favourite. A French courtier, Madame Bavière, wrote that they 'made a clandestine marriage' soon after the King's execution.

The diarist Sir John Reresby, who visited Jermyn and Henrietta Maria in 1659, believed a story that they were married and had had children. In 1662, Pepys heard the marriage had taken place 'for certain', adding 'her being married to my lord of St. Albans is commonly talked of'. In 1685, a story was printed that Cowley had witnessed the wedding. In the early nineteenth century, an antiquarian claimed to have *heard* of a marriage settlement between Jermyn and Henrietta Maria which Cowley had witnessed, adding that the signatures were subsequently – and most conveniently – cut off. In 1690 claims were made that one 'R. Osborne' had seen the couple 'solemnly married together' in Paris.

Historians remain divided over whether Jermyn and Henrietta Maria became husband and wife.

If she had married Jermyn, Henrietta Maria would not have been unusual in her family. She had shared her nursery with her father's numerous illegitimate offspring. Her mother's lover Conchini was loathed throughout France. Her widowed sister Christine of Savoy scandalised Europe with her affair with Count Philip San Martino d'Aglie. Her father-in-law James I shared his bed with the Duke of Buckingham and referred to him in private as his 'wife'. Her sister-in-law Elizabeth of Bohemia was rumoured to have married Lord Craven. Her nephew Rupert may have married his mistress Francesca Bard.

Of her own children, James and Mary were later to contract secret marriages with commoners, and Charles II may well have married his mistress Lucy Walter.

When considering the pros and cons of marrying the Count de Lauzun, her niece Mademoiselle de Montpensier wrote,

> I had read the history of France... in which I found examples of persons of inferior rank to [Lauzun's], having married the daughters, the sisters, the grand-daughters, and the widows of monarchs. Besides this, I decided that there was little real difference between men like these and those born of a more illustrious house; the one having far greater merit and elevation in their souls – the true measure of respective ranks.

Henrietta Maria, however, shared none of her niece's égalitari-anism. Earlier indiscretions with Jermyn were one thing, but marrying him was another. Truer to Jermyn's situation were the words put in the mouth of his alter-ego Theander in *The Platonic Lovers* by D'Avenant:

> If I should think t' enjoy
> Her by the tame and formal title of
> A wife, I were but simply gulled by my
> Ov'rweening and too saucy ignorance,
> As knowing well my birth, my fortune, and
> My years make me unfit for such a hope.

Besides, and contrary to much ill-informed gossip, Jermyn remained an Anglican all his life. However much she loved him, Henrietta Maria could not have countenanced marrying him without a proper Papal dispensation, and no evidence of any such document has ever come to light.

How Charles II and his siblings rated the likelihood of their being Jermyn's step-children, if not actually his offspring, is not recorded. The closest to a comment comes from a story written by the Baroness d'Aulnoy, based on conversations she may have heard first-hand in the 1670s. In her tale, Charles II's illegitimate son James, Duke of Monmouth argues with Jermyn about love:

> 'Ha!' cried the Duke, 'how ungrateful you are to complain, considering how your evils have been softened by the good that one cannot buy. I know sufficient of the History of the last Court to be aware of your antecedents, nor do I deny that you well merited your good fortune, that you are kind to me because——'
>
> At these words, Lord [Jermyn] laughed so loudly that Prince Rupert and the Duke of Buckingham hearing it, called them to come back.

Behind Jermyn's laughter is hidden the closest we may ever have come to hearing the truth.

The French army quelled the Fronde and, in June 1649, Prince Charles returned to Paris from the Netherlands, where he had been staying since the failure of the 1648 uprisings.

Since his father's death he was now Charles II, the nineteen-year-old exiled monarch of England and Scotland.

Although Jermyn was officially no more than a servant of Henrietta Maria's, his closeness to the Queen and his fatherly influence over the young Charles II made him the King's leading henchman, 'employed and trusted', as Secretary Nicholas was to write bitterly several years later 'as Premier Minister in the management of all his Majesty's greatest and most secret affairs'.

With the young King at his side, Jermyn was busy devising schemes to bring about the Restoration. Jermyn understood very well the importance of propaganda, and was fortunate in having a circle of extremely talented writers living under his patronage at the Louvre.

These included William D'Avenant, who was writing an epic poem, *Gondibert*, about an exiled prince's struggle to regain his throne, with a preface advocating an ideal society unified under strong, hierarchical government. The preface included a reply in which the young King's mathematics tutor, Thomas Hobbes, sketched out the philosophy of his own forthcoming book, *Leviathan*.

Published in 1651, *Leviathan* would eventually become one of the most influential philosophical works of the century. It was written in the Louvre, during the time when Jermyn dominated the royal household there, and, in parts, there is a remarkable overlap with the views he held. It argued the case for royalty at a time when Jermyn was desperately trying to use any means he could to restore the monarchy. It surely cannot be entirely coincidental that Hobbes just happened to write this extraordinary book in the very place and time when it could be of most use to Jermyn.

A further piece of indirect evidence that suggests Jermyn's close involvement in the writing of *Leviathan* is the readiness with which Hyde heaped condemnation on a book that in no respects contradicted his own efforts to restore the King. It makes considerable sense, in fact, to see *Leviathan* as the centrepiece of Jermyn's propaganda war against Cromwell's Commonwealth.

Hobbes argued that society was an uneasy truce between individuals seeking personal happiness, who agreed to surrender part of their freedom to a higher, sovereign authority, which he called 'the great Leviathan', in return for it protecting them against others. This sovereign authority could be a monarchy, autocracy or democracy.

On the whole, Hobbes thought a monarch, whose succession was not open to dispute in the way that a dictator's was, and who was far less likely than an assembly of men to disagree amongst himself, or to fall under the sway of demagogues (Pym and Cromwell, for example), was the best choice. In England, Hobbes argued, Charles I had been the sovereign authority. Parliament had been no more than a group of messengers acting as intermediaries between King and people.

Echoing what Charles I had said at his trial, nobody had the authority to try the King, because the King *was* the sovereign authority.

The arguments of Hobbes and D'Avenant gave a philosophical structure to Jermyn's views of the monarchy. Although Jermyn and most of his relatives had sat in the House of Commons, his own well-being had always depended on the strength of the Stuart monarchy. His and Henrietta Maria's mutual self-interest coincided with the doctrine of Divine Right, drummed into them both through court propaganda from their early childhoods. Besides, the only alternative to monarchy in Britain could not be classical democracy – which everyone at the time agreed could never work in anywhere larger than a Greek city – but Parliamentary power.

When the wealthy Parliamentarians tried to grasp power from the King, they acted in the interests of the middle and upper classes, not of the people as a whole. The majority of the English people were not represented in Parliament at all. Their liberties had been eroded by numerous laws imposed by Parliament, favouring landlords over tenants and employers over labourers. Parliament's Enclosure Acts continued to force small farmers out of secure tenancies and into an increasingly uncertain labour-market. Jermyn and Henrietta Maria's concern for the wellbeing of the English people was admittedly somewhat distant, but it was probably genuine. In their hearts, they believed the people would be better off living under a strong Stuart monarchy than under Parliament.

Though not normally associated with Jermyn, *Leviathan* was a central element of Jermyn's efforts to restore the King. Cowley likened the solid reasoning it contained to 'the Shield from Heaven, to the Trojan Heroe given'. Before Aeneas's monumental battle to secure his foothold in Italy, his mother Aphrodite asked her husband Hephaestus, the smith of the gods, to put his servants to work forging a magnificent suit of armour, and a shield, depicting the future glory of Rome.

That shield was given by mother to son, to protect him in the battle that was to come. Here, in *Leviathan*, was a shield of words, forged at Jermyn's behest, by which Henrietta Maria might hope to avert further bloody conflict and see her son safely enthroned at last in London.

The people whom Jermyn most wanted to persuade to restore Charles II to his throne were the Scots Presbyterians. For all their disobedience to Charles I, they had been incensed by Cromwell's execution of their monarch. So desperate was Jermyn to gain Scottish support, that he even tried behaving like a Presbyterian. Curbing his customarily flamboyant lifestyle, he attended services at the austere Huguenot chapel at Charenton, just south of Paris, prompting the Anglicans to start calling him 'the Louvre Presbyter', and 'the Baal of the Louvre' – or sometimes just 'His Greatness'.

His postal diplomacy with Scotland led to a successful

meeting between Charles II and the Scottish delegates at Breda in the Netherlands in May 1650.

Here, the young King agreed to uphold the Presbyterian Covenant, in return for the Scots' military support. With Jermyn's blessing, he sailed away to join Lord Argyll at the head of the Covenanting Army. Meanwhile, Jermyn's spies and agents primed the networks of Royalist conspirators in England, concentrating on the English Presbyterians and perhaps utilising networks of Freemasonic Lodges to mobilise support as well.

Jermyn planned to support the rising with troops transported from France in ships loaned by Henrietta Maria's son-in-law William of Orange. But this plan was thrown awry when, in October, the Prince suddenly caught smallpox and died. His wife Mary, who was only nineteen, was left heavily pregnant and, on Monday, 4 November, she gave birth to a son.

Jermyn made a hasty journey over the frozen roads of northern Europe to The Hague, where he found Mary's Buitenhof Palace draped in heavy mourning. Through Stephen Goffe, whom he employed as his political agent in the Netherlands, Jermyn tried to cajole the Dutch States General into honouring the late Prince's promise of ships, but they would not do so. But thanks to Jermyn, they did confirm the right of Mary's son to succeed his father, and arranged for her to be co-regent until the boy came of age.

While he was there, Jermyn also oversaw the baby's baptism. The child was named William Henry. The second name was well used in both the English and French royal families, but its use here may also, perhaps, imply Mary's tacit acknowledgment of Jermyn's role as defender of the Stuarts. Much later, the boy would become England's king, remembered in history as 'William of Orange'.

Having settled Mary's affairs in Holland, Jermyn returned to

Paris. He planned to join Charles II in Scotland, where he intended to assume the office of the King's principal Secretary of State. However, the work of co-ordinating the different risings in England kept him in Paris, unless it is true, as Sir Christopher Hatton alleged, that Henrietta Maria would not let him go for fear of the dangers he would face there.

She was right to be apprehensive. Cromwell's agents discovered and prevented the English risings. Instead of triumphant dispatches containing news of Charles II's victories, Jermyn and Henrietta Maria heard what happened next from the stream of broken refugees who came stumbling back to Paris.

At Worcester on Wednesday, 3 September 1651, Scottish claymores and dirks were pitted against the pikes and rapiers of Cromwell's army.

The pikes and rapiers won. When the bloody encounter was over, Cromwell was the unquestioned master of England. The young King fled, making his famous escape in disguise, hiding in the oak tree at Boscobel whilst Roundhead soldiers sniffed around below him. When he reached the Louvre two months later, Charles's shirt stank so badly that the first thing Jermyn did was to send for one of his own for the lad to wear.

In June 1652, Jermyn and Charles became embroiled in a new bout of France's on-going civil-war, the Fronde.

The Prince of Condé and Henrietta Maria's own brother the Duke of Orléans had hired the Duke of Lorraine's mercenaries to make another assault on Mazarin's forces, led by the Marshal de Turenne.

Jermyn, who was banking heavily on Mazarin's gratitude, proposed Charles as a mediator in the dispute. As the two armies drew closer in meadows just south of Paris, however, it was Jermyn who found himself galloping to and fro' between the two commanders, trying to obtain Lorraine's agreement to withdraw.

Finally, with the front lines less than a cannon-shot apart, Lorraine agreed. Jermyn spurred his horse across the now very familiar stretch of meadow, brandishing the signed treaty above his head. Peace had been restored, but when he and Charles returned to Paris, they found that the city itself had fallen into Frondeur hands.

For an uncomfortable few weeks, the English royal household found themselves trapped, yet again, in the Louvre, with dwindling food supplies. Outside, in the stinking streets, the mob chanted anti-English slogans, accusing Jermyn of a catalogue of misdeeds, from sleeping with the Queen to plotting to sell France to Cromwell.

Finally, the Duke of Orléans himself smuggled them out of the city at night. As dawn broke over the Seine valley, they rode up, cold and exhausted below the comforting ramparts of Saint-Germain, where the French royal family was waiting to welcome them to safety.

It was not until Thursday, 21 October 1652, that Jermyn could join the Bourbons and Stuarts at the balustrades of the palace gardens to watch the final showdown between Turenne and the Frondeurs. Even at such a distance they could see the flashes of the cannons firing and heard the booms echoing over the water meadows. Eventually, the noise stopped and the anxiously-expected messenger came pounding up to the palace. Turenne had won.

They had packed their meagre belongings already. Charles was given a place of honour in the procession, with Jermyn not too far behind, riding next to Henrietta Maria's carriage as they started their triumphant journey back to Paris.

Since 1649, Jermyn had spent almost four years as the effective 'Premier Minister' of the exiled court. For the first two, he had continued, as before, to hold absolutely no official government post at all. It was not until spring 1652 that he was even appointed to the Privy Council – which shows how effective the entirely notional position of *privado* was, and how ineffective the Privy Council could be.

Throughout this period, Jermyn's old adversary, Sir Edward Hyde, had been tirelessly seeking ways to oust him from the new King's affections. Playing on the young King's bad habit of agreeing with whoever was talking to him at the time, Hyde successfully (and quite falsely) made Charles suspect that Jermyn's ally Sir Robert Moray was a traitor. He insinuated (probably rightly) that a plan of Jermyn's for Charles to marry a French princess would alienate support from otherwise loyal Englishmen.

Hyde also contrived the somewhat perverse (and incorrect) argument that Hobbes's *Leviathan* was really a pro-Cromwellian tract. Following his arguments through to their logical conclusion, Hobbes had stated that 'the obligation of subjects to the sovereign is understood to last as long, and no longer, than the power lasteth by which he is able to protect them'. It was a logical but foolish thing for Hobbes to have written, and which Jermyn had failed to correct, and a gift to Hyde's rhetoric – but it was ridiculous to suggest that Hobbes (and Jermyn) were closet Republicans and, in any case, the offending lines applied just as much to Cromwell as to Charles.

It greatly helped Hyde that Charles, now twenty-three, was becoming increasingly intolerant of his doting but rather overbearing mother. Because she and Jermyn so often spoke with one voice, it was not difficult for Hyde to transfer some of Charles's irritation with her onto Jermyn himself. And ironically, the fact that Hyde so often disagreed with Henrietta Maria and Jermyn suddenly began to count in his favour with the independent-minded young King.

Jermyn's reaction to this was to make one of the most stupid blunders of his entire career. At Christmas 1653, without bothering to check any of the evidence, he and Prince Rupert came to the Privy Council and accused Hyde of being in treasonous correspondence with none other than Oliver Cromwell.

Both Hyde and the King reacted with incredulity. Under Hyde's ruthless cross-examination, the witnesses who were supposed to have firm evidence of this treason crumbled, and were forced to admit they were acting on mere hearsay. The affair ended with Hyde and the King closer than ever, and Jermyn's credibility in shreds.

We do not know why Jermyn made such an uncharacteristic blunder. He may simply have followed the impetuous Rupert's lead. There is also the possibility that Jermyn was ill: in June 1653, we know for sure that he suffered a severe fever, from which Rupert is reported to have cured him using charms brought back from his recent voyage to Africa. It is possible that the cure hadn't been as complete as was thought, and that Jermyn's customarily sharp mind was still out-of-sorts. Whatever the reason, Jermyn, normally so politically shrewd, was capable of making mistakes, and this was the worst of them.

And now greater misfortunes contrived to play into Hyde's hands as well.

For a long time, Cardinal Mazarin had been negotiating a peace treaty with Cromwell, whose naval power he had every reason to fear. As part of the treaty, all the Royalists in Paris, except for French-born Henrietta Maria and her immediate household, would have to leave. Jermyn was supposed to be the Royalists' most adept negotiator at the French court. When he finally had to admit that he could not persuade Mazarin to continue supporting Charles II, his favour with the King plunged yet further.

It was with great delight that Hyde arranged for Charles and his Royalist followers to settle in Spanish-occupied Flanders, where they would be able to preserve their honour by serving in the Hapsburgs' army. In July 1654, therefore, King Charles II, Hyde and almost all of the English Royalists rode away from Paris. Jermyn could not go with them, for his duty was to remain with Henrietta Maria. In any case, Charles was so fed up with both of them now that he probably would not have taken Jermyn anyway.

Relations between Jermyn and Charles seemed at their lowest ebb, yet, amazingly, there was still worse to come. That autumn, Henrietta Maria gave up hope of a Restoration and decided to convert her youngest son, Prince Henry, to Catholicism. Jermyn disagreed with this strongly, yet had no choice but to obey her commands and take the boy to the abbey of Pontoise, to be indoctrinated by its English abbot, the ex-courtier Walter Montagu.

When news reached Charles's court, Hyde knew how to make brilliant use of it. In a vituperative letter echoing Hyde's insinuations, the King accused Jermyn of covering up the Queen's efforts to 'pervert' Prince Henry. Provide proof of your innocence, Charles told his former mentor, or 'you must never think to see me again, and... this shall be the last time you shall ever hear from me'.

Relations between Jermyn and Henrietta Maria themselves were now under severe strain. We hear of them rowing. Wasn't associating the Royal family with Rome, Jermyn may have suggested, the best way of ensuring that the Restoration would never happen?

Henrietta Maria could have pointed out that the Restoration

was as unrealistic a dream as the conquest of Madagascar. In any case, wasn't saving Prince Henry's immortal soul more important than earthly considerations? Yes, Jermyn might have replied, but you'll alienate your eldest son for good in the process. 'Get out!' she reportedly shrieked at Jermyn, 'you are too impertinent!'

The argument between Jermyn and Henrietta Maria was quickly resolved and forgotten. To Charles, Jermyn wrote that his prime duty was to obey his mistress, whatever she ordered. Once Henry himself had told Charles how much Jermyn had disagreed with Henrietta Maria's plan, the King backed down and wrote rather lamely that 'all's well'.

All was not well, however. Over the next few years, in his political despatches to Charles, Jermyn tried unsuccessfully to repair the breach between mother and son. 'You are not to judge of the queen's affections', he told Charles in a note added to the end of a cold letter from Henrietta Maria in January 1656, 'no more by her style than by her words, for they are both sometimes betrayers of her thoughts and have sharpness, that in her heart she is not guilty of'.

However hopeless the situation seemed, Jermyn knew that the route back to power and influence lay through reconciliation with the King. So he waited, Jermynesque, constantly alert for the opportunity he needed to achieve his goal.

XIV

THE CHÂTEAU OF COLOMBES
1656 – 1660

I cannot chose but embrace some faint hopes that things are so disposing themselves in England that old friends may think of meeting again once [more] before they die.
Jermyn to Sir Marmaduke Langdale;
Senlis, France, 22 November 1654

Once Charles II and his retinue had abandoned Paris, there was little point in Jermyn and Henrietta Maria rattling about the echoing chambers of the Louvre.

A month after Charles's departure they had moved over the road into smaller apartments in the Palais Royale, a modern, classically-styled palace built by Cardinal Richelieu.

But living there was inconvenient, for it was much in use by the French court. Sometimes they even bumped into Cromwellian envoys in the corridors. 'Lord Jermyn', the English ambassador reported to Cromwell on one such occasion, 'did cast an angry eye upon me'.

In November 1654, therefore, the Queen bought a mansion at Chaillot and turned it into a convent for the Poor Nuns of the Visitation of Mary, with a small suite reserved for her personal use. For the rest of her life the convent, with its beautiful views out to the blue hills of Meudon and Châtillon, would be Henrietta Maria's favourite place of retreat.

In 1657, Queen Anne bought Henrietta Maria a new home. The Château of Colombes lay in the low-lying oxbow of land where the Seine makes its great semi-circular sweep from north to west before running down towards the ramparts of Saint-Germain.

Five miles from the centre of Paris, Colombes had been owned by Basil Fouquet, brother of the French finance minister. It was a grand neo-classical chateau, two stories high with a third row of shuttered windows in the mansard roof, ranged around a central courtyard whose high, ornamental iron gates faced out onto the little town of Colombes. Behind, stretched Italianate ornamental gardens. Inside, its main feature was a magnificent ceiling painted by Simon Vouet, showing Venus (Aphrodite) and Bacchus (Dionysius) – the goddess of love, and the god of wine, a combination that could lead to all manner of trouble.

Henrietta Maria as a widow

Back in the 1630s, it would have been an almost shockingly appropriate ceiling for Henrietta Maria and Jermyn to have dined beneath. Now, the diminutive Queen Mother and her stout Lord Chamberlain were little different to any of the other middle-aged married couples whose villas dotted the water meadows and hunting parks around them.

Colombes was an elegant, comfortable residence, but it was a far cry from the world of flamboyant luxury that Jermyn loved. They made periodic returns to their apartments in the Palais Royale, and Jermyn maintained his office there. There must have been dark days when he wondered whether all his efforts were for nought, but despite that Jermyn never gave up hope that one day all things might be restored to their proper order.

The Chateau of Colombes was demolished in 1793. No pictures survive of it, but next door stood a secondary mansion that was also part of Henrietta Maria's estate. This is a picture of the courtyard of the latter, which was itself demolished in the 1960s

In December 1653, Oliver Cromwell's ascendancy was made official when he became Lord Protector of England. The Rump Parliament, so-called because it had been purged of all possible dissenting members, had been dissolved eight months earlier. In

1655, the country was divided into eleven divisions, each run by an authoritarian Major General.

The government became infamous for its repressive Puritanism. Plays were banned and the celebration of Christmas was forbidden for being too pagan. In Canterbury, the initial enforcing of this ban by Parliament back in 1647 had provoked an outright riot during which the mayor was pelted with Christmas puddings in the city's Butter Market. Now, under Cromwell, this ban was enforced again.

Thereafter, Christmas celebrations could only be held surreptitiously. D'Avenant, who had returned to London hoping to make a living for his family, tried to find a way around the ban on plays by setting the words of his dramas to music, thus inventing the opera. But despite such furtive efforts, life in 'Merrie Englande', especially for the well-to-do, had become martial, mechanistic – and miserable.

Of this, Jermyn was well aware. To Jermyn, the Commonwealth was not an exciting experiment in forging a new world: it was merely an abortive experiment in doing without a King. But, perhaps more importantly, he was not the only Englishman who yearned for the bright days of plenty before the Civil War.

Throughout Britain, an increasing number of people who had once taken sides against the King in the hope of a better future were becoming disillusioned. Very few people had ever believed the execution of Charles I was right, and now an increasing proportion of the population began to long for the Stuarts to return.

Using smuggled correspondence and secret agents, both Jermyn and Hyde were in contact with many such disillusioned people. Hyde's main point of contact was the Sealed Knot, a group of staunchly Anglican conspirators. Jermyn's network of agents established their own contacts, particularly with Presbyterians, encouraging them not only to rise up against Cromwell but also to look to Jermyn, and not Hyde, for leadership.

Everything was surreptitious and furtive. Each agent had a code-name, often more than one. Over the years, Jermyn, the spymaster, had many, of which we know but a few – 'Mr Jackson'; 'Mr Juxley', 'Mr Welworth' and, possibly, 'Nemo' and 'Lord Clancarrl'.

One of Jermyn's successes, that put anybody off writing his biography three centuries after his death, was the volume of information about his own activities and those of his agents which he managed to keep secret. We know he had a spy network, but the vast majority of his underground connections remained forever where he intended them to be, in darkness.

Occasionally, a fortuitous hole, such as his dealings with Colonel Joseph Bampfield (1622-1685), exposes a tiny part of the whole. In the 1650s, Bampfield became a double-agent, selling Jermyn information about the Commonwealth government in London, and at the same time selling the Commonwealth government information about his conversations with Jermyn. Before then, Bampfield had been a Royalist spy, ostensibly, at any rate, though the nature of his true loyalties is impossible to fathom, unless they were simply to himself. Hyde had picked up on Bampfield's unreliability by 1653, yet as late as 1657 Jermyn was protesting the colonel's loyalty to the Crown, and risking being branded as a double-agent himself as a result. Had he been duped, or was he trying to play both Bampfield and Hyde along? What we do know is that, when Jermyn found out about Cromwell's prospective treaty with Spain in 1657, it had been Bampfield who had alerted him.

D'Avenant was almost certainly an agent-cum-spy of

Jermyn's. Abraham Cowley certainly was. Another, more surprising one, was the young Duke of Buckingham.

Born in 1628, in the very year when his father, that volatile favourite of James I and Charles I, had been murdered, young Buckingham was a close friend of Charles II, boisterous, extravagant and utterly irresponsible. Like Jermyn's poets, he returned to London, pretending that he had abandoned all hope of Restoration, and was prepared to live now under Cromwell.

In 1658 Cromwell, obviously suspicious of Buckingham's real motives, slung him into the Tower of London. When news of this filtered back to the Palais Royale, Jermyn visited Mazarin at Fontainebleau, the royal palace 60 miles up the Seine from Paris, to ask him to intercede with Cromwell for young Buckingham's release.

The night of 2 September 1658 must have seemed like Jermyn's nadir.

Overhead, a terrible storm howled across Europe, rattling the windowpanes and ripping branches off the trees in the palace gardens of Fountainebleau. The King of England held him in contempt thanks to the machinations of Hyde: the King of France's First Minister was so frightened of upsetting Cromwell he would not even intervene for young Buckingham.

For a man who had based his career on his ability to influence others, Jermyn was not doing very well at all.

What Jermyn did not know was that, in London, Oliver Cromwell lay helpless in bed, listening to the storm winds moaning along the corridors of Whitehall, his warty face drenched with feverish sweat.

The following day, 3 September, while Jermyn watched the gardeners clearing the fallen debris away from the ornamental gardens, Cromwell died.

* * *

What Jermyn was astute enough to know was that, like so many dictatorships, Cromwell's regime had been based on his own force of character. Now that force, like the September storm, was spent, so the regime was doomed.

True, the 'great Hell-cat' had forced Parliament to vote him authority to nominate a successor and, being a typical seventeenth century gentleman at heart, he had nominated his son, Richard. But Richard, in common with so many other sons of domineering fathers, was weak, feckless and hopeless with money. His attempts to run the republic lasted eight months, before he was forced to resign by the recently restored Rump Parliament. But even as Oliver was being lowered into his grave, Jermyn knew there was a good chance that the English upper classes, hankering after the good old days, might soon ask Charles to return home.

Mazarin was no less politically astute than Jermyn. On Thursday, 9 September 1658, the Cardinal put on his best scarlet robes and came hurrying to pay his personal respects to Henrietta Maria. The next day, Jermyn wrote to Charles, triumphantly anticipating the end of the alliance between France and Cromwellian England – 'the engagements contracted with the dead monster [Cromwell]', he wrote, 'expire suddenly'.

Charles II was now twenty-eight. He had long since gained his independence from Henrietta Maria and Jermyn, and forgotten his youthful resentment towards them. She was, after all, his mother, and Jermyn – whatever Jermyn really was in relation to him – was working harder than anyone else to help restore him to his throne. And this was, let us remember, an extraordinary situation. The King and his ministers were in the Low Countries. Nothing on paper suggested that his mother's Lord Chamberlain in Paris should necessarily be playing any role in politics at all, let alone blazing the trail towards the Restoration.

The new developments in England offered the King a perfect excuse to send a very friendly letter to his mother, urging her and Jermyn to seek any diplomatic, financial or military backing that Mazarin might be willing to give. Delighted to shine in use once more, Jermyn talked the Cardinal into loaning him the services of Marshal Turenne and a small army to send to England the following summer, to support a Royalist rising.

Jermyn and Henrietta Maria spent their last pennies on a frigate to carry the King home. But in doing so they acted prematurely. A member of Hyde's Sealed Knot group of conspirators betrayed the planned rising to the Council of State in London, who promptly arrested the rebellion's leaders. Neither the frigate nor Turenne's troops ever crossed the English Channel.

Now that he had lost his alliance with Cromwell, and the backing of the powerful English navy, Cardinal Mazarin was anxious to make a peace treaty with his old adversary, Spain. Talks were opened at Fuentenarabia in the Pyrenees in the summer of 1659. Only once the treaty was concluded would the Cardinal devote himself to helping the Royalists in earnest. Frustrating though the delay was, both Charles and Jermyn agreed that their best hope now lay in persuading both France and Spain to include an agreement to promote the Restoration in the peace treaty.

As soon as news of the failure of the English rising reached Charles, he set off with a handful of attendants to join the French court at Toulouse, and sent a message to Jermyn, ordering him to join him there as well.

Jermyn left Paris on Wednesday, 5 October. His coach and horses pounded through Orléans, Bourges and Limoges, the high peaks of the Massif Centrale jolting past outside the window. They passed through the warm vineyards of Cahors and thundered through the gateway of the ancient city of Toulouse, ending a journey of 350 miles.

Here, Jermyn had an audience with the increasingly plump Queen Anne. But he was too late to reach Mazarin before the Peace of the Pyrenees was signed. Contrary to all hopes, it contained no special provisions for aiding Charles's restoration.

The King sent for Jermyn to join him near Biarritz. Jermyn clambered back into his coach and set off west along the foothills of the Pyrenees. On Friday, 4 November, with the smell of the Atlantic tingling in his nostrils, he reached the village of Saint-Vincent and was spotted by Lord Colepeper. 'I see we carry our lousy fate with us wheresoever we go', grumbled the Kentish Cavalier in a letter to Secretary Nicholas, 'we all of us (except one) being as beggars here as we were at Brussels, and I in particular being…in an old thread-bare French suit for want of money'. That 'except one', of course, was the ever-dapper Jermyn.

The excited villagers told them Mazarin was on his way. As soon as the Cardinal's entourage lumbered into the village, Jermyn approached him and asked for an audience. The outcome was that Mazarin agreed to draw up a special agreement with Spain, independent of the peace treaty, agreeing to support the Royalists.

Travelling north, Jermyn reached Bordeaux on Friday, 11 November. After an anxious five days' wait, the King arrived. The two men had not met for five years. As Jermyn knelt to kiss Charles's hand, he knew his future, as well as the Queen's, depended on how the grown-up King treated him. But the younger man's frustrated anger had long-since dissipated. Instead, he was only too happy to accept the fatherly embrace of a man he knew would give his life to serve him. To Jermyn's delight, Charles said he wanted to visit his mother at Colombes. That extraordinary relationship between Jermyn and Charles II which had flourished in the early 1650s had been reaffirmed.

Jermyn reached Paris on Wednesday, 23 November, two days ahead of the King. Henrietta Maria, through a misunderstanding, was spring-cleaning their old apartments at the Palais Royale instead. She received the news that Charles wanted to see her in the more intimate surroundings of Colombes 'with mighty joy'.

There were tearful scenes when Charles was reunited with his mother at Colombes on Friday, 25 November. It had been so long since he had seen his sister Henrietta Anne that he almost kissed one of the Queen's ladies in waiting by mistake. It did not matter. The Royal Family was united again and Jermyn was exultant, and relieved, as he ushered his surrogate family indoors, out of the bitterly cold November afternoon.

While the snow fell heavily outside, Jermyn and Charles spent many hours shut away by a blazing fire in Jermyn's offices, deep in conference. Their select companions included a young Presbyterian Royalist, John Mordaunt. Mordaunt belonged to a network of English conspirators called 'The Trust'. The last time Mordaunt had visited Paris, Jermyn had recognised his potential value and made friends with him.

Mordaunt was now staying in Jermyn's personal apartments, 'the best quartered of anybody', as he told his wife, 'and my Lord Jermyn treats me dinner and supper'.

Jermyn had acted wisely because the young man had the most exciting news from England. The recently-restored Rump Parliament had been dissolved. The old Cromwellian regime was disintegrating. Martial law had been declared. Only General Monck and the remains of the Cromwellian army retained any real power. Mordaunt's contacts included friends and relations of Monck's. He felt sure the General could be persuaded to declare his loyalty to the King, especially if the French would back him up with a promise of armed support. Securing the latter, of course, would be Jermyn's job, whilst Charles returned to his home-in-exile in Brussels.

Jermyn had regained a great deal of Charles's confidence, but Hyde, recently made Baron Hyde and promoted from Chancellor of the Exchequer to Lord Chancellor, the titular head of the legal profession, was still the King's chief advisor – the 'First Minister'.

Jermyn understood the reason for this only too well, explaining to Lord Aubigny that when Hyde had the King 'with him among his papers, and shows him this and that letter of intelligence, and comments upon them, and that the king, who likes not to be over pressed with such knotty and intricate things, would divert himself, he may lead him to a resolution'. So, whilst England was the primary focus of his attention, Jermyn also gave considerable thought to what was happening in the King's court in Brussels, and how he might be able to prise the limpet Hyde off the great rock that was the King.

Before he left Colombes, Charles had signified his renewed confidence in Jermyn by granting him an earldom. Jermyn chose the title of Earl of St Albans.

Jermyn chose this partly in memory of his kinsman Francis Bacon, who had been Viscount St Albans. But St Alban himself was the legendary founder of English Freemasonry, and it may be significant in this context that, whilst history remembers Jermyn as Earl of St Albans, he himself always signed himself 'St Alban'. It was to the English Freemasons that Jermyn may now have looked for support in his bid to oust Hyde and become First Minister himself.

Besides Freemasons, Jermyn definitely sought support from the English Presbyterians. He told them truthfully that, after the Restoration, the staunchly Anglican Hyde would be 'implacably bitter' against them, whereas he, Jermyn, would strive for religious toleration. He hoped these groups would create a groundswell of opinion against Hyde, which would help convince Charles to give Jermyn his old position back.

Jermyn's main weapon against Hyde, however, was to build the Restoration on a French guarantee of Charles's well-being which Jermyn, not the Chancellor, had negotiated. 'Otherwise', as Hyde's friend Dr Morley commented sardonically, 'the Lord Chancellor cannot be put out nor Jermyn brought in'.

In March 1660, after his customary prevarications, Cardinal Mazarin agreed to Jermyn's request for military backing. It was not until April, however, that the Cardinal granted permission for Charles to return to France, whence he could launch his triumphant return to England.

As soon as Jermyn knew that permission had been granted, he raced off to deliver the good news to the King, who was now staying with his sister Mary at Breda, on the border between the Netherlands and Spanish-controlled Flanders.

Meanwhile, however, the diplomatic strategy set in motion via the English agent Mordaunt had worked. The former Cromwellian General George Monck now believed that the restored monarchy was all that could save England from anarchy. Under his aegis, a full Parliament was called, and it voted to restore the King.

The very same day as Jermyn reached Breda Castle, full of plans to bring Charles back to France, the messenger arrived from London to bid the King come home.

Suddenly, there was no need to go to Paris. Instead, Charles processed triumphantly to The Hague, where an English ship, hastily renamed the *Royal Charles*, awaited him. At Colombes, and despite the disappointment at the change of plan, Henrietta Maria heard the news 'with all the marks of joy imaginable'. Carriagefuls of French nobles rolled up to her little chateau to congratulate her. Returning to the Palais Royale, she held a grand ball to celebrate the amazing news. She invited every Englishman in Paris to the ball, and as many French nobles as would fit in.

And Jermyn? His place was with the Queen, and his duty was to convey the King's apologies to Mazarin for not taking up his offer. With fireworks and toasts behind and ahead of him, his solitary coach rumbled back over the potholed roads of northern France.

He had done an amazing amount to achieve the Restoration of the monarchy, yet in his latest efforts to supplant the power of that most tenacious of adversaries, sharp-minded Lord Chancellor Hyde, he had failed.

Charles II entered London on Tuesday, 29 May 1660. Passing regally through the crowds with Hyde not far behind, he reserved a particularly cheery wave for Mordaunt's wife, whom he spotted watching from a balcony. The same morning, Henrietta Maria sat at her bureau at Colombes, gazing out with tearful eyes towards the distant ramparts of Saint-Germain. To her eldest son she wrote, 'you may judge of my joy, and if you are torn to pieces over in England, I have had my share here in France'.

Finishing her letter, she set off with Jermyn for Chaillot to hear her nuns singing *Te Deums*. Afterwards, they processed into Paris, the Queen coughing triumphantly as the crowds cheered and waved. That evening, Jermyn and Henrietta Maria watched as celebratory fireworks exploded over the high roofs of the Palais Royale.

* * *

The Restoration had been a major goal of Jermyn's. The lost world of his early years had been miraculously regained. The fight for his own power and influence, however, was still to be resolved: and the battlefield where that fight would be waged was no longer in France, but in the corridors of power in Whitehall.

XV

RESTORATION!
1660 – 1662

Where's now the royal mother – where?
To take her mighty share
In this inspiring sight,
And with the part she takes,
to add to the delight!

Ah, why art thou not here,
Thou always best, and now the happiest queen,
To see our joy, and with new joy be seen?
How well thy different virtues thee become,
Daughter of triumphs, queen of martyrdom!
Abraham Cowley, 'Ode on the Return and
Restoration of Charles II' (1660)

At the beginning of June 1660, Henry Jermyn, Earl of St Albans, set foot on English soil for the first time in sixteen years.

On the quayside around him he heard a sound that had become thoroughly unfamiliar – men and women speaking English.

The dashing Cavalier colonel who had sailed away from Pendennis Castle with Henrietta Maria had changed a great deal. Despite all their money worries, sixteen years of French soup and gold had added considerably to his waistline, although his upright stature and broad shoulders still preserved him from looking too overweight.

The goatee beard and moustache he had sported so gallantly

in his youth had vanished: his lined face was now shaved fashionably clean.

Since 1624, when Louis XIII started wearing artificial hair over his thinning locks, periwigs had become commonplace amongst mature European gentlemen. Worn initially to defy signs of aging, they had developed to become the height of fashion for men of all ages. Now the sumptuous curls of Jermyn's new wig clustered around his furrowed brows and cascaded lustrously down over his shoulders.

At the Palace of Whitehall on Wednesday, 6 June, Jermyn took his seat at the Privy Council (to which he had been appointed in 1652), the body through which the newly restored King ruled England. A few members were good friends of his, such as Prince Rupert, the young Duke of Buckingham – who had survived his spell in Cromwell's gaol – and Jermyn's young cousin, Charlie Berkeley, a talented soldier and high-spirited drinking-companion of the King, who was also a close friend of Jermyn's nephew Harry Jermyn.

But the Council was dominated by Lord Chancellor Hyde, now a late-middle aged man like Jermyn, his flaxen hair turning grey and perhaps already hidden under a wig similar to Jermyn's, his waistline also much enlarged, but in no respects any less sharp or energetic in his work than he had been twenty years earlier.

The majority of members shared Hyde's lofty anti-French, pro-Anglican sentiments.

One of the first things Hyde proposed was to dismiss the French ambassador, because he had previously served under Cromwell. It was a move calculated to offend Cardinal Mazarin, so Jermyn objected. Not one person backed Jermyn up.

The ambassador's dismissal was part of Hyde's policy of

aligning Britain with the Hapsburg countries of Spain and Austria and against France. If Jermyn had not been in London, these policies would have been fulfilled.

Yet Jermyn's personal relationship with Charles II still counted for a great deal. The King had known Jermyn all his life. He knew the rumours that this tall, clever, incredibly well-informed and profoundly reliable man was his father, but more than that he remembered and valued the fatherly role Jermyn had played in his life. Therefore, even as Hyde's Privy Council thought they were deciding on one set of policies, Jermyn had a quiet drink with the King and persuaded him to take on a completely different set – based around a closer alliance with France.

Throughout the Commonwealth period, Jermyn had struggled to preserve friendship between the English and French royal families. He did so partly at Henrietta Maria's behest, for she belonged to both; partly because he felt that France was the exiles' strongest potential ally; and also because he knew that such a friendship was the surest footing on which his own power could rest.

In the very different world of Restoration England, Jermyn continued to press for Anglo-French unity, and for the same reasons. The policy of Anglo-French co-operation was known as the 'Closer Union', a term Jermyn first used himself in a letter to Charles in April 1661. Its details emerge through the correspondence and events of the ensuing decade, leading up to the Secret Treaty of Dover in 1670.

In its grandest form, as it emerged over the next decade, Jermyn's scheme promoted a Europe dominated by Henrietta Maria's family, particularly her son Charles, her grandson William of Orange and Louis XIV, who was (the likelihood of his really being Mazarin's son aside) her nephew. If these three could rely on one another's armed support, they could quash their national parliaments and count on one another's support if any of their subjects rebelled. United, they could overcome the Hapsburg powers: this in turn would lead to their joint domination of central Europe and the carving up of the fabulous wealth of the Hapsburg colonies in South America.

It is impossible to say precisely when any individual element of this plan was first considered, or by whom. But all the evidence suggests that, even if the original idea was not Jermyn's – though it may well have been – it was a plan that he embraced and promoted wholeheartedly.

It does not seem unlikely that Jermyn could indeed have been the man who first dreamed up such an audacious scheme as the Closer Union. Early documentary evidence of Jermyn's enthusiasm for the scheme, in its most basic form of the English and French crowns' pledge of mutual assistance against enemies, external and internal, includes a letter he wrote in July 1662. Here, Jermyn wrote that Charles and Louis 'will be preserved so very much by the happy union that is now between them which continuing they will have very little to fear either from foreign enemies or domestic embroilments'.

The plan clearly appealed to Charles more than a Hapsburg alliance precisely because of the importance it placed on his own, immediate family ties. In June 1660, therefore, and without consulting Hyde, the King sent Jermyn's nephew Harry Jermyn to apologise to Mazarin for the ambassador's dismissal.

Charles also agreed to appoint Jermyn as Ambassador Extraordinary to France, to renew the ancient Anglo-French treaties and sign a new treaty with France, each side promising to send armed assistance should the other be attacked. Charles also concurred with Jermyn that his little sister Princess Henrietta Anne should marry Louis XIV's brother Philippe, who had recently inherited the title of Duke of Orléans. Charles himself would marry Catherine of Braganza, the daughter of France's ally, the King of Portugal, thus bringing Portugal into the anti-Hapsburg coalition.

All of these policies ran contrary to those of Hyde's government. Thanks to the extraordinary, almost father-son relationship that existed between the King and his henchman, it was Jermyn himself who now directed England's foreign policy.

When Jermyn set foot back on English soil, he did so alone. The Queen simply could not face seeing her desecrated chapel at Somerset House or the collapsing roofs of her other palaces. The thought of being amongst the very crowds who, as she imagined, had jeered her husband as he went to the executioner's block, filled her with horror.

Yet in the autumn, she summoned Jermyn back to collect her, and they landed safely at Dover on Friday, 26 October.

The Queen had changed her mind because her second eldest son James, Duke of York, had just announced his previously secret marriage to a commoner, none other than Chancellor Hyde's own daughter, Anne. The Queen's aim in returning was to force Charles to dissolve the marriage, but nothing she could say could persuade him to do so.

Worse events then unfolded, for first her youngest son Henry and then her daughter Mary contracted smallpox and died.

Mary, who had come over to England that autumn as well, was a widow and had, for several years now, been conducting a semi-illicit romance with Jermyn's twenty-four-year-old nephew, Harry Jermyn.

An unflattering description of Harry, the second son of Jermyn's quiet older brother Thomas, states that he had a big head and thin legs. But he was also very athletic, an accomplished swordsman and an enthusiastic soldier, who had spent most of the previous decade serving in the French and later the Spanish army, alongside James and Harry's equally high-spirited cousin, Charlie Berkeley.

Copy of an old photograph of a portrait of Jermyn's rakish nephew Harry Jermyn

A series of diplomatic missions to Holland on behalf of his uncle, and his accompanying of the Duke of York on visits there, had brought Harry into frequent contact with Mary who, according to her advisor Daniel O'Neill, was 'pleased with Harry Jermyn's love'. Once Mary knew she had smallpox she decided, according to the veteran gossip, Samuel Pepys, to marry Harry.

If this marriage really took place, it was on or about Thursday, 20 December 1660. Regardless of the truth or not of this, there is no doubt at all how Mary felt about Harry's uncle. She had always regarded him as her family's defender. Now, in her will, the princess made Jermyn one of the executors of her estate.

Mary's death shook Henrietta Maria into making her peace with James, his new wife Anne, and even with Lord Chancellor Hyde himself. She did so on New Year's Day, 1661. Then, she left Whitehall with Jermyn immediately, embarking from Portsmouth nine days later under a brooding sky.

As soon as they left the shelter of the harbour a gale struck, tearing at the sails and driving the ship and its terrified occupants back onto Horse Sands. They ran aground with a sickening crunch, convinced they were about follow Mary to the grave. But, as Henrietta Maria had always been fond of commenting, no English queen had ever been drowned. They were rescued and brought safely to shore. Their next attempt was more successful and they crossed safely to France.

Mary of Orange, daughter of Charles I and Henrietta Maria, young widow of
William II of Orange and mother of William III of Orange.
By 'van Honthorst', and reproduced with very kind permission of the present owner

Early on the morning of Saturday, 16 March 1661, Jermyn's

coach crunched down the frost-encrusted gravel of Colombes's driveway and out onto the rutted road towards the distant smog of Paris. Instead of his own coat of arms, the doors of his coach were emblazoned with those of Charles II. This was the day of his official *entrée* into Paris as the King's Ambassador Extraordinary.

After the formal procession of carriages sent by the other foreign ambassadors and dignitaries, Jermyn reached the French court at the Louvre.

Here, under the eyes of the French nobility, he proceeded past the scarlet-liveried musketeers and into the great audience chamber. Jermyn swept the long plume of his black velvet hat across the inlaid marble floor before him and crooked his knee in an elegant bow.

He was in the presence of Louis XIV, the most powerful man in Europe, a monarch so exalted that, if courtiers saw his dinner being carried down the palace corridors, they were obliged to salute it.

The twenty-three-year-old King, with his narrow eyes, Roman nose and arching eyebrows, was wearing black. Seventeen days ago, Cardinal Mazarin had died. Rather than appoint a new First Minister, Louis had surprised everyone, including Jermyn, by deciding to rule France personally. Mazarin and Richelieu before him had created the Absolute Monarchy in France. Now Louis had become France's first truly Absolute Monarch, the Sun King, radiating glory from the centre of his great domain.

Though conducted in the most ritualised, courtly fashion, Jermyn's conversation with Louis would have been very different to most dialogues between kings and new ambassadors, who may never even have met face to face before. Besides being absolutely fluent in French, Jermyn had, most unusually, spent some sixteen years at the French court. He had known Louis from the time when the King, as a small boy, used to march up and down the courtyard of the Palais Royale, beating his toy drum. His effectiveness as an ambassador therefore had the potential to be immense.

On his deathbed, Cardinal Mazarin had urged Louis to foster closer ties with Charles. Jermyn now told Louis that the creation of such closer ties with France was exactly what Charles wanted.

Jermyn had already completed the negotiations for the marriage of Henrietta Anne and Louis's brother Philippe. Four days after his *entrée*, Jermyn returned to the Louvre for the formal signing of the contract. After the signatures of the French royal family appears his own title, Earl of St Albans, translated into French – 'Comte de St Alban'.

Henrietta Anne had grown up with the Queen and Jermyn in France. She had never known Charles I. Jermyn was the closest person she had known to a father, and she (the vexed question of Eleanor Villiers' baby aside) was the closest he had known to a daughter. Henrietta Anne's wedding, on Sunday, 31 March 1661, was a proud day for him personally. And Jermyn was delighted too when Louis told Charles that the marriage would be 'a new tie which will draw still closer the bonds of our friendship'.

At Fontainebleau, on Midsummer's Eve, Sunday, 23 June 1661, Jermyn and Louis signed a renewal of the ancient treaty between England and France, and began discussing a new treaty whereby each monarch would send armed help should the other be attacked either by foreign enemies or domestic rebels.

Because the marriage of Charles II and Catherine of Braganza was so politically important to France, Mazarin had agreed to pay the dowry. The negotiations over the amount, and which colonies Portugal would give Charles in return, were conducted in Paris.

According to some sources, the Portuguese marriage had been Jermyn and Henrietta Maria's idea. Regardless of who first thought it up, it was now an integral part of their greater scheme for Anglo-French friendship, and Jermyn did all he could to make the negotiations run smoothly.

The discussions were made rather complicated by Hyde. Unable to prevent the marriage going ahead – he would have preferred a Protestant or, at a pinch, a Hapsburg princess – Hyde had decided, in the manner of pompous men, to pretend the Portuguese marriage had been his idea all along, and thus take the credit away from Jermyn.

Therefore, while Jermyn negotiated openly at the French court, Hyde was in secret correspondence about the same thing with Louis's finance minister, Nicholas Fouquet. It was therefore a combination of both negotiations that produced the finished contract, although ultimately Jermyn does deserve the credit – not least because in August, Hyde's efforts were curtailed.

On 17 August, Fouquet gave a sumptuous ball at his newly-completed Chateau of La Fontaine. The whole French court was invited, and also Henrietta Maria and Jermyn. During the proceedings, someone, probably the Queen's old friend the Duchess of Chevreuse, mentioned to Louis, seemingly casually but really quite deliberately, that the only way Fouquet could possibly have afforded such magnificence was by embezzling the King's money. Four days later, Fouquet was flung into the Bastille. Was Jermyn behind this? We do not know.

The following May, 1662, when swallows flitted over the glittering waves on their way back to England, Jermyn's nephew Harry escorted Catherine of Braganza up the Channel to Portsmouth. Jermyn arrived back from France to be present at the royal wedding, which was celebrated in Portsmouth Cathedral on Wednesday, 21 May.

The marriage dowry that Jermyn had negotiated brought England Tangiers, which proved worthless, and the province of Bombay, Britain's first possession in India. Almost three thousand miles of the Arabian Sea separated Bombay from Madagascar, yet in Jermyn's mind this may have seemed some fulfilment of that old, 1630s dream, that one day the English would rule the Eastern oceans. His plans to transform London into a new Rome were already in hand, the acquisition of Bombay was a major element of that yet more audacious dream – to gain for Britain an empire to rival that of Rome's.

As things turned out, Jermyn's wildest dreams were fulfilled – and vastly exceeded. At the height of its empire, Rome may have controlled as much as three million square miles. When Britain's empire was at its height at the start of the twentieth century, it was larger by four and a half times.

Jermyn had achieved all his aims, except the signing of the new defensive treaty between England and France. But the brilliant lawyer's mind of Hyde, whom Charles had now made Earl of Clarendon, was already working on a counterattack, and of course it was he, and not Jermyn, who had access to the King's ear in London.

Hyde took every opportunity he could to create diplomatic incidents between England and France, such as by ordering the navy to interfere with French fishing boats and demanding that French ships should salute English ones. Although Jermyn made a special journey to London in December 1661 to see Charles, he still could not prevent Hyde from continuing to damage England's relations with France.

From Louis's point of view, and however much Jermyn tried

to persuade him to the contrary, what Jermyn said about Charles's affection for France was simply not reflected by the actions of Charles's government. Although Louis thanked Jermyn for his efforts as ambassador and gave him a large diamond, he refused to sign the new defensive treaty with England.

Instead, the Sun King accepted a very similar one offered him by the Dutch States General. Despite all Jermyn's efforts, France became allied to Holland under its republican States General, and specifically not to Britain. The consequences for Britain and, ironically, for Hyde in particular, were to be appalling.

XVI

'GRAND MASTER OF THE FREEMASONS'
1662

We are graciously pleased at the humble suite and petition of our right
trusty and well beloved Cousin Henry E[arl] of St Albans to ratify and
confirm... the said several grants for or concerning the said field
or close called Pall Mall Field...

Charles II's confirmation the grant of what
would become St James's Square, 1662

On Monday, 28 July 1662, a flotilla of magnificently gilded
barges glided up the River Thames, carrying Jermyn, Henrietta
Maria and their household.

It was the end of a traumatic journey back from France. As
their ship was crossing the Channel, a violent storm had
whipped up the waves, driving them up past the White Cliffs and
into the North Sea.

Greenwich, showing the old palace and the Queen's House, drawn by Wenceslaus Hollar in 1637

They had narrowly escaped being shipwrecked on the
treacherous sandbanks off the east coast of Kent, and had
finally come ashore at Deal. They must have been extremely

relieved when the barges rounded the last bend in the river and they saw their destination – Greenwich.

Since the Restoration, Jermyn, in his joint capacities as the Queen's Lord Chamberlain and – by Henrietta Maria's new appointment – High Steward of Greenwich, had organised the repair and improvement of her palace.

When they stepped ashore, painters and gilders were putting the last touches to the restored Queen's House, the white, classically-styled mansion in the palace grounds, that had been designed by the great Inigo Jones.

Greenwich Park, which had degenerated into a wilderness during Cromwell's rule, was being landscaped to designs they had commissioned from André Le Nôtre, the designer of the gardens of both Fontainebleau and Henrietta Anne's new home in the Parisian suburbs, Saint-Cloud.

Meanwhile, masons were toiling in the July sun to demolish the old Tudor palace and replace it with a new classical one. Inigo Jones had died in 1652, and nobody knows which of two architects Jermyn had hired for this purpose – it was either Inigo Jones's protégé John Webb, or Sir John Denham, who had been one of Jermyn's secret agents during the Commonwealth.

From the front door of the Queen's House, Jermyn and Henrietta Maria could look north over the piles of rubble and imagine what the view would be like in the future.

In the distance the lush green grass of the water meadows of the Isle of Dogs was already turning into golden hay. In the middle-ground was the Thames, its rippling surface glinting and flashing in the summer sunlight.

In the foreground, when all was finished, would be ornamental gardens rounded off with neat stone balustrades. And on either side of their vista would be two massive square buildings of fine stone, pillared and corniced like English versions of the Louvre.

It would be like a grandiose stage-setting, and indeed Greenwich seems to have been planned thus, as a magnificent real-life stage, on which the King could receive foreign ambassadors.

As ambassadors landed, they would see the same view, but in reverse, the great classical blocks of the palace framing the emerald background of the landscaped park, and, in the foreground, the shining whiteness of the Queen's House.

Late in the summer of 1662, Jermyn and Henrietta Maria travelled further up-river in their splendid barges from Greenwich to Somerset House. Here, too, Jermyn had been busy renovating and innovating.

He and the Queen had altered some old designs made by Inigo Jones for extending the palace. A large block of rooms was being built in brick along the Strand, enclosing the Great Court inside. A gallery supported by white marble pillars was being constructed on the south side, overlooking the Thames. The land between the palace and the river was being laid out as an Italianate garden, complete with a set of marble stairs leading down to the water.

They made Somerset House so beautiful that Jermyn's poet Abraham Cowley wrote a poem in which the palace itself sings of its gratitude to the Queen.

Cowley, who had lived in London since 1654 in order to spy on Cromwell for Jermyn, now rejoined the Queen's household as Henrietta Maria's secretary. He served until 1667, when Jermyn wrote sadly of the death of 'poor Cowley'. Shortly before he died, Cowley asked his friend the Bishop of Rochester to publish his collected works and dedicate them to Jermyn. 'I doubt not', the Bishop wrote in the preface

> but according to his usual humanity, he [Jermyn] will
> accept this imperfect legacy, of the man whom he

long honoured with his domestic conversation. And I am confident his Lordship will believe it no injury to his Fame, that in these Papers my Lord St Albans and Mr Cowley's name shall be read together by posterity.

The masons whom Henrietta Maria and her Chamberlain watched toiling in the July sunshine were only some of the hundreds whom he was employing all over London, and with whom he had a very special relationship for, according to a later source, Jermyn was Grand Master of the Freemasons.

The frontispiece of Anderson's 'Constitutions', published in 1738, gives a hint of the world of Freemasonry, with its emphasis on classical architecture and the inspirational connection between heaven and earth symbolized by the flying chariot, that Jermyn may himself have experienced some 70 years earlier.

During Jermyn's lifetime, Freemasonry went through a major change. Until the seventeenth century, Freemasonry consisted of meetings, or 'lodges', of working masons, builders and architects. Their purpose was chiefly to maintain and pass on standards and techniques, including the detailed knowledge of geometry necessary to construct such wonders as the medieval cathedrals.

In the sixteenth and seventeenth centuries, when the church-dominated universities still viewed new ideas with deep suspicion, Freemasonic lodges started to attract non-masons who were interested in geometry. Particularly, it attracted people inspired by Francis Bacon's new ideas of exploring the world through scientific investigation.

There was a spiritual element as well, for science and religion had not yet become divorced. Because the world was believed to have been created by God, science – the exploration of the world – was regarded as an investigation into the mind of the creator, the great architect of the Universe.

By the eighteenth century, Freemasonry would become an organization for esoteric, spiritual studies, coupled with complicated grades of rituals, and a substantial social element as well.

Thus, in Jermyn's day, Freemasonry was somewhere in between old and new – it was gaining a strongly spiritual element, but it was still rooted in practical, working masonry.

Jermyn's Freemasonry is attested by a single source, the 1738 edition of Dr James Anderson's *Constitutions of the Antient and Honourable Fraternity of Free and Accepted Masons*. Published by the authority of Grand Lodge, this book includes a history of Freemasonry in England, alleging some measure of continuity from Roman times onwards, and listing Grand Masters from the Middle Ages up to and beyond the foundation of Grand Lodge in London in 1717.

It is a controversial list because its earlier sections seem rather fantastic and because it was not included in the first edition of the book, which came out in 1723. Further, it was dropped in 1841, since which time the Craft has denied that any form of organised Freemasonry existed in England before 1717, and thus that there were any earlier Grand Masters at all.

When the matter has been debated, arguments have tended to focus on Sir Christopher Wren. Wren is said to have become one of Jermyn's two Grand Wardens during Jermyn's term of office, rising to become Deputy Grand Master by 1678, and presiding over Freemasonry as Grand Master for many years.

Detractors of Anderson point out that Wren was alive in 1723, so Anderson did not dare publish his 'false' history of the Craft, but he did so in 1738, once Wren was safely dead and unable to deny this 'false' story.

Another interpretation of these events, however, is that seventeenth century Freemasonry was hedged in with so many oaths of secrecy that Wren, who had been involved since the 1660s, may not have countenanced seeing its true history published. Once he was dead, however, this obstacle was removed, and the correct story of seventeenth century Freemasonry could appear in print.

It is significant that, when Wren's son published his monumental biography of his father in 1750, he did not refute Anderson's allegations. Indeed, his text and Hawksmoor's illustrations for the book are full of Freemasonic references. But it was not only Wren's son who kept silent: when the 1738 edition came out, we hear of no protests from the heirs of any of the other earlier, alleged Grand Masters. Nobody spoke out in protest, perhaps because everybody knew that they were reading the truth.

Wren's involvement has been much debated, and on the

outcome of that argument Freemasonic historians have been content to rest the fate of history up until that point. Never have the alleged seventeenth century Grand Masters, such as Jermyn, been studied in their own right, to see if what Anderson said about them might hold any water.

Several aspects of Jermyn's life suggest that he might have been a Freemason, and I still remember my astonished delight when I first leafed through a copy of Anderson's book and found his name listed, not just as a Freemason, but as a Grand Master. The circumstances that had drawn me to look in the first place also help bear out the veracity of Anderson's history, for the seventeenth century, at least.

First, Anderson relates that, having served as deputy Grand Master under several aristocrats, Inigo Jones eventually became Grand Master shortly before the Civil War broke out, and remained so until his death in 1652. We know that Jones's work on the Queen's buildings, especially Greenwich and Somerset House, brought him into contact with Jermyn, and there is no doubt that Jones's work was a clear inspiration for Jermyn's own grand-scale development of St James's. We have also seen how Jones's work on court masques brought him into collaboration with Jermyn's poet, Sir William D'Avenant.

There are tantalising hints of Freemasonry in the writings of both D'Avenant and Cowley, especially when they wrote about spiritual flights in which their souls soared above the earth. These can be linked to a Medieval form of Cabalism called *Merkavah* mysticism, which purported to enable its initiates to do just that, and which was one of the acknowledged, spiritual roots of esoteric eighteenth century Freemasonry. In 'Madagascar', too, D'Avenant wrote that Jermyn was inspired by 'mighty Numbers', in other words, by geometry.

No Grand Master was appointed during the Interregnum.

During this period, Jermyn had fascinatingly 'cloak-and-dagger' dealings with Sir Robert Moray, whose membership of Scottish Freemasonry is an established fact. Whilst the theory cannot be proved, it seems highly likely that Jermyn used his contacts with English Freemasonic lodges as part of his spy-network, gathering information, planning uprisings and spreading Royalist propaganda.

In 1659, as we saw, Jermyn chose the title 'St Alban', which he always spelled without an 's', perhaps harking back to the name of the legendary founder of English Freemasonry, St Alban. Another reason may have been Jermyn's family connection to the long-dead Viscount St Albans, Francis Bacon, but Bacon himself was widely rumoured to have been a Freemason in any case.

Was his adoption of this title a signal to English Freemasons that Jermyn wanted to become their Grand Master? He took office, says Anderson, on the Restoration in 1660. As a man set to develop the West End and with control of the restoration of the Queen's dower palaces, and with the strong possibility (at that stage) that he would become First Minister, Jermyn was indeed an ideal candidate to become the Freemasons' leader.

Anderson tells us that, half way through Jermyn's six year Grand Mastership, he held a national assembly of Freemasons in December 1663. The location was designated by Anderson by thirteen dashes, which *could* denote Somerset House, where the masons working on the renovations would certainly have formed a Lodge. There, Jermyn issued a set of pragmatic rules to reorganise Freemasonry after the disruption of the Cromwellian era.

Such an action is not at all out of character for Jermyn. The rules are not at all dissimilar in character to those he drew up, once he had become the King's Lord Chamberlain, to regulate the ceremony of the Touching for the King's Evil (a ceremony of Medieval origin based on the belief that the King's touch could cure his subjects from scrofula), which are in the State Papers for 1 May 1674.

Anderson's list does not suggest any ties between Jermyn and the other officials who appear at the same time, yet such connections exist. Jermyn's alleged Deputy Grand Warden, Sir John Denham, turns out to have been a spy for Jermyn during the Interregnum. Jermyn's Grand Wardens were John Webb, Jones's son-in-law and Wren.

Jermyn first met Wren in 1665, when the then thirty-five-year-old had travelled to Paris to study Louis's great classical building works. The diarist John Evelyn had given Wren a letter of introduction to Jermyn, who in turn introduced him to many of the most renowned architects of his day, including the great Gianlorenzo Bernini, who was then redesigning the Louvre. This was the year before Jermyn's Grand Mastership ended, giving Jermyn plenty of time to install Wren as a Grand Warden and thus ensure his future as a prominent member of the Craft.

Jermyn's resignation of the office in 1666 ties in with his deep embroilment in the Anglo-Dutch peace-process, which required him to stay almost full-time in Paris. The man who replaced him as Grand Master, Earl Rivers, was in fact a distant cousin of his.

None of this is conclusive evidence that Anderson's list was correct, but let us look at the problem from the other way around. If Anderson had made his list up, and Jermyn was not Grand Master, then he was pretty lucky to have picked someone whose life, when placed under the microscope of historical research, just happens to fit the story so well.

Also, if Anderson was making his list up, then Jermyn was a pretty bad choice. By the eighteenth century, Jermyn and his successors, Rivers, Arlington and even Buckingham were all associated with the sort of pro-French policies that were anathema to the Hanoverian regime, which was then facing very real dangers from pro-French, pro-Stuart conspiracies and rebellions. Anderson's list gives Freemasonry some unpalatably 'Jacobite' roots – exactly the sort of public image that the Craft was seeking to avoid. Hyde would have been a much better choice than Jermyn, if the list was made up.

Anderson's work relied on a number of sources that were later destroyed, and it is hardly his fault that they are not available to us today, to verify his work. Indeed, his narrative almost certainly preserves material that would otherwise have been irrevocably lost.

Anderson also relied on living memory and, when he was writing, very old Masons would still have remembered Jermyn's era. Significantly, Deputy Grand Master Martin Folkes, one of those who officially oversaw Anderson's work, was the son of Jermyn's lawyer. Folkes may have had access to many of Jermyn's papers, that are now lost. The fact that Folkes approved Anderson's list is again pretty good circumstantial evidence that it is true.

On the whole, there seems to be no very good reason to dismiss Anderson's assertion that Jermyn had been Grand Master of the Freemasons. Yet it is quite possible to see how Bacon, Jones and D'Avenant had all inspired Jermyn with the idea that the Golden Age of classical antiquity could be recreated in Stuart England. That is why Jermyn supported the poets D'Avenant and Cowley. It is why he agreed to guide Freemasonry through the first years of the Restoration. And it is why he promoted classical building work at Greenwich, Somerset House and, as we shall see, at St James's, Westminster.

Shortly after the Restoration, Jermyn and Charles were talking in

a chamber at Whitehall when a servant came in to announce a
visitor, who had come to ask for a very lucrative sinecure which
was vacant. Charles could not be bothered dealing with the man,
so he passed Jermyn his hat and told him to pretend to be the
King.

The man came in and bowed low to Jermyn, who listened
very regally to his petition. When the man finished, Jermyn told
him that he clearly deserved the sinecure. But, he continued, as
soon as he had heard it was vacant, he had granted it to his
faithful friend, the Earl of St Albans. After the man had left,
Charles roared with laughter and told Jermyn he could indeed
have the sinecure for himself.

The story does not state what the sinecure job was. But it was
only one of several which combined to bring Jermyn an
enormous income. These included being a Commissioner for
Prizes; a Commissioner for the Coronation; a Justice of the
Peace for Middlesex and Surrey; Engrosser of the Great Rolls
and Governor of Jersey, none requiring any work except for
instructing his lawyer Martin Folkes to collect the fees due to
him.

As Registrar in Chancery, Jermyn received £900 a year in fees
from the portly judges who in turn reaped an income from
people disputing wills and pursuing unpaid debts. Translating
old money into meaningful modern values is very difficult, but a
rough equivalent is about £69,000. A further £1,000 a year
(about £76,500 now) was his stipend for his main job – for
which he did work very hard – of Lord Chamberlain to
Henrietta Maria. As her Lord Chamberlain, Jermyn presided
over her enlarged post-Restoration household and oversaw the
work of her Treasurer and Steward.

While Jermyn was ambassador in Paris he also received £400
(roughly £31,000 in modern money) a month to offset the vast

entertainment expenses the job entailed.

Besides jobs, Jermyn collected an enormous income from land. This included a handful of East Anglian manors he had inherited. By a royal grant of 1649, Jermyn had become a co-proprietor of the Northern Neck of Virginia, where Chickahoan Indians menaced the bold settlers who hewed clearings in the deciduous forests by the shores of Chesapeake Bay. Another royal grant made Jermyn seigneur of the windswept fiefs of Saint-Germain, L'Islet and Saint-Helier in Jersey, all of which paid their feudal dues to him and gave him the right to appoint clergymen to all the island's churches (and charge for the privilege).

The poor tenants of the fertile fields and soggy meadows of an enormous tract of County Antrim in Ireland paid Jermyn an income as well. Jermyn had used his influence with the King to help the Earl of Antrim regain estates that Cromwell had confiscated. In return, Antrim had granted Jermyn a share of the estates' revenue for life. Jermyn's prosperity had been restored in abundance. But there was yet more to come.

Just before he joined Charles at Breda in April 1660, Jermyn had calculated how much money he had raised for the war effort since 1643. The total was 647,416 *livres Tournois*, about £45,000, or about £3.5 million in modern terms.

To put this in context, Charles II's government had an income of only £773,700 in the first year after the Restoration.

Because the King could not repay the debt in cash, he granted Jermyn leases out of the Queen's estates instead. In Surrey, the crumbling edifice of Oatlands Palace and its overgrown deer-park became Jermyn's by a royal grant in 1661, together with the lush water meadows of Byfleet and Weybridge, including valuable, fur-producing rabbit warrens, producing a total of £466 a year.

Of more value to Jermyn was Byfleet Lodge, one of Inigo Jones's earliest classical houses. Significantly, it and the Silk House at Oatlands, another of Jones's designs, were the only parts of his Surrey estate he did not sub-let. The Duchy House, one of the most impressive buildings on the Strand besides Somerset House, became Jermyn's, its rents adding to Jermyn's brimming coffers. Finally, there was the Bailiwick of St James's stretching, in modern terms, from Green Park in the west to St Anne's, Soho in the east.

It was back in 1640 that Jermyn and Henrietta Maria had organised a survey of the almost entirely undeveloped fields of the Bailiwick of St James's. Jermyn and Henrietta Maria surely had grandiose plans for the area before Civil War intervened. By the time Jermyn returned to England in 1662, a series of royal leases, set to run until the mid-eighteenth century, had made the entire Bailiwick his.

On its scrubby fields, especially the area in front of St James's Palace where courtiers practised archery, Jermyn planned a new magnificent addition to London, all built on classical principles, which would bring the capital, and himself, both wealth and prestige. 'The beauty of this great town and the convenience of the court', he wrote to the King, 'are defective in point of houses fit for the dwellings of noblemen and other persons of quality', and he proposed the construction of 'great and good houses' in St James's Fields'.

Standing in the shade of St James's Palace later that summer, Jermyn and Henrietta Maria could watch the builders and surveyors hard at work, marking out the new streets and the grand central square with ropes. The labourers had even started digging the foundations of the first houses in what was to become Jermyn Street.

Jermyn had laid magnificent foundations for London's West

End. The area was inevitably going to be built up as London expanded. Yet it was Jermyn who determined its nature: not the ramshackle medley of residential streets that was spreading out north and east, or the later suburban sprawl that would engulf the lovely fields south of the river, but a truly grand, uplifting area of elegant squares and broad streets, worthy of, if not eventually exceeding, the magnificence of Rome itself.

And a new Rome, rather than yet more old 'New Troy', was surely what Jermyn and Henrietta Maria had in mind. It was visions of this that surged through their minds as they stood gazing out over what was to be a bright Restoration future for London, echoing the prophetic words of Virgil's fourth *Eclogue*, whose text was then well-known to every educated European:

> Ours is the crowning era foretold in prophecy:
> Born of Time, a great new cycle of centuries
> Begins. Justice returns to earth, the Golden Age
> Returns...

London was set to become a city worthy of Virgil, thus achieving one of Jermyn's major goals. Yet his other great ambition, the attaining of high political power would, as in Virgil's Rome, prove far harder to achieve.

XVII

SOMERSET HOUSE
1662 – 1663

So they loved as love in twain,
Had the essence but in one,
Two distincts, Division none...
Francis Bacon, 'The Phoenix and the Turtle'
(*Love's Martyr*, 1601)

After suppers eaten to the accompaniment of musicians and singers, the golden candelabras of Somerset House would be kept burning into the early hours while Jermyn, Henrietta Maria and their guests chatted over the card tables.

Whatever the game, the excitement of gambling was the same. Hyde characterised Jermyn's love of gambling as 'the sponge that sucked in, and the gulf that swallowed up all he could get'.

But Jermyn was only marginally worse than most of his contemporaries. Even Henrietta Maria sometimes had to borrow a few pounds from Jermyn in order to be able to carry on playing after having lost everything in her own purse.

The fashionable card games they enjoyed included *Crimpo, Whisk* (later called Whist) and *Ombre*, a Spanish game in which the trump cards were the three *Matadores* – *Spadille* (ace of spades), *Manille* (seven of trumps) and *Basto* (ace of clubs). Both within the game, which they played insatiably, and in their political intrigues, Jermyn and Henrietta Maria sought to hold such trumping 'Matadores' as frequently as possible.

The Queen's salon at Somerset House soon became a popular

meeting place for all those disaffected with Hyde's government.

Recently ennobled as Lord Clarendon, Hyde was determined to restore the Church of England to the position of dominance it had enjoyed under Charles I, through a series of pro-Anglican laws nicknamed the 'Clarendon Code'.

In March 1662, his Act of Uniformity made it illegal for anyone to be a teacher or minister without first swearing to use the Anglican Book of Common Prayer.

The law effectively outlawed teaching or preaching any doctrine except Anglicanism, and it was detested by all those who did not conform to the Church of England. Jermyn and Henrietta Maria's supper guests included Privy Counsellors and Members of Parliament of all denominations who opposed it. Catholics such as Jermyn's old adversary George Digby, now Earl of Bristol, rubbed elbows around the *Ombre* table with the Presbyterian Lord Holles and even Jermyn's Anglican cousin, the excitable young Charlie Berkeley.

Another visitor was the pro-Catholic Henry Bennet, soon to become Lord Arlington. Thirteen years Jermyn's junior, Arlington's most distinguishing feature was a little black patch that he wore over the bridge of his nose covering, he claimed ostentatiously, a Civil War wound. Arlington owed his first official appointment – to the household of James, Duke of York – to Jermyn. Sympathetic to Catholics and later to become one himself, Arlington was another opponent of the religiously intolerant Hyde.

Also at the *Ombre* tables were the young Duke of Buckingham and his salacious twenty-one-year-old cousin Barbara Villiers, Countess of Castlemaine. Barbara had become Charles's mistress shortly before the Restoration. Hyde was deeply disapproving of Charles having a mistress, and as a result Barbara detested him.

Charles's recent marriage to Catherine of Braganza had done nothing to diminish Barbara's ability to influence the King. Shrewd politicians like Jermyn had been quick to recognise her as a formidable tool to use against Hyde.

Out of this cabal of courtiers and politicians, of which Jermyn was a – if not *the* – leading member, was launched a fresh assault on Hyde's party. Charles was still too dependent on the Lord Chancellor to dismiss him, but it was possible to weaken Hyde by removing his allies.

In bed with Barbara, Charles innocently agreed to replacing the elderly Secretary of State, Edward Nicholas, with Arlington. Arlington's vacant post of Keeper of the Privy Purse went to Charlie Berkeley, bringing another member of the Somerset House party into the government.

Arlington became Secretary of State in October. That December, he persuaded Charles to issue a Declaration of Indulgence, temporarily suspending the penalties imposed by Hyde's Act of Uniformity.

'The design aims higher' the cashiered Nicholas warned his Anglican colleagues. And he was right, for Somerset House planned to replace Hyde's friend, Lord Treasurer Southampton, with Jermyn himself.

Whilst all these machinations were unfolding, Jermyn's nephew Harry was indulging in some court intrigue of his own by starting an affair with Barbara. Their romance was described in salacious detail both in the memoirs of the Comte de Gramont and in the *New Atlantis* by Mrs Delarivierre Manley (1663-1724), in which she calls Harry 'Germanicus'. Mrs Manley related how Barbara already had a lover apart from the King. Wanting to seduce her himself, Harry arranged for her to come to a room where she thought she was going to meet this lover, but instead, she saw something quite different:

> The weather was violently hot... the curtains of the
> bed drawn back to the canopy, made of yellow
> velvet, embroidered with white bugles... Upon the
> bed were strewed, with a lavish profuseness, plenty
> of orange and lemon flowers.
>
> And to complete the scene, the young Germanicus
> in a dress and posture not very decent to describe. It
> was he that was newly risen from the bath, and in a
> loose gown of carnation taffety, stained with Indian
> figures. He had beautiful long flowing hair, for then
> 'twas the custom to wear their own tied back with a
> ribbon of the same colour. He had thrown himself
> upon the bed, pretending to sleep, with nothing on
> but his shirt and nightgown, which he had so
> indecently disposed, that slumbering as he appeared,
> his whole person stood confessed to the eyes of the
> amorous Duchess...

Inevitably, Barbara succumbed to this temptation. Their affair
was discovered, and Harry was banished from court, 'for
courting Lady Castlemaine', in December 1662. Charles II
allowed him to return the following year, however, and their
affair continued on and off until 1670.

During her affair with the King, Barbara had a number of
children, of whom Charles acknowledged five as his: Anne
(1661); Charles Duke of Southampton and Cleveland (1662);
Henry Duke of Grafton (1663); Charlotte Countess of Lichfield
(1664) and George, Duke of Northumberland (1665). Anne's
paternity was originally claimed by Lord Chesterfield, and only
later by Charles. Another of these, according to Mrs Manley was

Harry's: so indulgent of Barbara was the King, wrote Mrs Manley, that 'he suffered a great belly of the Duchess (due to that happy amorous rencounter of the bugle-bed) to pass in the esteem of the world (as the rest of hers had done) for his'.

Mrs Manley was writing a novel, based on thinly disguised facts, but her father was second-in-command to Harry Jermyn's brother, Governor of Jersey from 1684, and in the same decade she was Barbara's lesbian lover. On the subject of Barbara and the Jermyn family, Mrs Manley knew more than most.

Her story, however, clearly condenses events that took place over a period of years into a much smaller time-period, for she suggests that the child who was really Harry's was conceived when he and Barbara first slept together, before December 1662. However, it was not until July 1667 that Pepys recorded 'the King hath declared that he did not get the child of which she is conceived at this time, he having not as he says lain with her this half year; but she told him – God damn me! but you shall own it. It seems he is jealous of Jermyn [Harry] and she loves him'.

Barbara had no surviving children born in that year. But was Mrs Manley correct in saying that one of Barbara's children was also Harry's? Over the years, various suggestions have been made as to who this child may have been. One was Dame Cecilia FitzRoy, a daughter of Barbara's of unknown parentage, who became a nun in Dunkirk. But Cecilia, by their own estimation, was not born until about 1670. Another more intriguing possibility is Henry, Duke of Grafton, who was born on 20 September 1663, nine months after Harry's pre-emptory banishment from court. The King hesitated a long time before acknowledging the boy as his. Evelyn wrote suspiciously that, unlike the King's other children, Grafton had been 'rudely bred', and observed that he was 'exceedingly handsome, far surpassing any of the King's other natural issue'. Harry was very handsome, and was also an excellent soldier; so was Grafton.

In 1672, the boy was created Duke of Grafton, Earl of Euston, Viscount *Ipswich* and Baron Sudbury. In 1688, William of Orange invaded and Grafton, then one of James II's principal generals, did the Jacobites dreadful damage by defecting to join the usurper. During his Irish campaign the following year, James II broke the cardinal law of honours – not using the same territorial designation twice – when he granted Harry Jermyn a number of titles, including Baron *Ipswich*. This was clearly a well-deserved snub to Grafton, and a barbed indication of what James, at least, may have thought of the Duke's true paternity.

That all lay, of course, in the future. Back in December 1662, Harry's banishment from court for courting Barbara had a serious impact on his uncle's plans. Barbara's influence with the King suffered a substantial, albeit not long-lasting setback. For now, she could no longer intermingle Somerset House's political plans with the sweet nothings she whispered into the King's ear at night. Hyde's portly frame remained for now parked between the King and Jermyn, and Jermyn's promotion to become Lord Treasurer was never mentioned again.

In March 1663, the intemperate Digby launched a premature attack on Hyde himself. As had happened before, Charles stood loyally by his Lord Chancellor, greatly strengthening Hyde's position.

Jermyn's failure to oust Hyde's grip on the government coincided with the first of many spasms of pain, which shot through Jermyn's feet like red-hot musket bullets. His decades of eating and drinking the finest food the courts of England and France could offer had debilitated his health.

At fifty-eight, Jermyn's bountiful acquisition of soup and

gold had brought him gout. For the rest of his life he would spend days or weeks on end suffering agonizing bouts, affecting first his feet, then his legs and eventually his whole body.

On one occasion in the 1670s, 'a large fit of the gout' affected his hand, forcing him to dictate his correspondence. He joked that it was a good excuse to use a secretary, but the crabbed handwriting of a note he scrawled at the end of the same letter remains a silent testimony, to this very day, of the pain that had become part of his daily life.

The disease was caused by a build-up of uric acid in his joints. Today, there are pills to disperse the acid and remove all discomfort, but in Jermyn's day it was incurable. To alleviate the agony, some doctors recommended beating the affected areas with bunches of nettles. Others advocated burning cones of dried moss on the most painful area of skin. The sensation of a small area of flesh being burned raw was apparently a welcome relief from the excruciating pain of the gout itself.

The combination of gout and age forced Jermyn to reappraise his future. With younger men like Arlington and Charlie Berkeley energetically seeking ever higher office, Jermyn realised he was too old to succeed Hyde.

The goal he had pursued for decades had finally eluded him. But with this acceptance came a moment of epiphany when he realised he had no need to be seen as 'Premier Minister' after all. If he could succeed again in influencing Charles as he had done in the past, it was possible that he could exercise more power than men constrained by the responsibility of high office. There was still a way forward, Jermyn realised, after all.

XVIII

THE SECOND ANGLO-DUTCH WAR
1664 – 1666

Well he the title of St Albans bore,
For never Bacon studied nature more;
But age allaying now that youthful heat,
Fits him in France to play at cards and treat.

.....

France had St Albans promised (so they sing),
St Albans promised him [Hyde]*, and he the King;*
The Count [Jermyn] *forthwith is ordered all to close,*
To play for Flanders and the stake to lose
While, chained together, two ambassadors
Like slaves shall beg for peace at Holland's doors.

from *Last Instructions to a Painter* (1681), attributed to
Andrew Marvell (1621-1678)

By a royal charter dated Tuesday, 18 December 1660, Jermyn, Henrietta Maria, Prince Rupert and sixty-three leading courtiers became colonial proprietors of the Guinea coast of West Africa.

The extensive rights of their new 'Company of Royal Adventurers into Africa' included being able to trade with the native Africans. It seemed that all the spice, ivory, gold and gems that D'Avenant had dreamed up for the fantasy-island of Madagascar would now be theirs in reality.

There was another commodity, however, that D'Avenant would never have advocated: slaves. Every month, English galleys left the Guinea coast carrying closely packed cargoes of manacled Africans to the plantations of the Caribbean. Unwittingly or not, Jermyn and Henrietta Maria had become early profiteers from the slave trade.

Their Company's ships and traders soon came into conflict with the Dutch, who also claimed a monopoly of the lucrative trade in human cargo. Soon fleets were sailing for Africa from both countries, each attacking and recapturing slaving-posts from the other.

In spring 1664, Charles II's younger brother James, Duke of York, escalated the conflict by sending a fleet to north America, capturing the village of New Amsterdam and renaming it New York.

In London the mob, Parliament and the City merchants bayed for full-scale war with the Dutch. At court, Charles and his younger companions – Arlington; Rupert, Barbara and particularly Charlie Berkeley, now Earl of Falmouth, rubbed their hands in anticipation of the pride, pomp and circumstance of glorious war.

Though no lovers of the Dutch republic themselves, Jermyn and Henrietta Maria could not support the war. When Hyde had scuppered Jermyn's proposed defensive treaty with France in 1662, Louis had signed a similar one with the Dutch. If Charles declared war on Holland, Louis would have to side with the Dutch against England.

Over the *Ombre* tables at Somerset House, Jermyn and Henrietta Maria tried to promote peace. To win back the high-spirited Charlie Berkeley, they arranged for the Queen's daughter Henrietta Anne, now Duchess of Orléans, to start corresponding with him.

His chivalrous loyalty to the beautiful princess aroused, Charlie dutifully changed sides and joined Jermyn's 'Peace Party'.

Henrietta Anne, Duchess of Orleans

Two unexpected recruits to the 'Peace Party' were Lord Chancellor Hyde and Lord Treasurer Southampton. It was clear to their mature minds that England's navy could not prevail against the combined fleets of Holland and France.

And if the war was lost, it was they, the senior members of the government, who would receive the blame. Hyde and Jermyn were probably both as surprised as each other to find themselves on the same side at long last.

Louis also wanted to prevent war. He had plans to drive the Spanish out of Flanders and had no desire to waste his military resources attacking England. He sent the Marquess of Ruvigny to bribe leading Members of Parliament to join Jermyn's Peace Party. Louis also offered to mediate between the English and Dutch. Overcoming his pride, Hyde proposed sending Jermyn to Paris as Ambassador Extraordinary to represent England in the talks.

Unfortunately, the Secretary of State, Lord Arlington, still sporting his ostentatious nose-patch, had by now become as adept as Hyde and Jermyn in influencing the King. In the matter of war, Arlington had the upper hand, and overruled the Lord Chancellor.

In November 1664, Parliament voted Charles a quarter of a million pounds to attack the Dutch.

On Wednesday, 22 February 1665, Jermyn and Henrietta Maria listened despondently as the crowds in the Strand cheered the official opening of hostilities. The Second Anglo-Dutch war – so called to distinguish it from Cromwell's conflict with Holland in the previous decade – had begun.

Jermyn's diplomatic efforts to prevent outright conflict continued. Early on the evening of Thursday, 6 April, Jermyn, his excitable cousin Charlie Berkeley and the French ambassador, Gaston de Cominges, waited on the river-steps of Exeter House in the Strand to greet two special ambassadors from Louis – Honoré Courtin, a seasoned diplomat, and Henrietta Maria's illegitimate half-brother, the Duke of Verneuil.

But despite Jermyn presenting the *Célèbre Ambassade*, as it was known, to the King personally, and giving all his encouragement to the subsequent talks, the desire of Arlington and Charles for war would not be shaken.

The Dutch and English navies met on Saturday, 3 June, off the coast of Suffolk near Lowestoft. Commanding the English fleet on board his flagship, the *Royal Charles*, was James, Duke of York, accompanied by Jermyn's nephew Harry Jermyn and Charlie Berkeley who, however much he had been against the war, was as keen to defend his country from the Dutch as anyone else.

The English attacked the Dutch flagship, their cannon balls ripping at the planks of the Dutch vessel until it exploded with a deafening blast.

In London, Jermyn and Henrietta Maria listened anxiously to the booms. Without the incessant noise of motorised traffic to mask it, the roar of the cannons was clearly audible over the hundred miles of gently undulating countryside that lay between them and the battle. In the evening, messengers brought news of what had happened.

Twenty-six Dutch ships had been destroyed. But the victory came at a terrible price. Harry and James were unharmed but their finely embroidered coats were stained with the blood of three of their friends who, standing next to them, had had their bodies ripped open by a single Dutch bullet. One of the three dead friends was the Earl of Falmouth – Jermyn's young cousin Charlie Berkeley.

Lowestoft was a victory for the English, but it had been a hard-fought one. The King, his battle-fever checked sharply by Charlie Berkeley's death, imagined the consequences of his battered navy being confronted by a superior French force. On Friday, 24 June 1665, with Hyde rubbing his podgy hands in agreement, Charles appointed Jermyn as his Resident Minister in Paris. His instructions were simple: keep Louis out of the war.

Henrietta Maria announced that she would go too. Her excuse was that she wanted to drink the medicinal waters at Bourbon, to combat her worsening bronchitis. But the truth was that she simply wanted to be with Jermyn.

Leaving England was no hardship for her, either. The stench of the streets of London that summer was worse than anyone could remember. Open sewers swarmed with flies. Rats, some the size of small dogs, were everywhere. Plague stalked London's alleys in one of the worst epidemics since the Black Death of the 1340s. As it ravaged Londoners, it caused the lymph glands or 'buboes' in their armpits, necks and groins to bloat up into agonising swellings, whilst fever ravaged their generally undernourished bodies, torturing them with cramps and seizures, bleeding and comas until the cold hand of death snatched them inevitably away.

People had not died like this in such numbers since the dark days of the Middle Ages. Meanwhile, down the few narrow streets where the Great Plague had not cast its fetid shadow, the London mob was out, hollering for the blood of Dutch and French alike.

Jermyn and Henrietta Maria crossed the Channel under heavy escort to protect them from Dutch attack. Their old apartments in the Palais Royale were occupied, so they leased the Hôtel de la Bazinière on the Quai Malaquais, just over the Seine from the Louvre. Despite its name, it was a private house, belonging to a nobleman currently serving a spell in the Bastille. Built in classical style in 1644, the Hôtel de la Bazinière was a typical Parisian residence, with an arched gateway leading into a central courtyard, completely enclosed from the murderous streets outside. In the dispossessed Bazinières's sumptuously furnished staterooms the Queen could receive the obligatory stream of visiting French Princes of the Blood, and Jermyn could entertain his fellow diplomats and officials to large meals and long evenings of Ombre and Crimpo.

Amongst the guests alternately winning and losing piles of gold livres with them, and on their many evenings out in the fashionable salons of Paris, were leading members of the Sun King's cabinet, including the fifty-six-year-old Hugues de Lionne, 'who hath', wrote Jermyn, 'more particularly than the other ministers, the Foreign affairs in his repartition, and is appointed, to treat with me'.

Widely acknowledged as a political genius, Lionne was also intensely lazy, cramming his work into short periods of frenzied exertion, followed by long days slouched drunkenly round gaming tables, such as those of the Hôtel de la Bazinière – a *modus operandi* that brought him into frequent, easy contact with Jermyn.

Jermyn's tactics were twofold. First, he argued that the renewal of the ancient treaties between England and France, which he and Louis had signed in 1661, prohibited Louis from attacking Charles. To Jermyn's dismay, Lionne denied this.

The treaties had to be renewed within a year of the accession of a new monarch, argued Lionne. Jermyn and Louis had signed the renewals in 1661, just over a year after the Restoration. But because Charles himself insisted that his reign had begun when Charles I was executed in 1649, then the treaty, Lionne, concluded with a smug smile, had been signed twelve years late and must therefore be invalid!

Jermyn's second tactic was to out-bid the Dutch by offering Louis a new, more beneficial treaty. If France kept out of the Anglo-Dutch war, England would not interfere with Louis's attack on Flanders. Better still, Jermyn suggested, they could invade the entire Netherlands together, keeping part of it each and letting Charles's nephew William of Orange rule the rest, not as a Stadtholder – effectively an employee of the Dutch States General – but as a sovereign prince.

After a summer of negotiations, Jermyn and Henrietta Maria retired to Colombes to await Louis's decision.

On Monday, 21 August, a magnificently gilded state-coach rolled up their gravel driveway, pulled by six white horses plumed with gold feathers and escorted by a heavily-armed troop of musketeers.

Out stepped the athletic twenty-seven-year-old Sun King, his long hair curling down the edges of his handsome face like the scroll of a Baroque picture frame. In the cool interior of the château he had a long conversation with his aunt and Jermyn. Although he loved his cousin Charles, he could not trust him while he did the bidding of his Francophobic Parliament and ministers like Arlington. If Charles persisted with the war, he must inevitably come to blows with France.

Having failed to bring Charles back to a truly pro-French stance by correspondence, Jermyn returned to see him in person in November. The plague was still rampaging through London: by the time it abated the following year 100,000 Londoners – about a tenth of the city's population – would be dead. The court had escaped to enjoy the cleaner air of Oxford, carousing in the college buildings, just like they had during the Civil War.

It was not the Plague, though, but the impending war with France that dominated everyone's thoughts. Jermyn swapped his governorship of Jersey in exchange for a £1,000 pension, to allow for the appointment of a resident governor, who could prepare the island against a French invasion.

The fleet was being re-equipped. Arlington was seeking new alliances with the Hapsburgs. Yet despite the state of panic, Jermyn could not convince Charles that Louis would actually attack England. It therefore came as a genuine shock to Charles (though not perhaps to Jermyn himself) when, on Wednesday, 17 January 1666, France declared war on him.

In fact, this was Louis's bluff. Anxious to devote his energy to invading Flanders, the Sun King had no intention of fighting England, but he did hope to scare Charles into accepting French mediation. Exactly as planned, Charles agreed, instructing Jermyn to return to Paris to open new talks.

But while Charles and Hyde dithered over the exact nature of Jermyn's instructions, the war escalated. Although the French navy remained at anchor, the French colonies now joined the bewildering maelstrom of attack and counter-attack that the

English and Dutch had been playing amongst themselves. War raged across the globe, from the west coast of America and across the Caribbean to the troubled shores of Africa and the rich spice islands of Indonesia.

When Jermyn was finally able to return to Paris in April, his journey was widely interpreted as a sign of Charles's desire for peace. Yet because they were framed by the cautious lawyer Hyde, who still did not fully trust his erstwhile enemy, Jermyn's powers to negotiate were severely and frustratingly limited.

Very, wisely, Jermyn did not tell the French this. On Easter Monday, 16 April 1666, he and the Queen invited the leading players to meet under the watching eyes of Aphrodite and Dionysius, whose lively images dominated the ceiling of their great painted hall at Colombes.

Considering the personalities involved, it is not hard to understand why the French and Dutch were at war with the English. Representing Louis was the genial but chronically lazy Lionne.

For England, besides Jermyn and the Queen, was the regular ambassador Denzil Holles. Although he was one of Jermyn's old Presbyterian allies, Holles's natural disdain for the French had been made worse by having to deal with them diplomatically. He refused to speak French, and insisted that, as Charles's ambassador, he was entitled to keep his hat on in Louis's presence – which, to the protocol-obsessed French court, was anathema.

The Dutch were represented by the forty-four-year-old Conrad van Beuningen, a vigorous xenophobe, who regarded the war as a just crusade against the English, whom he loathed.

The main issues for an Anglo-Dutch peace treaty were who should pay compensation for losses incurred in the war, and whether captured colonies should be handed back to their original owners.

Van Beuningen demanded maximum compensation for the Dutch, and continued possession of all the English colonies they had seized. When Jermyn and Lionne gently suggested that there might be scope for compromise, the Dutchman became enraged and the talks halted.

Jermyn made better progress with Louis that August. Playing on the Sun King's unwillingness to attack England, Jermyn suggested he should make a token show of aggression to appease the Dutch. In return, Charles would make peace with the Dutch and would also sign a secret agreement promising not to interfere with Louis's planned invasion of Flanders.

Louis agreed, but, due to his limited powers, Jermyn could not finalise this agreement. He had now to persuade Charles to agree, and to do that, he had to make another trip to London.

As Jermyn left Paris on his return journey to London, he knew that the fate of Europe depended on his ability to influence that most fickle of monarchs, King Charles II.

XIX

THE ROAD TO BREDA
1666 – 1667

But Louis was of memory but dull,
And to St Albans too undutiful,
Nor word nor near relation did revere,
But asked him bluntly for his character.
The gravelled Count did with the answer faint
His character was that which thou didst paint
And so enforced, like enemy or spy
Trusses his baggage and the camp does fly.
from *Last Instructions to a Painter* (1681), attributed to
Andrew Marvell (1621-1678)

The London to which Jermyn was about to return was already appreciably different to the city into which he had been born.

His new building work at St James's had already increased the size of London, shifting the focus away from the City of London, and creating new areas in the west, both for social and political life, that had never existed before.

Jermyn Street was now finished and had in turn stimulated others to build along the rutted lane that ran parallel to it – Piccadilly. Pall Mall was completely lined with neatly built classically-proportioned brick houses. St Albans Street and Bury Street (named after Bury St Edmunds, near his family home of Rushbrook) were nearing completion, followed closely by King Street, Duke of York Street and Charles Street.

Only St James's Square itself was substantially unfinished. Jermyn had hoped to lease out plots for 'thirteen or fourteen great and good houses, fit for the dwelling of persons of quality and needed for the beauty of the town and convenience of the Court'. But so far only he and Arlington had built themselves houses in the square. Its frontage, like that of Arlington's, was part of what Jermyn hoped would become a uniform façade running right around the Square, with three classically-proportioned stories, punctuated by regularly placed sash windows.

The design seems unremarkable to us now because we are so used to seeing it repeated all over cities across the world. But in Jermyn's day, it was startlingly new. Compared with the jumble of Jacobean and Tudor architecture that it superseded, the houses' simple, clear proportions, combined with the scale of Jermyn's plans for St James's, were truly revolutionary.

Jermyn left Calais by frigate on Monday, 3 September. If he looked into the skies to the north, he would have felt a tremendous foreboding at the sight of a lurid orange glow filling the sky over London.

It was caused by the third night of the Great Fire of London. The blaze had started on the parched floor of a bakery in Pudding Lane in the eastern side of the City. Fanned by the breeze, the flames had consumed the timber wharves nearby and then hissed through the narrow streets, leaping gleefully across the high-pilled thatch of the cluttered roofs.

By the time Jermyn's coach rattled into London, there was little of the city left. Old St Paul's Cathedral had been physically blown to pieces by the heat, the molten lead from its roof congealing in puddles all the way down Ludgate Hill. The magnificent Royal Exchange, the pride of Elizabethan London, was a smoking mound. The house where Jermyn had been born in St Margaret's, Lothbury was a pile of blackened timbers.

Jermyn's ever-active mind would have seethed with

questions. Had the terrible inferno spread from the City to blaze westwards down the Strand? Had its searing heat razed the stones of his beloved Somerset House to rubble? Had venerable old Whitehall Palace, together with Inigo Jones's magnificent Banqueting House, been reduced to ash? Had Jermyn Street and the rest of St James's been left smouldering?

Miraculously, the answers were no. While the City merchants piled their belongings into barges and fled the conflagration, the court had turned out to fight the flames.

Charles; the Duke of York; Prince Rupert and Jermyn's nephew Harry had all joined soldiers throwing buckets of water onto the flames and blowing up houses to make fire-breaks to contain the destruction. The dreadful inferno had reached the east end of the Strand. Everything to the west had been saved.

On Tuesday, 2 October 1666, Jermyn entertained King Charles II to dinner in his magnificent new mansion in St James's Square. Built at a cost of £5,000, Jermyn's new house was one of the finest in London 'hung with gilded leather containing tapestry, pictures, andirons [log-holders], chairs of velvet and damask... the great dining-room with a suite of green damask hangings with yellow borders, six chairs with arms and seven others of red velvet'. It was, literally, 'fit for a King'.

Though Charles had pushed Jermyn away at several points in his life, he always came back to his faithful henchman in the end. The older man was, it seemed, politically indestructible. In part, it was Jermyn's engaging character alone that ensured his continued success. Jermyn's intricate web of political connections in France made him indispensable on the diplomatic front. He was an intimate part of the King's mother's life, and any dealings with her automatically involved Jermyn.

Yet was there more to it even than that? Was there, lurking at the bottom of Charles's inconstant, but ultimately life-long affection for Jermyn, a genuine belief that this aging courtier might actually be his father – or a hope, even, that he was? Surrounded by fawning career-politicians and their buxom wives, each on the make, half of them as turn-coat perhaps as Charles I had found the preceding generation, did Charles II long for a connection based on something stronger than mere lip-serving loyalty?

The King had recently started copying Jermyn's habit of dressing in sombre black satin. Aged thirty-five, he was no longer the exuberant young man who had galloped away from Paris to join the Spanish army, just over a decade before. Now the cynical arcs of his eyebrows were accompanied by furrowed brows and the shadows of bags were edging their way under his deep brown Tuscan eyes.

For a year, the City had been starved of commerce by war and plague. Now it was a smoking ruin. A Franco-Dutch attack now could destroy the navy, overrun the colonies and probably precipitate another revolution. The substance of the conversation between Jermyn and Charles II that evening has not been recorded, but it is not hard to envisage Jermyn outlining his peace plans, as only Jermyn could, and the King listening very attentively indeed.

Secretary of State Arlington, however, with his ostentatious little black nose-patch, had almost finished negotiating a treaty with the Hapsburgs. Alarmed by the King's change of heart after the dinner in St James's Square, Arlington stalled Jermyn's return to France by offering their indecisive master a series of alternative plans.

Deeply frustrated, Jermyn had then to use his own powers of persuasion, again, to draw Charles back to committing himself to accept French mediation.

Jermyn succeeded, but the powers to negotiate which Jermyn carried back to France, written grudgingly by Arlington and approved by the ever-cautious Hyde, were vexingly restrictive. Yet we should remember, in judging what follows, that had Jermyn and his unique influence over the King not existed, there would never have been any negotiations at all.

Jermyn finally set sail for France on Tuesday, 29 January 1667. He crossed the Channel unmolested by Dutch ships, but when he stepped ashore he heard that Henrietta Maria had died.

Then, as the grieving Jermyn's carriage pounded through the snow-bound forests of Normandy, robbers leapt out from the trees and plundered his chests, taking £20,000 in gold, an instalment of the Queen's English pension. The loss of the gold was irrevocable, but before he reached Paris he learned, to his immense joy, that the news of the Queen's death had been false, and the two were happily reunited again.

Jermyn's arrival in France was again interpreted as a clear indication of Charles's willingness to end the war.

Louis summoned him to Versailles, then merely a hunting lodge in the chestnut woods outside Paris. But when Jermyn was forced to admit how limited his negotiating powers were, Louis was immensely disappointed. Nevertheless, Lionne stirred himself to discuss Jermyn's terms with van Beuningen. A week later, he gave Jermyn two sealed draft treaties to send to Charles. Either of them, said Lionne, would be acceptable to the Dutch.

With the treaties safely dispatched to London, Jermyn and Henrietta Maria relaxed, attending a grand carnival at Versailles together. While fireworks exploded like rising suns, Lionne and Jermyn had a chat.

During the course of this, Lionne realised he had omitted

from both treaties the critical English demand that the Dutch should return Pularoon (or Pulau Run). The recovery of this miniscule member of the Moluccas (the Spice Islands), that lay between New Guinea and Sulawesi in the Indian Ocean, had been one of Charles's stated objectives in going to war. Barely two miles in length, the island was not just a spot on the map, though: its plantations brimmed with cloves and nutmeg, that commanded astronomical prices in Europe. Pularoon's plantations might just as well have grown gold: a treaty without its inclusion would never be accepted in Whitehall.

Lionne rather wretchedly suggested taking Jermyn to discuss the matter with the volatile van Beuningen. Jermyn's powers did not include negotiating directly with the Dutch. In these extraordinary circumstances, however, it seemed wise to follow Lionne's impromptu plan.

When they met on Monday, 18 February, van Beuningen was civil. When Lionne mentioned Pularoon, however, the Dutchman's face flushed. When Jermyn explained that the return of Pularoon was essential if peace was to be made, van Beuningen went scarlet. Didn't Jermyn realise that England was in no position to stand up to the Franco-Dutch alliance? How dare he try to dictate terms in this manner!

As Jermyn opened his mouth to speak again, van Beuningen's tirade degenerated into a barrage of guttural Dutch. His arms flailing like windmills, he threw himself at Jermyn. With great difficulty Lionne managed to drag van Beuningen away and help Jermyn escape.

The strain of the negotiations had a dreadful effect on Jermyn's gout. He spent March negotiating with Lionne from his bed in the Hôtel de la Bazinière.

His constant pain added a blunt edge to his normally courtly letters home. He told Hyde that letting peace depend on a tiny island was ridiculous. If the French could not calm van Beuningen down, Charles would simply have to accept the loss of Pularoon. 'Pray be pleased to tell me', Jermyn added fractiously, 'whether there be in the treaty of [sixteen] sixty two anything, besides the article of Pularoon, that makes you affect the observation of it for the future'.

Jermyn's ultimatum had a surprising affect. On Friday, 22 March 1667, Hyde authorised him to set the question of Pularoon aside. Negotiations for a formal peace treaty could now go ahead. The place chosen for the talks was Breda.

In the fifteen months during which England and France had been at war, their forces had not clashed. Now, with peace in sight, the Dutch demanded that Louis should honour his promise to attack. When Jermyn visited the Sun King at Versailles on Tuesday, 2 April, they discussed the matter frankly and agreed their countries would not attack each other in the next month. This was just as well as, a week later, van Beuningen appeared at Versailles, demanding an immediate French naval strike on England.

On the basis of his agreement with Jermyn, Louis refused. As Jermyn was able to report triumphantly to Hyde, Beuningen promptly 'fell into flames of passion'. The next day, Louis came to Colombes to collect a secret promise which Jermyn had persuaded Charles to sign just in case, agreeing not to intervene against Louis's invasion of Flanders.

Confident that the Anglo-Dutch war was almost over, Louis assembled his armies for what Jermyn described as his 'open-faced' invasion of Spanish-owned Flanders.

Alarmed at the build-up of French soldiers on the border, Sir William Temple, Charles's diplomatic representative in Flanders, wrote to Jermyn,

> We are so amazed with the number and bravery of
> the French preparations to invade this country, that
> we can hardly lift up our eyes against the rising of
> this sun, that, it is said, intends to burn up all before
> it.

On Wednesday, 8 May, Jermyn and Lionne watched rank after rank of soldiers marching out of Paris.

With them went the nobility and Princes of the Blood, their ornamented armour glittering in the brilliant spring sunshine. And at their head, his shining breastplate moulded like the chest of Apollo, rode the Sun King himself.

Jermyn had hoped to be one of the negotiators at Breda. But when Hyde and Arlington decided to send Denzil Holles and an up-and-coming diplomat, Henry Coventry, instead, Jermyn accepted the decision gracefully.

Instead, he asked to be Ambassador Extraordinary to Louis's court, so as to oversee the formal signing of the resulting treaty. Unwilling to allow Jermyn any more power, Hyde prevented this. And because he was not an Ambassador Extraordinary, Jermyn could not leave Paris with Louis and the French court.

Instead, he had to communicate with Holles and Coventry in Breda, and with Louis at the Flemish front, by post. This, as he warned, was bound to lead to misunderstandings.

He was right. Honoré Courtin, one of the French negotiators at Breda, received a letter from Paris suggesting Jermyn had agreed to England fulfilling all the conditions contained in the Anglo-Dutch treaty of 1662, whereas the King had agreed to no such thing. When Coventry queried this with Jermyn, he wrote back denying it.

But the Dutch refused to accept that Courtin had been wrong, and insisted on England standing by what Jermyn had been reported to have said. When Louis heard about this, he told the

Dutch to be reasonable, or he would withdraw his military support for them.

When news of this sudden escalation of tempers at Breda reached England, Charles panicked. Hyde wrote to Jermyn, urging him to catch up with Louis and clear the misunderstanding up personally. Had Jermyn been appointed Ambassador Extraordinary as he had wanted, he would already have been with Louis.

Instead, he was now he faced with a long journey on his own. And hurrying mile upon weary mile over sun-baked ruts in an unsprung seventeenth century carriage was agony for a late-middle-aged man with severe gout.

As he jolted north-east towards the Flemish border, Jermyn heard that Louis was laying siege to the border town of Douai. But when he reached the market town of Arras he could go no further. The twelve mile hinterland between Arras and Douai was infested with hostile Spanish soldiers.

So he waited in a down-at-heel tavern in Arras until, on Thursday, 20 June, he received a letter from Hyde. As he started to read, a sickening sense of horror crept through him.

The Dutch had hoped to make peace only after the English navy had been destroyed. On Monday, 27 May, when it was clear Louis was not going to do this for them, the leader of the Dutch States General, Jan De Witt, sent the Dutch fleet to sea. On Wednesday, 12 June, it sailed up the Thames estuary.

Taken by surprise, the fortress at Sheerness was quickly overrun and the boom across the mouth of the Medway was blasted to pieces. The English fleet lay defenceless.

On the shore, James, Duke of York and Jermyn's nephew Harry ran about ordering the sailors to defend the ships. But it was too late. Dutch cannon balls and firebombs crashed repeatedly into the English ships.

The sailors on the *Royal Charles*, unable to move the great vessel out of the way of the Dutch fire ships, abandoned it. Clambering on board, Dutch sailors hoisted their own flag and sailed away, singing triumphantly. When breathless messengers spread the news through the charred ruins of London the citizens panicked. The *Royal Charles* was captured, the fleet destroyed, and all was lost.

Having sent Jermyn this dreadful news, Charles's government was finally prepared to grant Jermyn what he had wanted all along – authority to use his own discretion to end the war. But, cut off from Douai and Breda by the war, he could only send an intrepid messenger galloping towards Louis's camp. Jermyn then hurried back to Paris, where he could use the secure and speedy military postal links to communicate more freely with Louis and the ambassadors at Breda.

Jermyn's return to Paris was widely misinterpreted. Unaware that he had been cut off from Douai by the fighting, false reports circulated throughout Europe asserting that he had reached Douai, where Louis had accused him of lying about Charles's intentions, and banished him from the French court, in the ignominious manner related in the poem at the start of this chapter. Despite this later being known to have been palpably untrue, the story remained stuck to Jermyn's reputation. He is often seen now as the incompetent ambassador, who 'repeated on gilt-edged paper the formulae drafted by Lionne, sank cosily into the French atmosphere in which he felt at home, and staked his life on the pacifism of France', who was eventually sent packing by Louis in disgrace.

Nothing could be further from the truth. In fact, Jermyn's message had reached Douai safely and was forwarded to the English ambassadors in Breda. Although the peace treaty allowed the Dutch to keep Pularoon, the danger of further attacks on England had at last been averted. On Sunday, 30 June

1667, the terms of the Anglo-Dutch peace treaty were finally concluded.

But that was just the start of it.

XX

THE GRAND DESIGN
1667 – 1668

Most fears he [Jermyn] *the Most Christian* [Louis] *should trepan*
Two saints at once, St Germain and St Alban,
But thought the Golden Age was now restored,
When men and women took each other's word.
from *Last Instructions to a Painter* (1681),
attributed to Andrew Marvell (1621-1678)

From the safety of Colombes, Jermyn heard anxiously that
Parliament and the London mob alike were baying for a
scapegoat for the loss of the fleet. In some quarters, he was
being blamed as the 'author of these misfortunes'.

Parliament accused Hyde of corresponding with Jermyn
without the King's knowledge, and of passing on secrets that the
French had in turn told the Dutch. But the King had authorised
the correspondence, so this false accusation was dropped.

In the scathing political satires circulating London, Jermyn
was portrayed as 'full of soup and gold' – incompetent, but not
downright treacherous:

St Alban's writ to, that he may bewail
To Master Louis, and tell coward tale,
How yet the Hollanders do make a noise
Threaten to beat us, and are naughty boys

Ultimately, however, Jermyn was not a leading royal minister,
and the furore soon passed him by.

Jermyn, Earl of St Albans, as a Knight of the Garter, painted by Sir Peter Lely

Goaded by Arlington, the storm of voices demanding vengeance gradually focused on the King's First Minister, Hyde. Hearing this from Lionne's agents in London, Jermyn warned his old enemy to take care for the sake of 'the King's service and your own quiet'.

But it was too late. Parliament decided to accuse Hyde of treason. Desperately dissociating himself from the failed war, Charles was forced to abandon his old mentor. Hyde was sacked on Friday, 30 August. Three months later, the storm not having abated, the King had no choice but to send him into exile.

As he trailed disconsolately away from Whitehall, the last thing Hyde saw was the King's mistress, Barbara Villiers, taunting him from her balcony.

The first thing Hyde did when he landed in France was to write to Jermyn, asking him to use his influence with Louis to find him somewhere to stay.

Despite everything he had done to them, Jermyn and Henrietta Maria could not help but feel sympathetic to the gouty old lawyer. But to help Hyde would risk criticism and maybe even guilt by association. Consequently Jermyn sent a curt reply, refusing to help.

Hyde wandered through France until he reached Montpelier, where he settled down. He occupied himself until his death in 1674 writing an autobiography, which became one of the most influential histories of the period.

Not surprisingly, when he mentioned Jermyn he did so in the most critical terms. He portrayed him as a man who grasped greedily at power, yet could never have wielded it effectively had he succeeded. It set the tone for the way Jermyn has been viewed ever since, and has been followed rather slavishly, even by most academic historians. But you, reading this book, now know the truth.

For all his vitriol, the bookish Hyde was unable to disguise a sneaking admiration for Jermyn, who was as happy laughing with his drinking companions in St James's as he was joking with his gambling-partners at Versailles, and who could treat the King both as a close friend and, even, as a son.

Hyde's last word on Jermyn was written in April 1669: 'if he dies without some very signal calamity, he may well be looked upon as a man of rare felicity'.

Louis's invasion of Flanders was repulsed by the Spanish. But even as the autumn frosts put an end to the campaigning season, the Sun King resolved to try again the following year.

Temporarily appointed Ambassador Extraordinary in Paris, Jermyn negotiated a treaty whereby Charles and Louis would launch a joint attack on Flanders in 1668. But after he had sent the treaty to be signed in London he had a terrible shock.

With Hyde in exile, Arlington had seized the opportunity to step into the role of First Minister. Having done so, he concluded an alliance with the Dutch and Swedes, aimed at preventing further French expansion.

The Triple Alliance, signed on Monday, 13 January 1668, was a massive setback to Jermyn's long-term plans. But his response was deft. Having agreed a strategy with Henrietta Maria and Louis, Jermyn made a flying visit to London to see Charles personally.

As ever, Jermyn's long-standing and complex relationship with the King enabled him to do what nobody else could do so well. Probably over a few bottles of fine Burgundy, he talked Charles into changing his mind. All of a sudden, the King's policies became quite different – and perfectly harmonised with the objective for which Jermyn and Henrietta Maria had been striving. Declaring that the Triple Alliance had been Arlington's idea, not his own, Charles now agreed to follow a new version of Jermyn's Closer Alliance – the Grand Design.

The Grand Design was to be an alliance between Charles and Louis for the joint conquest of Flanders and Holland. The Dutch trading empire would be carved up. The Dutch parliament, the States General, would be disbanded and William of Orange would be elevated from being a mere salaried Stadtholder, or military leader, to the status of a sovereign prince.

To show his permanent commitment to his alliance with

Catholic France, Charles would convert to Catholicism and declare freedom of worship for all denominations. To safeguard Charles against Parliament, Louis would guarantee military assistance if and when needed, and pay him an annual subsidy of two million crowns (about £25 million now, but again, comparisons in value are fraught with difficulty: government spending was vastly less than it is now, so this sum basically guaranteed that Charles would be able to rule perfectly effectively without needing Parliament to vote him any tax revenue).

It was a bold policy, aimed at changing Britain and Europe forever. It was also a perilous one. If Parliament found out before the agreement was concluded, revolution would be inevitable. Besides Arlington, only a handful of Catholic courtiers were told the secret.

At the end of 1668 Jermyn ceased to be Ambassador Extraordinary. This did not imply loss of any real power on his part: it was simply so that, if the plan was ever found out, nobody could claim that it was being promoted by one of Charles's officials.

A new permanent ambassador, Abbé Walter Montagu's young cousin Ralph Montagu, was appointed to replace Jermyn as ambassador. Charming, apparently irresistible to women and deeply spiteful towards those whom he disliked, Ralph was told nothing of the Grand Design.

Although Arlington was strongly sympathetic to Catholicism, he was still passionately anti-French, so Louis sent Charles Colbert de Croissy to be his ambassador in London, with special instructions to cultivate Arlington with a bribe of 200,000 gold pieces. Charles's sister Henrietta Anne had already started corresponding with Arlington as well, trying to draw him, as she had done so successfully with Charlie Berkeley, into the pro-French

280 THE KING'S HENCHMAN

camp. But what really changed Arlington's mind was Charles himself.

With a rare show of fortitude, the King told Henrietta Anne – and by implication Arlington himself – that the notion that 'my ministers are anything but what I will have them' was untrue. By the end of 1668, Arlington had become an enthusiastic promoter of Jermyn's Grand Design. The question now was this. Could Jermyn bring his grandiose plans for Europe to fruition?

XXI

SAINT-DENIS
1669

And thou, my love, art sweeter far
Than balmy incense in the purple smoke;
Pure and unspotted, as the cleanly ermine ere
The hunter sullies her with his pursuit;
Soft as her skin, chaste as th' Arabian bird
That wants a sex to woo, or as the dead
That are divorced from warmth, from objects,
And from thought...

Theander (Jermyn) to Eurithea (Henrietta Maria),
Sir William D'Avenant, *The Platonic Lovers* (1636)

By April 1669, Jermyn was indeed enjoying the good fortune –
the 'rare felicity' – that had inspired so much envy in Hyde.

Through the French windows of his study at Colombes he
could have looked out to see the swathes of spring flowers, such
as pale yellow narcissi and bright red tulips, in the château
garden.

Years of peering at ciphered correspondence by candlelight
had strained his eyes so much that the flowers were no more than
a blur. All the same, he could still have filled in from memory the
other details of the landscape: the cattle grazing quietly in the
water-meadows, the broad sweep of the Seine, and the purple
silhouette of spires and towers of Saint-Germain on the horizon.

The plans Jermyn had formed years before were now
blossoming. With the exception of St James's Square, his new
classically-inspired developments in London were virtually

complete. His rivals were exiled or brought to heel. The Closer Union of England and France was close to fruition.

There was only one pressing worry. Henrietta Maria had been ill for the last quarter century with an alternating succession of migraines, toothaches, coughs and attacks of bronchitis. Now, her condition had grown suddenly worse. On Saturday, 10 April Jermyn wrote to Arlington, who was expecting him back in London,

> she is not yet near so well as we wish to see her. She hath, since my last, taken very little rest at nights, and consequently recovered very little strength... yesterday [her physicians] let her blood, for the third time since this sickness, in her foot; her rest this night hath not been so good as we hoped her bleeding would have procured.

> She had a little fever in the night, which is not yet totally gone, and therefore they have again, this morning, let her blood in the arm. Her fever is so little, that it can scarce be discerned whether she have any or no; and if it increase not, there is cause to be as confident as we have been that the danger is past; if the fever increase, as nobody is safe in such assaults, so she that is of so delicate a constitution, will be more to be apprehended than other in the like case.

> You will easily conjecture that, in this state of the matter, I am not like to remove from hence until I see a change of it, and her health perfectly established.

Jermyn was relieved when Henrietta Maria started to recover. A week after her recovery started he wrote, 'she coughs not much, and the matter she spits is not ill-conditioned; she takes asses' milk, and I believe to-morrow she will be purged, from whence is expected the last hand of her recovery'.

Jermyn had to return to London to help Charles and Arlington persuade the Privy Council to agree to a treaty with France that would serve as a cover for the secret Grand Design.

His movements, so often taken as a barometer for Anglo-French relations, caused much speculation in the City. 'You cannot imagine what a noise Lord St Alban's coming has made here', Charles told his sister Henrietta Anne.

Jermyn, as the Venetian ambassador observed, presented his most inscrutable face to the public. His business finished, he hurried back to Henrietta Maria, who had gone to her nunnery at Chaillot with her friend Madame de Motteville.

What he found there concerned him deeply. Henrietta Maria was thinner and greyer than ever. She was eating much less than before. But besides taking her home to Colombes, there was little Jermyn could do to help her.

In August, the Duke of York's podgy four-year-old daughter Anne came to stay, so that she could be treated by a French eye specialist. Jermyn hoped the presence of Henrietta Maria's granddaughter might give the Queen some energy back. It did, but only very briefly.

When Henrietta Anne and her husband the Duke of Orléans came to see the young princess, they too were gravely concerned by Henrietta Maria's health. Jermyn, who had been with her every day, had now grown used to her slow decline, but to the Duke and Duchess the deterioration was more starkly apparent. They summoned Louis's doctors at once.

The doctors came hurrying up the gravel driveway of Colombes on Saturday, 28 August. Two days later, on Monday,

30 August, as the greyness of dawn seeped through the gaps in
the heavy velvet curtains, Jermyn sat down at his ornate desk,
picked up a quill pen in his trembling hand and told Charles
what had happened next:

> If that which hath happened here could or ought to
> be concealed from you my hand should not be the
> first in giving you notice of it. It hath pleased God
> to take from us this morning, about 3 o'clock the
> queen your mother and notwithstanding her long
> sickness as unexpectedly and with as much surprise
> as if she never had been sick at all.
>
> On Saturday last she had a consultation of
> physicians at which assisted M. Vallot, M. D'Acquin,
> M. Esprit and M.Evelin. The result of the consulta-
> tion was to give her the usual remedy on Sunday
> night for preparing her against Monday morning to
> be purged with a certain opiate designed for that
> purpose. It was also a result of the consultation to
> give towards night in order to the quieting of the
> humours in her body from whence they conjectured
> the great disorder came with some rest a grain of
> Laudanum. About ten o'clock she was in too much
> heat to venture the grain of Laudanum and the
> resolution was taken not to give it all. She caused
> thereupon her curtains to be drawn and sent us all
> away just as she used to do for several nights before,
> fearing herself no more than she had done nor
> indeed imprinting in any of us the least imagination
> of that which immediately followed.
>
> Not being able to sleep of herself, she called to M.
> D'Acquin for the grain. He contrary to his former

resolution and as he said to his opinion when he did it suffered himself to be over-ruled by the queen and gave it her in the yolk of an egg. She fell presently asleep he sitting by her perceiving her to sleep too profoundly and her pulse to alter, endeavoured by all the means he could to wake her and bring to herself but could effect neither by all the several remedies used in such cases. She lasted thus till between three and four o'clock and then died.

That which doth further concern this matter I shall give my Lo[rd]: Arlington an account of. God of heaven give you all necessary consolations in it.

Jermyn had sent word to Louis at once, but was still surprised when, at six o'clock in the morning, a carriage and six horses came pounding up the driveway.

It was the Duke of Orléans, hurrying there not out of concern for Henrietta Maria, but to lay claim to her belongings. Abruptly, Orléans told Jermyn that Louis was sending two officers to seal the Queen's apartments, to stop her servants stealing anything.

Jermyn protested that this intrusion on the Queen of England's house by French officers would offend Charles, and asked the Duke to speak to Ambassador Ralph Montagu first. Impatient and unsympathetic, Orléans told the old man he was imagining things and that Charles would have nothing to complain about.

When the French officers arrived, Jermyn hobbled out and asked them if they had spoken to Ambassador Montagu. Bemused, the officers said they knew nothing about ambassadors: their orders came direct from Louis. Deflated,

Jermyn gave in. The soldiers sealed Henrietta Maria's apartments and the offices of her principal officers, Jermyn's included.

Orléans now started harassing Jermyn because Henrietta Maria's will could not be found. She had made one before she left England in 1665 but, although Jermyn knew she had intended to cancel it, he did not know if she had done so, or if she had made a new one.

It soon emerged that Henrietta Maria's 1665 will was intact. It appointed Jermyn as one of her executors. She left everything she had to Charles. Yet in the short period before the will was found, Jermyn had the upsetting task of trying to fend off Orléans' claims.

The next morning Jermyn went to Saint-Cloud. Henrietta Anne was in tears, and at last the two of them could benefit from each other's genuine sympathy. Ambassador Montagu was there as well, putting on a show of concern. But Montagu disliked Jermyn, probably because he suspected the older statesman of being involved in secret talks with Louis, from which he had been excluded.

It turned out that the idea of sealing the apartments at Colombes had originated with Montagu, who revealed his sneering contempt for Jermyn in a letter to Arlington. 'I am sure without this,' he told the Secretary of State, 'my lord St Albans would not have left a silver spoon in the house'.

While Jermyn was at Saint-Cloud, surgeons visited Colombes to remove the Queen's heart from her body and place it in a silver casket. Jermyn returned soon afterwards. As the cool of evening settled over the Seine valley, he led a slow procession of household staff from Colombes to Chaillot.

Here, at Henrietta Maria's own desire, the casket was placed above the altar of the convent chapel.

Over the next few days, Jermyn raised a £27,000 loan to pay

for the official mourning and funeral. He asked Arlington if the English government would guarantee the loan as 'the easiest way of carrying on things here with decency... You ought to pity me', he told Arlington,

> as much as to lament yourself, that you receive this trouble from my hand. I have no more pleasure in the matter than I am like to find in others, but receiving no reproaches from my own heart for not having done my duty to the queen during her life, so I would have that [which] I owe to her memory of the same peace.

Instead of allowing himself time to come to terms with his loss, Jermyn found as much as possible to do. As soon as Henrietta Maria's body had been laid out in state at Saint-Denis, the ancient sepulchral church of the Bourbon dynasty, he hurried over to England. He found Charles at Hampton Court, told him in detail about the funeral arrangements, and fussed over the English court's mourning.

Understanding Jermyn's need to be involved, Charles appointed him as one of the four commissioners responsible for settling Henrietta Maria's estate.

Somerset House and Greenwich became part of the dower lands of Queen Catherine, Charles II's much-neglected Portuguese wife. The rebuilding of Greenwich Palace, a project Jermyn had set into motion in 1661, was brought to a stop with only one of the planned two blocks finished, for Catherine lacked the desire or money to continue the project. Colombes and the Queen's property at Chaillot were given to Henrietta Anne.

For the next three years, Jermyn was kept busy arbitrating disputes over wages from Henrietta Maria's servants, claims by creditors and settling arguments over leases for parts of her estate.

Years later, the occasional dispute still had to be referred to him. He never complained: long after Henrietta Maria's death, he could feel, through such work, that he was still able to serve her.

On Monday, 27 September, after a month of nervous confusion, Jermyn collapsed. Charles's doctors put him to bed in his chamber at Hampton Court and diagnosed a massive attack of gout.

For a few days they made Jermyn stay lying down, but he was determined to go back to France, so that he could be involved in the arrangements Louis was making for the funeral.

Henrietta Maria de Bourbon, Queen Mother of England and Scotland, was buried at Saint-Denis on Wednesday, 10 November 1669.

At ten o'clock that morning, the congregation began to proceed solemnly into the ancient cathedral. On entering, they heard the angelic voices of the royal choristers way up in the choir loft, speeding prayers for the Queen up to Heaven.

The procession began with members of the French government and the ambassadors of Venice and Savoy. Following them came the Queen's household, led by her senior lady-in-waiting and long-standing friend the Duchess of Richmond. Amongst the Queen's ladies was Rebecca Jermyn, Jermyn's sister-in-law (and mother of young Harry Jermyn), as disconsolate as the rest at the loss of her beloved mistress.

Next came a hundred paupers dressed in grey, twenty-four criers carrying bells, and then the French heralds, in magnificent gold-embroidered tabards.

And after them all, a plaintive figure shuffled up the aisle, alone. Because of his gout, he leant heavily on the white wand that denoted his office of Lord Chamberlain to the Queen.

No elegant hat or vain wig concealed his cropped grey hair or the deep wrinkles of his sorrowful jowls. Abandoning his customary black satin suits, Jermyn had dressed himself in the sackcloth habit of a Capuchin monk.

He was not a Catholic, but this donning of humble Catholic vestments was his way of paying homage to the piety of the woman he had loved continuously since his youth.

Behind Jermyn came the principal mourners, led by the Duke and Duchess of Orléans. Henrietta Anne's tears were obscured by her heavy black lace vale: behind her flowed the long black train of her mourning dress.

In the centre of the cathedral stood a temporary monument. Eight marble pillars supported a cupola, surmounted by a pyramid decorated with fleur-de-lys and topped by a globe bearing a replica of the Crown of England. Within the mausoleum lay a coffin containing Henrietta Maria's tenderly shrouded body.

The congregation took their places. The Archbishop of Reims began the service, assisted by four bishops. The Queen's coffin was removed from the mausoleum and lowered gently into a vault to lie next to her mighty father, Henri IV.

Will Crofts, the captain of her guard, stepped up to the entrance to the vault. Taking his staff of office in both hands, he broke it in two and threw it in, symbolising the end of his service.

Rising from his seat, Jermyn hobbled forward. Holding up his own wand of office between his large hands, he cracked it in two, and let the pieces fall down onto the coffin. Then, with the same tenderness with which he had held her pale white hand so often in life, Jermyn picked up Henrietta Maria's crown and handed it to one of the French heralds, who took it down into the vault to place it on the coffin.

It was never a farewell, and nor was the Queen truly dead. Her spirit did not truly pass away until the last time Jermyn himself closed his eyes, many years later, in his house in St James's Square.

In mid-December, as the winter snow fell in gentle flurries, Jermyn, his sister-in-law Rebecca and the rest of the disconsolate household boarded a ship at Calais and embarked for England.

In the Channel a terrible gale struck, throwing them about below decks and blowing the ship right past Dover and up the Kent coast. Their ghastly nine-day ordeal ended on Christmas Day when their ship foundered on the infamous Goodwin Sands.

A fishing boat put out from nearby Deal, braving the towering waves to haul the travellers off the ship, one by one. Jermyn and Rebecca came ashore shivering violently, their mourning clothes drenched in icy brine, but miraculously still alive.

XXII

THE SECRET TREATY OF DOVER
1669 – 1678

We have a pretty, witty King,
Whose word no one relies on;
Who never said a foolish thing,
Nor ever did a wise one
John Wilmot, Earl of Rochester, 'Impromptu on Charles II'

The day Henrietta Maria died, Jermyn revealed to Arlington the depth of his grief.

'You will believe me easily', he wrote, 'when I tell you no man can labour under the weight of more affliction than it pleased God to lay upon me in this occasion. I hope for some support from the same hand'.

Writing about him later, Jermyn's friend the Baroness d'Aulnoy put a short speech into his mouth, which she may actually have heard him utter. Addressing a group of friends, Jermyn told them, 'I have no tears in reserve... Love has cost me too much that all your pains together cannot in the least approach what I have suffered'.

Back in London, aged sixty-four, with failing sight and partially disabled by gout, Jermyn embarked on what seems to have been a futile search for a substitute for Henrietta Maria.

First he developed an infatuation for Katherine Crofts, sister of his former colleague Will. Her London salon, with its blazing fires and merry company, was far more homely than the soulless chambers of his palatial mansion in St James's Square. Soon Jermyn decided to marry Katherine but was prevented, according to gossip, because his debts were so great he could not raise the dowry. More likely, Katherine realised that Jermyn's heart would always belong to the dead Queen alone and turned him away as kindly as possible.

After Katherine, he became obsessed with the much younger 'Miledy', who may actually have been Lady Falmouth, widow of his young, bellicose cousin Charlie Berkeley. He played court to 'Miledy' and she played at being courted. Amused and slightly contemptuous of this old man who found her so attractive, she led him on, arranging trysts she had no intention of keeping and laughing with her friends as he made a fool of himself.

It seemed to be open-season on Jermyn's sex-life. Marvell sniggered that Jermyn was 'membered like a mule' (though very well endowed, male mules cannot reproduce) while Lord Rochester jested that Jermyn's only real sexual satisfaction came from a modern innovation recently introduced from Italy:

> St Albans, with wrinkles and smiles in his face,
> Whose kindness to strangers becomes his high
> > place,
> In his coach and six horses is gone to Borgo
> To take the fresh air with Signior Dildo.

Only Jermyn's friend and gambling-companion Charles de Saint-Évremond came to his defence.

The Frenchman was a Protestant – a Huguenot – and as such an exile, living in England. Charles had taken a liking to him, giving him the ridiculous post of Governor of Duck Island, in the middle of the lake in St James's Park, but with a small salary to go with it.

Saint-Évremond alone seems to have understood that Jermyn's emotions were in turmoil, and that behind his false gaiety lay the terrible, open wound caused by the loss of a woman he had loved all his life, yet had never been able to marry.

That, of course, he could not say openly, but in an open letter, 'To Monsieur ———, who could not endure that the Earl of St Albans should be in love in his old age', Saint-Évremond wrote,

> At this age all the springs of ambition leave us, the desire of glory no longer fires us, our strength fails us, our courage is extinguished, or at least weakened... Love alone supplies the place of every virtue; it averts all thoughts of those evils that surround us, and the fear of those that threaten us. It turns aside the image of death, which otherwise would continually present its self to our eyes.

No wonder Jermyn had been seeking love. But, thus counselled, Jermyn started coming to terms with his own emotions and could recognise his distracted infatuations for what they were.

In another speech put into his mouth by the Baroness d'Aulony, he reflects on Miledy: 'it is true that I have greatly loved this lady, and had she wished she might have turned me round her little finger... [but now] I am in a position to view what passes with a tranquil mind'.

And on beautiful girls in general he was wise enough to conclude that 'I admire their Beauty, without any design, heaven knows, of making any impression upon their hearts. I only endeavour to please my own self, and study rather to find tenderness in my own breast, than in theirs. 'Tis by their charms and not by their favours, that I pretend to be obliged'.

There was still one woman to whom Jermyn could give, and from whom he could receive, unconditional love.

Although there can be no certainty whether or not she was his biological offspring, Henrietta Anne, Duchess of Orléans, was certainly Jermyn's daughter in all other respects. Of all the tears shed over the Queen's grave, those of Jermyn and Henrietta Anne had been the most plentiful. Now they provided each other with a continued emotional connection to Henrietta Maria.

A cathartic outlet for them both was their work on the project that had been so dear to Henrietta Maria – the Grand Design. By corresponding with Charles and Arlington and talking directly to Louis, Henrietta Anne was able to resolve all remaining obstacles. Soon, the secret treaty was ready to be signed.

It was decided that Henrietta Anne should bring the treaty to England for Charles to sign, disguising her journey as a family visit. Initially the obstreperous Duke of Orléans, who did not suspect his wife of being a secret agent, refused to let her go.

Even Louis could not persuade his stubborn younger brother to change his mind, but letters, both pleading and flattering, from Jermyn, Charles and James, Duke of York, finally had the desired effect. Jermyn attended to every detail of Henrietta Anne's journey, reaching Dover with the court on Sunday, 22 May, and even embarking that evening to collect her from Dunkirk himself.

This time, the sea was calm and a strong breeze filled the sails of his frigate, speeding him across the Channel to be reunited with his surrogate daughter.

They sailed back on Wednesday, 25 May, enjoying the sight of rosy-fingered dawn bathing the cliffs of Dover in pink and orange. They stepped ashore beneath the ramparts of Dover

Castle, and Jermyn reunited the remnants of Henrietta Maria's family for the last time.

Ensconced in Dover Castle, Charles and Henrietta Anne agreed the final points of the treaty. It was to remain absolutely secret until Louis sent the money that would safeguard Charles from having to call Parliament to ask for permission to raise taxes. Louis was planning to attack Flanders again once its overlord, the sickly king of Spain, had died. At that point, Charles would become a Catholic and send 50 ships and 6,000 soldiers to join Louis's forces.

The Secret Treaty of Dover was signed behind the closed doors of Dover Castle on Wednesday, 1 June 1670, by French ambassador Colbert de Croissy; Secretary of State Lord Arlington and three Catholic royal officials, Lord Arundell, Sir Thomas Clifford and Sir Richard Bellings. Because Jermyn and Henrietta Anne were not royal officials, their names do not appear amongst the signatories (thus giving historians the completely false impression that they were not closely involved – which is exactly the sort of subterfuge they intended).

They spent a happy sojourn in Kent, including a ballet and feast at St Augustine's Abbey, Canterbury, where Henrietta Maria had been married. Then, Henrietta Anne sailed back to France on Sunday, 12 June. At the quayside, they said farewell and parted, she for Paris and Jermyn for London.

After supper at home on Wednesday, 29 June, Henrietta Anne suddenly felt an acute pain in her side. She cried out in agony and fell to the ground. Her attendants carried her to bed as gently as they could and summoned Louis's doctors. As courtiers and friends crowded round her bedside, she spotted Ralph Montagu, the English ambassador. In a weak voice she told him to take some of her money to repay her debts, including one she said she owed Jermyn. At 3 am on Thursday,

30 June, the lovely eyes of Henrietta Anne, Duchess of Orléans, daughter of Queen Henrietta Maria of England, were closed by the indifferent hand of death, never to shine in life again.

Henrietta Anne had in fact died of acute peritonitis contracted whilst swimming in the Seine a few days earlier.

Gossips spread the story that the Duke of Orléans had poisoned her, and to allay such stories in England, Louis sent the Marshal de Bellefonde over to London.

In an attempt to keep loneliness at bay, Jermyn had recently moved into a suite of rooms at the end of the Matted Gallery in Whitehall Palace. Here, on the warm evening of Thursday, 14 July, Jermyn entertained Bellefonde, Charles and a select group of guests who had known and loved Henrietta Anne, including the poet Edmund Waller, to dinner.

Having accepted Bellefonde's assurances that the princess had not been murdered, they relaxed over their wine, reminiscing about Henrietta Anne's life, Jermyn no doubt describing the dramatic circumstances surrounding her birth in Exeter only twenty-six years ago.

Jermyn went back to France to see Henrietta Anne buried in great solemnity next to her mother at Saint-Denis.

He took with him the young Duke of Buckingham, whom he had primed to perform a piece of political intrigue. In order to maintain the secret of Charles's proposed conversion, Arlington had presented the predominantly Anglican Privy Council with a pretend version of the Grand Design, for their eyes only, but without the clause about Charles's conversion to Catholicism.

In France, Jermyn and Louis fooled Buckingham into 'nego-tiating' this pretend treaty with the French government. After some mock-arguments, Louis agreed to it and Buckingham returned to London triumphantly, believing he alone had achieved this splendid Anglo-French treaty.

After the funeral, Jermyn travelled back to England with Buckingham. What memories crowded his mind as the sails billowed above him and the French coastline receded from his blurred vision? The last time he saw the Queen alive? His life with her at the Louvre and Colombes? Or maybe the first time Henrietta Maria's young Tuscan eyes, sparkling in the candlelight of the Louvre, had settled on him in the days when they were both young and had all their lives in front of them.

On Wednesday, 21 December that year, back in England, Buckingham's pretend treaty was signed by all the King's principal ministers. Later the same day Charles, Arlington and Colbert de Croissy secretly signed a confirmation of the real one.

The plan which Jermyn, Henrietta Maria and Henrietta Anne had worked so hard to fulfil was now official government policy. By 'joining together to surpass all others', as the Venetian ambassador had written, France and England would be unbeatable.

'The Earl of St Albans', wrote a courtier in May 1671, 'is grown young again... and will be as youthful when he gets the white staff and blue ribbon as when he was Harry Jermyn'.

Despite his increasing infirmity, Jermyn was as unwilling to retire into obscurity as Charles was to lose his sage advice. In the spring of 1671, Charles granted Jermyn the highest-ranking office in the whole court by appointing him Lord Chamberlain.

Jermyn could now fill up his days licensing plays; hiring and firing royal household staff; making sure the King's furniture was looked after properly, and dozens of other welcome distractions.

With the job came a new set of apartments at Whitehall

behind the Banqueting House, in the block leading up to the Gothic towers of the Holbein Gate. From his narrow windows, Jermyn could peer out across the box hedges and bright flowers of the Privy Gardens to the pavilion in which the elderly Freemason Sir Robert Moray performed mysterious chemical experiments.

On Sunday, 30 June 1672, Charles further honoured Jermyn by making him a Knight of the Garter. Jermyn now joined Charles; James, Duke of York; Prince Rupert, a handful of European sovereigns and the foremost luminaries of the English government in membership of England's most elite order of chivalry.

Jermyn's main concern remained the Grand Design. Typically indecisive, Charles had chosen not to rule through a First Minister but through a group of five ministers: Clifford; Arlington; Buckingham; Ashley and Lauderdale, whose initials conveniently spelled out the word for a group of conspirators and gave rise to the nickname of the 'C.A.B.A.L. ministry'.

Rivalries emerged at once, the now pro-French Arlington pitted against the feckless Buckingham who, simply to spite him, decided to become the leader of the pro-Spanish faction. In a wider sense, Arlington represented the court party, willing to suspend their personal preferences in obedience to the King, while Buckingham stood for the majority anti-French, pro-Anglican views of Parliament.

As before, the main battlefield was Charles's bedroom, where two new mistresses, Louise de Keroualle and former orange-seller Nell Gwyn, vied with each other to influence the King on behalf of Arlington and Buckingham respectively.

Twenty-two-year-old Louise, with her alabaster skin and beguiling eyes, had been brought over from France by Henrietta Anne in 1670, specifically to become a royal mistress-cum-

French agent. It was naturally enough with Louise, Arlington and Colbert de Croissy that Jermyn spent much of his time, working out how to counteract Buckingham's increasingly bold assaults on the Grand Design.

To prepare for the momentous announcement of Charles's conversion, Jermyn held secret talks with Dr Innes, the leader of the English Presbyterians. Faced with Jermyn's astute powers of persuasion, Innes agreed to support Charles, come what may, in return for a promise of increased religious toleration.

In March 1672, Charles issued a Declaration of Indulgence, greatly increasing religious freedom in England. Meanwhile, Arlington provoked war with the Dutch by accusing them of damaging the East India trade and the English fisheries.

On Saturday, 6 April, Louis's 110,000-man-strong army stormed into Flanders. At the same time, a great fleet of Dutch ships sailed across the North Sea to attack England.

The Dutch encountered the English fleet in thick fog at Solebay (also referred to as Southwold Bay) off the Suffolk coast on Thursday, 6 June. James, Duke of York and Lord High Admiral of England, destroyed many Dutch ships and chased the rest back across the North Sea. Meanwhile, Louis's armies burst through the Flemish defences and ploughed on into Holland, the Sun King's hawk-like eyes now set on the spires of Amsterdam, only twenty miles distant.

Far from siding with Charles and Louis against the Dutch States General, however, the twenty-one-year-old William of Orange took command of the Dutch forces and fought back against the invasion.

As the Sun King's troops bore down on him, William ordered his men to open sluices and cut dikes, flooding the approach to Amsterdam. Boldly ignoring Louis's indignant calls for a truce,

William attacked the retreating French forces and sent his
remaining ships back to menace the English coast.

The predominantly Anglican Parliament now demanded an
end to the war. When the King asked for money to continue
fighting, Parliament, goaded by Buckingham, would only agree if
the King cancelled the Declaration of Indulgence – which he
had no choice but to do.

They also made him sign the Test Act, forcing all non-
Anglicans out of office: although technically exempt from it, the
King's Catholic brother James, the Lord High Admiral was
forced, nonetheless, to resign his post soon after.

Then, in January 1674, feckless Buckingham revealed the
details he knew of the Grand Design. When Charles slung
Buckingham out of the Privy Council, Parliament retaliated by
accusing Arlington (whose Catholicism was still secret) of
treason. Terrified of suffering Hyde's fate – or worse –
Arlington persuaded Charles to abandon the Grand Design and
make peace with the Dutch later the same month.

By a cruel irony, it was the Lord Chamberlain's job to
proclaim the Anglo-Dutch peace. Standing unsteadily in his
heavy robes of office, his new white staff of office clutched in
his trembling hand, Jermyn announced to the world that Charles
would give no further aid to the French.

Every time the crowd cheered, more of Jermyn's dreams disintegrated. Nine months later, when Arlington was finally able to
resign as Secretary of State, Jermyn sold him his office of Lord
Chamberlain and retired.

Earlier that year, according to Baroness d'Aulnoy, Jermyn had
joked with Epicurean stoicism that 'a poor old man such as I, is
good for nothing, not even to scare the crows'.

Now the loss of Henrietta Maria; the death of Henrietta
Anne; the failure of the Grand Design; the derisory laughter of

'Miledy' and his increasing ill-health crowded in on him. He bade farewell to Charles, though doubtless still urging him to remember Henrietta Maria's dream of harmony between England and France. As the autumn rains splashed the newly-laid pavements of St James's Square, Jermyn's coach rattled out of the mews behind his house and set off towards Suffolk. The old crow was flying home at last.

Rushbrook Hall, Jermyn's old family home near Bury St Edmunds in Suffolk, now belonged to his eldest nephew, Thomas Jermyn. Thomas, who lived in Spring Gardens near Charing Cross, had agreed readily to his uncle moving back there.

From his house in St James's Square, Jermyn brought his furniture, including two cabinets intricately inlaid with Henrietta Maria's monogram, which Henrietta Anne had probably given him out of the contents of Colombes.

There was also a chest bearing Charles I's monogram, containing two of the late King's shirts and a night cap: cherished relics of the past. In addition, Jermyn brought his collection of portraits. Over Rushbrook's dark Tudor panelling, his servants hung bright portraits of Charles I; Strafford; Hamilton: Nell Gwyn; Louise de Keroualle; his long-standing friend Rupert and his old kinsman and mentor, Francis Bacon. Amongst these friends hung Van Dyck's portrait of Jermyn's younger self, proud and confident in his black satin suit and white lace collar, and Sir Peter Lely's portrait of him wearing his Garter Robes, the paint barely dry on his old, careworn head placed, according to the practise of the day, onto the body of a much younger model.

Most precious of all, though, was his personal copy of one of Van Dyck's most lovely portraits of Henrietta Maria, dressed in blue silk decorated with gold, and holding in her hand two pink roses.

The countryside around Rushbrook was teeming with wildlife, but Jermyn was too old now to ride with hounds or aim a musket at whirring clouds of partridges and pheasants.

His eyesight was too poor for him to see much of the autumn countryside, where the River Lark snaked through the brown fields. But even though he could hardly see it, the drizzly emptiness of the Suffolk countryside could only enforce his feelings of failure and desolation.

Jermyn's many friends in London missed his genial presence. His friend Saint-Évremond wrote him two long letters, entreating him to come back and offering to 'suffer myself to lose at chess' for Jermyn's gratification. Ormonde promised him a game of 'tick-tack without odds'; Mary of Modena, the new, Catholic wife of James, Duke of York, offered a *vole* of Ombre and the French ambassador, Honoré Courtin would provide news of foreign affairs.

And Cardinal Mazarin's beautiful niece Hortense Mazarin, who now lived in London as yet another of Charles's mistresses 'will ease your scruple about Visits; she will not take it ill that you just sit by her without seeing her'. Saint-Évremond continued:

> A man of honour and politeness ought to live and die in a capital City; and, in my opinion, there are but three capital Cities in Europe, Rome, London, and Paris. But Paris is no longer a place for your Lordship to live in; of the many friends you had there, some are dead, and others are imprisoned; Rome cannot suit with you; nor can the Disciple of St Paul like a place, where St Peter's successor is the sovereign; this goodly and great City, called London,

daily expects you; and here, my Lord, you ought to fix your abode.

Free conversations at table, with a few guests; a game of Ombre at Her Royal Highness's [Mary of Modena], and Chess at home, will make you as easily wait the last period of life at London, as Monsieur des Yveteaux did at Paris. He died at eighty years of age, causing a Saraband to be played to him, a little before he expired, 'that his soul', as he expressed himself, 'might slide away the easier'. You'll not pitch upon Music to soften the hardships of that voyage. A Vole at Ombre, and three aces eldest hand against three nines at Crimpo, will determine your days with as great satisfaction.

Saint-Évremond knew Jermyn was determined to stay in the countryside, but was clearly concerned about it.

I'll not give you six months life, if you stay in the Country with those melancholy thoughts you have taken up there. But why, my Lord, should you resolve to pass winter in a Country where the Horses are a hundred times better looked after than we are? Where there are Mayernes [i.e., doctors] to cure the diseases of the Race-horses, and little better than Farriers to cure those of the men.

You will tell me now, that you are scarce able to see, and that you are troubled with so many indispositions that the World is weary of you. My Lord you take the thing wrong; 'tis the Country, and not the World that is weary of you. In the Country, people judge of you by the weakness of your sight;

your Infirmities there are taken for faults; and you can't imagine what a despicable opinion your robust Country Gentlemen have of an infirm Courtier. Here in Town, my Lord, you are valued for the strength of your Judgement; your Infirmities are pitied, and your good Qualities reverenced.

As winter set in, Jermyn travelled fifteen miles east to his nephew Harry Jermyn's new house, Cheveley Park. Now a Catholic and soon to marry Will Crofts' niece Judith Poley, Harry had at last stopped behaving like a reckless teenager.

Under Jermyn's guidance, he had bought an old Tudor manor close to Newmarket racecourse and rebuilt it as a classical mansion, with beautiful flower gardens and terraces modelled on those at Saint-Germain.

On Saturday, 2 January 1675, huddled cosily by a blazing fire in the great drawing room at Cheveley, Jermyn scratched a letter to his old friend the Duke of Ormonde, the former Lord Lieutenant of Ireland in the days of the Civil War, 'to give you a little account of my self...

after having been these three months at my own house in this neighbourhood I am come hither and am going with the master of it to London within five or six days for some domestic affairs.

I think when I go to Clarendon House and miss you there and find my own deprived of the honour of your presence which it had some times the delight of with so much satisfaction, I shall come as quickly back as if I had nothing to do there, and in all events not be very long from retiring to these quarters.... as long as there remains with me any

taste for the things of this world, meeting you again
at London... I think would give me the most
contentment and am with all forms of truth and
respect as is the mark of this I am, My Lord, Your
Grace's most humble and most obedient servant,
  St Alban

Ultimately, Jermyn did indeed return to London – but not
because of Saint-Évremond's letters. At the beginning of 1678,
three months before his 73rd birthday, something more
enervating shook Jermyn out of the torpor of his old age.

Charles II had decided to revive the Grand Design.

XXIII

'JOINING TOGETHER TO SURPASS ALL OTHERS'
1678 – 1685

Fill the Bowl with rosy Wine,
Around our Temple Roses twine,
And let us cheerfully awhile,
Like the Wine and Roses smile.
Crowned with Roses we contemn
Gyges wealthy Diadem.

To day is Ours; what do we fear?
To day is Ours; we have it here.
Let's treat it kindly, that it may
Wish, at least, with us to stay.
Let's banish Business, banish Sorrow;
To the Gods belong Tomorrow.
Abraham Cowley, 'The Epicure'

Jermyn's new development of St James's was now virtually complete. Standing in the square, a man with better eyesight than Jermyn could look north up Duke of York Street to where it ran into Jermyn Street, and see beyond that the rising walls of St James's Church.

Jermyn was still struggling with the Anglican authorities to have St James's made into a parish – it was at the time merely part of the larger parish of St Martin-in-the-Fields – but in the meantime, on his brief return trip to London in 1676, he had laid the foundation stone and commissioned his long-standing friend Sir Christopher Wren to build his church.

St James's Square as Jermyn left it, drawn by Sutton Nicholls in the early 18th century

Wren repaid his mentor handsomely with his design for St James's Church. The barrel-vaulted roof was a prototype for the style Wren later used on St Paul's Cathedral. For the tops of the pilasters towering above the altar, Wren had designed bosses decorated with Jermyn's coat of arms, which can still be seen there today.

The magnificently carved pulpit was the work of the most talented carver in London, Grinling Gibbons, a protégé of Evelyn's, and who had recently been promoted to become a Grand Warden of the Freemasons.

By 1678, St James's Square was fully built. Jermyn had overcome the problem of persuading people to build his planned 'thirteen or fourteen great and good houses' by dividing the plots into smaller ones, and selling them off freehold.

He sold his original house and built another – and better – one in the north-west corner of the square, at a cost of £15,000 (roughly £1.2m in modern money). Now, twenty elegant houses, inhabited by an eclectic mixture of royal mistresses, royal officials and relations of Jermyn's, stood behind the unified façade of the completed Square.

The discerning John Evelyn was certainly impressed. Jermyn's 'large and magnificent structures', he wrote, had brought about 'a renaissance' in English classical architecture.

Despite this triumph, St James's Square was not precisely as Jermyn had intended. Practicalities of costs and the annoying habit of builders changing his plans led to the square not being fully symmetrical. He had wanted four roads to enter the square at the exact centre of each side, but instead only three did so, the fourth being replaced by two side-roads leading down to Pall Mall, that broke the square's southern corners.

Fully unified squares were a new architectural development in northern Europe. They were introduced to Paris by Henrietta Maria's parents and had been brought to England by Inigo Jones, who built the Piazza at Covent Garden in 1631. But these always combined houses with shops. Jermyn's innovation was in creating a square exclusively 'for the conveniency of the Nobility and Gentry who were to attend upon his Majesty's Person, and in Parliament'.

Unified squares denote social cohesion imposed on individuals. To men like Jermyn, they represented the defining power of monarchy. Richelieu made this explicit in Paris, placing a statue of Louis XIII in the middle of the Place Royale. In London, and with the same end in mind, Jermyn built his square as close as possible to St James's Palace.

Its enclosed, uniform design was intended to give the area the feel of a palace courtyard. For Jermyn, St James's Square was a physical embodiment of Hobbes's *Leviathan*, the book written under his ægis to give philosophical structure to monarchy. His aim in building St James's Square was to remind all who saw it, and any government ministers and Members of Parliament who might live there, that the King was in charge.

Since the collapse of the Grand Design, Charles's now exclusively Anglican Parliament had grown increasingly hostile towards the Crown. Whenever Charles asked for more money to govern the kingdom, Parliament increased its demands for the exclusion of the King's openly Catholic brother and heir, James, Duke of York, from the line of succession. Parliament favoured instead the brothers' courageous Protestant nephew, William of Orange who, in 1677, had married James's daughter Mary.

The only alternative to being beholden to Parliament was for Charles to have another source of income in the form of financial subsidies out of the brimming coffers of the King of France, a solution that had been much discussed before, but never implemented. Some money was forthcoming in 1677, but a permanent arrangement was needed. Nobody was better suited to guide Charles's ministers through the bewildering intricacies of French diplomatic etiquette, or indeed of the Sun King's devious mind, than Jermyn.

This is why the King had recalled his most trusted of henchmen back to London in 1678, and it is what kept Jermyn happily occupied over the next three years.

There were many times in this period when Jermyn, although a retired statesman with absolutely no official position, seemed to know the King's mind far better than any members of the government, as Ambassador Paul de Barillon observed. Indeed, without power or position, Jermyn seemed to exercise the most extraordinary, fatherly influence over the nation's future.

The French were obstinate. They wanted England to be Catholic and on their side, but at the least cost to them. Jermyn's quiet diplomacy continued, talking to French ambassadors and envoys in the salons of those two alabaster-skinned royal mistresses-cum-French agents, Hortense Mazarin and Louise de Keroualle.

Meanwhile, Protestant revolution simmered, mobs howled for Catholic blood and ministers rose and fell with alarming speed. Parliament even sent one Lord Treasurer, Thomas Osborne, to the Tower for what they perceived as *his* treasonous negotiations with France over the subsidies.

By 1681, England faced crisis. Charles's coffers were empty. Before it voted him a penny in taxes, Parliament wanted war with France and the absolute guarantee that the Protestant William of Orange would be the next monarch.

The consequences of both for Louis would be dire. In this game of diplomatic *Ombre*, Jermyn found himself holding the trumps. On Good Friday, 1 April 1681, French Ambassador Paul de Barillon agreed to a down-payment of 2,000,000 *livres* (about £12m in modern money), and a subsequent annual pension of 1,500,000 *livres*, conditional on Charles not summoning Parliament for three years.

Right back in 1662, Jermyn had written of his project for the Closer Union of the French and English crowns that

> If it please God to continue those beginnings...
> [Charles and Louis] will be preserved so very much
> by the happy union that is now between them which
> continuing they will have very little to fear either
> from foreign enemies or domestic embroilments.

Nineteen years later, Jermyn had turned this hope into reality.

Jermyn waited for a couple of weeks for Louis to thank him – in vain. On Thursday, 21 April, his courtliness tempered by the abrupt impatience of the elderly, he told Barillon that a token of France's gratitude would be appropriate.

Embarrassed, the ambassador consulted the Sun King, who told him to give Jermyn a diamond-studded box, worth 1,500 *livres* (about £9,000 in modern money), which the former ambassador to France, the Francophobic Denzil Holles, had turned down. So Jermyn received Holles' box, James returned from exile and Charles settled down to rule without having to summon Parliament, an Absolute Monarch within his own realms at last.

Jermyn's coat of arms, with the addition of the greyhound supporters that proclaimed his devotion to Henrietta Maria, granted when he became an earl, and the Garter riband inscribed 'Honi Soit Qui Mal Y Pense': 'shame on him who thinks this evil'. Missing from the scroll below is Jermyn's enigmatic family motto 'Ab orient nec ab occidente': 'Neither from the East nor from the West'.

In Jermyn's last years, the bright world retreated down a darkening tunnel as his eyesight continued to deteriorate. But surrounded by his nephews and friends like Saint-Évremond and Hortense Mazarin, he was not as lonely as he had once feared he would be.

Another friend, despite all their erstwhile political differences, was sixty-five-year-old Lord Arlington 'to whom', Saint-Évremond had written in 1677, 'you yielded the title of the first gouty Man in England'. Arlington was retired as well now, but still sported the black patch on his nose, ostentatiously concealing the Civil War scar he claimed was there.

Arlington's main residence was now Goring House at the west end of St James's Park. Many years later, rebuilt and enlarged, it would receive its present name – Buckingham Palace.

Late in the afternoon of Tuesday, 18 September 1683, Jermyn set out for Goring House in his coach, attended by his footmen liveried in black and silver, to visit his old friend and sometime adversary.

After eating and drinking with what his fellow guest John Evelyn considered 'an extraordinary appetite', Jermyn retired to the *Ombre* table. He was so blind now, Evelyn noted, that he needed a servant-boy to sit next to tell him what cards he was holding.

Thus Evelyn recorded the full, debilitating effect of a lifetime of almost unlimited soup and gold.

Jermyn and Arlington probably reminisced about the old days in France, when the younger man had cultivated Henrietta Maria's Lord Chamberlain with gifts of Piedmont wine and truffles.

They may also have speculated about the future. The foundation stone had just been laid for a new palace at Winchester, commissioned by Charles from Sir Christopher Wren. Conveniently near France, this would be an English Versailles, a new capital for the Absolute monarchy that Jermyn had created.

Like the conquest of Madagascar, however, the completion of Winchester Palace, and all it stood for, would prove an ephemeral dream. But that night in September 1683, its rising walls were a tangible manifestation of what Jermyn had achieved.

Jermyn stayed drinking at Arlington's as late as he could. Eventually he allowed his servants to take him home to the opulent splendour of his empty house.

When Lady Borlais died in France, Louis, citing the Medieval law of *droit d'aubains*, had claimed that her estate belonged to him. Her heir, Lord Preston knew that, in 1667, Jermyn had successfully overcome a similar claim made by Louis on the French estates of the Dukes of Richmond. So, in November 1683, Preston sought Jermyn's help and advice over how he should handle his personal conflict with the King of France.

One way or the other, Jermyn remained useful right up to the end.

And now the end had come.

A contemporary depiction of the Frost Fair, that was being held on the frozen Thames at the time Jermyn died.

The start of 1684 saw Britain in the grip of a mini-Ice Age. The timeless Thames, which Geoffrey of Monmouth had imagined lapping London's banks when the mythical Brutus traced out the perimeters of his 'New Troy', and which had watered the countless generations of real-life Britons, Romans, Saxons and

Normans who had lived and died in the city's cramped streets – that mighty river upon which Jermyn had travelled so often in high-sailed ships and gilded barges – was frozen solid. The Londoners were enjoying an 'Ice Fair', held on its crisp surface. Charles II went himself, to watch the extraordinary spectacle of a whole ox being roasted over a fire blazing on solid ice.

Detached from the excitement, up in his house in St James' Square on Wednesday, 2 January 1684, and two months short of his 79th birthday, Henry Jermyn died.

It is unfortunate for us that no record survives of Charles's reaction on hearing of the death of the man who had been so widely rumoured to have been his real father. Henry Jermyn had been a strong, surviving link with his mother, and had done so much, in so many ways, to make Charles the man he was. It was Henry Jermyn, more than anyone else, who had set him safe upon his throne in 1660, and had left him, financially and thus politically secure on the same seat, a quarter of a century later.

James, Duke of York, wrote, in his usual, somewhat detached, soldierly fashion, of an event he had clearly anticipated for some time:

> As for news, what is from foreign parts you will see in the Gazette; and for here there is none but that Lord St. Albans is dead, and that the river has been so frozen over these two days that people go over it on foot.

Rather than be buried in Westminster Abbey, Jermyn wanted a 'decent Christian burial amongst my ancestors in the church of Rushbrook' – evidence, if ever it were needed, that he had never become a Catholic.

Accompanied by his sorrowful nephews, his body was borne

speedily along the ice-bound roads to Rushbrook, where he was buried eight days later. An elegant classical tomb, which Jermyn had probably commissioned himself, was erected in the south chancel wall, showing a couple of cherubs, his coat of arms, and a simple Latin inscription, which reads:

> Here lies the noble Henry Jermyn, Earl of St Albans, Baron of Bury St Edmunds, second son of Sir Thomas Jermyn, Master of the Horse and Lord Chamberlain to Henrietta Maria, mother of Charles II and, after her death, Lord Chamberlain and Privy Councillor to His Majesty the Queen's son, created a Knight of the most noble Order of the Garter at Windsor the day before the Kalends of July [i.e., 30 June]1672.

Not 'to the King', but *to His Majesty the Queen's son*. All that ever really mattered to Jermyn was her.

This monument, however, was very far from being all that remained to remind the world of Jermyn's astonishing achievements.

XXIV

'THE FUNERAL OF GLORY'?
1685 – present

Next, painter, draw the rabble of the plot:
[Harry] Jermyn, Fitzgerald, Loftus, Porter, Scot;
These are fit heads indeed to turn a State,
And change the order of a nation's fate;
Ten thousand such as these shall ne'er control
The smallest atom of an English soul.

Old England on its strong foundation stands,
Defying all their heads and all their hands;
Its steady basis never could be shook,
When wiser men her ruin undertook;
And can the guardian angel let her stoop
At last to madmen, fools, and to the Pope?
No, Painter, no! close up the piece and see
This crowd of traytors hang'd in effigie
Edmund Waller, *Advice to a Painter* (1666)

Jermyn died leaving Charles II secure on the throne. The treasury was full; James's succession was assured, the monarchy was Absolute and Britain was well on the way towards full religious toleration.

Yet within five years of Jermyn's death Britain became a religiously-repressive state – ruled by a Dutchman!

How did Jermyn's plans go so dramatically wrong?

It started on Monday 2 February 1685 when Charles, who was waiting for his morning shave, suddenly bellowed with pain and collapsed.

Unaware that the King's kidneys were failing, his doctors spent the next few days bleeding him and feeding him a terrible cocktail of drugs, an estimated 58 in all, ranging from hellebore root and white vitriol (sulphuric acid) dissolved in peony water, to forty drops of 'extract' from a human skull and also some powder made of ground 'bezoar' stone taken from the stomach, it was recorded, 'of an eastern goat'.

Some of these 'medicines' were deadly poisonous; all were useless. When these drugs failed to make him any better, his doctors burned his feet and head with red-hot irons.

On Thursday, Louise de Keroualle told Barillon to fetch a Catholic priest, who baptised Charles into the Catholic Church. At noon on Friday the 6th, the Thames ran, unfrozen, at high tide and the man who had so often been taken for Jermyn's son was dead.

After Charles II's death, his brother James, Duke of York, succeeded to the throne as James II.

Fulfilling the Anglicans' worst fears, James soon brought a 'rabble' of Catholics into the government, including Jermyn's nephew Harry, whom he made Earl of Dover; a Privy Counsellor; Lord Lieutenant of Cambridge; a Lord of the Treasury and acting Lord Chamberlain.

When James's queen Mary of Modena gave birth to a Catholic heir, James Francis Edward, in June 1688, the patience of the Protestant establishment ran out.

A cabal of Protestant courtiers offered William of Orange the throne. William landed at Torbay in November. After a brief attempt to fight back, James II fled to France. It is extremely likely that Harry Jermyn had contracted a death-bed marriage to William's mother Mary back in 1660 and thus had been, technically, his father-in-law. Yet despite this, Harry's loyalties lay firmly with James, whom he followed quickly across to France.

In 1689, James and Harry landed in Ireland, backed by Louis's money and officers. Harry's view was that both were far too inadequate to be of any real use and that Louis, like Mazarin and Richelieu before him, was more intent on creating trouble in England than in providing genuine help for James. He appears to have been right.

James and Harry rode out of Dublin Castle on Sunday, 16 June 1689 at the head of an army of 26,000 men, nicknamed 'Jacobites' after the Latin version of James's name. Passing through Dundalk, they looked out across the waters of the River Boyne to see William's 36,000-strong army assembling for battle.

They fought their battle on Monday, 1 July 1689. Only 2,000 men were killed, three quarters of them on James's side, but the Jacobite army was thoroughly trounced. James and Harry galloped south to Waterford, where they parted. James sailed for France, dying in exile at Saint-Germain in 1703. After long months of waiting, Harry finally gained the permission of William of Orange to return to England. He lived quietly at Cheveley, troubled in his later years, like his uncle, by acute gout.

Harry's last word on the subject of Anglo-French relations was made to John Evelyn, who visited him at Cheveley in 1691. Louis had over-stretched himself fighting the Hapsburgs, he said. If William still wanted to attack him, now would be the right time. Not even Harry, it seems, retained Jermyn's firm conviction that England's future lay in a peaceful friendship with France.

Ultimately, the winners were the people against whom Jermyn had struggled the hardest. The spiritual heirs of the Parliamentarians and Roundheads, who rejected the idea of absolute monarchy, now govern Britain. And the statue of

Oliver Cromwell, though never a great friend of Parliamentary democracy stands, nevertheless, in pride of place outside the Palace of Westminster.

But had Jermyn been so wrong? His advocacy of absolute monarchy may not sit well with modern Liberalism, yet it was a widely-accepted form of government at the time. And let it be remembered that it was Jermyn, and not Cromwell or the post-Restoration Parliament, who favoured religious toleration.

In terms of foreign policy, it may be argued that friendship with France could have saved a great deal of trouble. In 1704, Queen Anne's favourite general John Churchill (later Duke of Marlborough), defeated Louis at the Battle of Blenheim. For the rest of the eighteenth century, Britain and its allies remained periodically at war with France. Impoverished by the demands of constant war, the French population eventually erupted into revolution.

And while Britain and Napoleonic France battled on into the nineteenth century, the power of Prussia grew, eventually becoming the German Empire and replacing France as the dominant power on the Continent. By the time Britain finally reverted to Jermyn's policy of co-operation with France, Germany had become so powerful that it was too late to prevent the two devastating world wars of the twentieth century.

That's not to say that, had Jermyn's policies been followed, there would have been no more war in Europe. Of course there would – but history would not have unfolded as it did, and maybe it would not have been quite as terrible.

For the eighteenth century, at any rate, and like his ephemeral hope of possessing Madagascar, Jermyn's desire that England and France could live in friendship and peace proved to be nothing more than a dream.

* * *

So what were Jermyn's real legacies to the world?

Jermyn's love of French wine was one of the defining passions of his life. Not only did he have it imported, but he paid extra to have bottles made bearing his family's coat of arms: the bottle-blower was given a copy of the family's seal, which was stamped into the glass whilst it was still soft.

One of the bottles, which had once seen Jermyn and his friends through a hearty meal, has long been on display in the museum at Mont Orgueil, Jersey.

The museum's curators looked on it as nothing more than a curiosity, until they were contacted in 2007 by Professor Martin Biddle of Oxford University, who was making a study of old wine bottles. 'If it belongs to Henry Jermyn's first governorship [of Jersey]...' he told them, 'it would be the earliest datable wine bottle'. There are of course many much older bottles: what makes Jermyn's unique in the world is that his is the oldest one, anywhere, that can be identified to a specific owner.

How entirely appropriate that Jermyn, having spent so much of his lifetime enjoying his wines, should have written himself into the history of wine itself.

That was one achievement he had not expected. The list of what he did achieve is impressive, even when only measured in terms of official positions. Jermyn was, at varying times of his life, a Knight of the Garter; Earl of St Alban; 1st Baron Jermyn of St Edmundsbury; Lord Chamberlain to Charles II; Lord Chamberlain, Gentleman Usher of the Privy Chamber, Treasurer, Receiver General and Master of the Horse to Queen Henrietta Maria; Governor and Captain of Jersey; Governor of Elizabeth and Mont Orgueil castles; Ambassador, Ambassador Extraordinary and Minister Plenipotentiary to the Court of

France; Colonel of the Queen's Regiment of Foot; High Steward of Greenwich and Kingston upon Thames; Registrar of the Court of Chancery; Co-coroner and Attorney of the Court of King's Bench; Joint Surveyor of the Petty Customs and Subsidies; Member of Parliament for Bodmin and Liverpool; Justice of the Peace for Middlesex and Surrey; co-proprietor of the 'Northern Neck' of Virginia; an original member of the Company of Royal Adventurers into Africa; Lord of the Bailiwick of St James's; Sieur de Saint-Germain in Jersey and Lord of the Manors of Rushbrook, Weybridge, Oatlands, Byfleet, Eldoe and Tofts, founder of the West End and reputed Grand Master of the Freemasons.

Jermyn was also variously rumoured to be, or tipped to become, various things that were either never to be or, at any rate, did not transpire. These include, particularly, Treasurer of the Household (1640); a viscount (1640); First Minister of State (various dates); Earl of Yarmouth (1645); Ambassador Extraordinary to the Netherlands (1645); a Duke of France (1646); Lord of Aubigny (1646); a Secretary of State (1641; 1649/50); Lieutenant General of the Channel Islands (1648); Lord High Admiral (1648); husband of the Queen of England (c. 1650); Governor of the Principality of Orange (1659) and Lord Treasurer (1662) – and that is to name but a few.

During the Civil War, Jermyn had accrued a debt of some £45,000 for the Crown. Charles had repaid this debt with leases, especially for the St James's estate, and the income they generated reached easily £8,000 a year by the time the land was all developed. Yet for all that, this income had barely covered the ever-increasing interest on the original debts.

Whilst Jermyn had a vast overall income, he also had enormous expenses due to gambling and entertaining. When the final calculations were made, Jermyn's nephews were stunned to find that he had died £60,000 in debt.

Jermyn's earldom became extinct when he died. By a special condition written into the grant, the title of Baron Jermyn went to his nephew Thomas Jermyn.

Of Thomas's numerous sons, only one boy survived beyond the cot. In 1692, the survivor, fifteen years old and as high-spirited as his great uncle was at his age, was messing about on a barge in the Thames when he was struck by a falling mast and killed. The baronial title passed, by a special arrangement made when it was created, to Jermyn's nephew Harry. When Harry died without children in 1708, it became extinct.

Once the various leases to Jermyn's estates ran out in the course of the next century, very little was left of his transient empire. The main properties, Rushbrook and the house in St James's Square, were inherited by the Hervey family.

The intermarriages of the Jermyns and Herveys produced some interesting connections. Jermyn's great aunt Susan Jermyn married Sir William Hervey of Ickworth. Their son John Hervey (d. 1679) was a trustee for some of Jermyn's London leases, whilst their grandson John became 1st Earl of Bristol. Felton Hervey, a younger son of the 1st Earl was, incidentally, an ancestor of the Randolph family, who were ancestors of the actor Hugh Grant, who is thus a not-too-distant cousin of Henry Jermyn's.

The 1st Earl of Bristol's eldest son, meanwhile, was John, Lord Hervey (1696-1743), whose career echoed Jermyn's. He became vice chamberlain to Queen Charlotte and thus a prominent, if generally unpopular, power behind the throne of her husband George II. Lord Hervey died before his father, and his sons became 2nd, 3rd and 4th Earls of Bristol in turn: the latter married Elizabeth Davers, who was herself a great granddaughter of Jermyn's brother Thomas. The son of the 4th Earl and Elizabeth Davers was Frederick William Hervey, who was made 1st Marquess of Bristol and was also granted the title of Earl Jermyn, to commemorate his family's inheritance from the Jermyn family in general, and from Henry Jermyn in particular. The 1st Marquess' senior heir today is Frederick, 8th Marquess of Bristol & Earl Jermyn. The 8th Marquess' sisters are the famously stylish Ladies Victoria and Isabella Hervey.

Two additional family connections of the Jermyns are worth mentioning too. From the 4th Earl's daughter Mary, Lady Erne, we can bring down a line (via the families of Wharncliffe, Chetwynd-Talbot and Ford) to the explorer and television presenter Edward Michael 'Bear' Grylls. The youngest British person ever to climb Everest, he is another well-known character who can certainly be considered a notable relative of Henry Jermyn.

Going further back into the Jermyns' past, Henry Jermyn's own great grandfather Sir Ambrose Jermyn had a daughter Susan, who was the ancestress (via the families of Tollemache and Allington) of the great naval commander, Earl Howe (d. 1799). Sir Ambrose's brother John Jermyn (d. 1606) went one better, for he was the ancestor – via the family of the poet Sir John Suckling, who appears in Jermyn's story – of none other than Horatio, Admiral Lord Nelson, the victor of Trafalgar.

Jermyn's mother's sister, Lady Elizabeth Berkeley, gave Jermyn a further interesting connection, for her great great great great grandson was the poet Lord Byron.

As to Henrietta Maria's blood, after the demise of the Stuarts in 1714, the crown passed sideways across the royal family tree, to George I of Hanover, whose grandmother Queen Elizabeth of Bohemia was the sister of Charles I. However, the blood of Henrietta Maria continued down several lines of dukes, sprung from the illegitimate progeny of Charles II and his brother James II. A line of descent from Charles II's natural son the Duke of Richmond leads us to Lady Cynthia Hamilton, whilst a line coming down from James II's natural daughter Henrietta, Lady Waldegrave, brings us to Lady Cynthia's husband, John 7th Earl Spencer. Through their granddaughter Diana, Princess of Wales, and her son Prince William, Henrietta Maria's blood has flowed back into the British royal family – and with it the tantalising suspicion of a dose of Jermyn's blood if either Charles II or James II were his offspring.

In terms of his physical impact on London, Jermyn remains a largely unsung hero.

Work on Greenwich Palace ceased when Henrietta Maria died in 1669. But at the end of the century Sir Christopher Wren was commissioned to complete what Jermyn had started. Wren expanded his design from two to four blocks, retaining Jermyn's original plans for the vista between the Thames and the Queen's House, but making the palace itself much bigger. The palace became the Royal Naval Hospital and is still one of the most beautiful and awe-inspiring buildings in London.

The Church of St James's, Westminster, which Jermyn had financed to the tune of £7,000, was finished soon after his death. Charles granted the freehold of the site to the Church of England and soon afterwards St James's became an independent parish as Jermyn had wished.

On Monday, 13 July 1685, while James II was still getting used to his new throne, the Anglican Bishop of London, attended by an impressive retinue of clergy, processed into St James's Square and up to the doorway of Jermyn's house.

On the steps stood Jermyn's faithful lawyer Martin Folkes, who handed over the title deeds of the church to the Bishop.

Having worked for so long with his master towards that moment, Folkes alone knew how proud Jermyn would have been of this achievement.

Thanking Folkes graciously, the Bishop rounded the corner and proceeded up Duke of York Street, crossed Jermyn Street and entered St James's Church. While the Bishop solemnly consecrated the church, Thomas and Harry Jermyn took their seats near Folkes and Sir Christopher Wren. They listened happily as the choir sent the first of very many hymns of praise echoing round the fine barrel-vaulting of Jermyn's church of St James's, Westminster.

The Great Fire of London of 1666, which Jermyn had feared might destroy St James's, actually stimulated its expansion.

From the start, the City fathers had feared St James's would draw new builders away from their Square Mile. In 1663 they had even lobbied Parliament, unsuccessfully, for legislation banning any further development by Jermyn in Westminster. Although the post-Fire building regulations issued by the Privy Council adopted many of the standards set by Jermyn at St James's, including wider streets, paving and a sewerage system – all hitherto unknown in the City – many Londoners chose to move to St James's and build their new houses there instead.

In his later years, Jermyn had the satisfaction of seeing many other developments taking place around St James's, all inspired by what he had done.

Jermyn's cousin Jack Berkeley, Sir Thomas Bond and Sir George Downing were amongst the many men who constructed their own classically-styled squares and streets – including Berkeley Square, Bond Street and Downing Street, nearby.

The foundations of King's Square, Soho, planned in direct imitation of St James' Square, were laid in 1680. After Jermyn's death, a chess-board of other squares based on St James's would spread out across the fields to the north and west to encompass the villages of Knightsbridge, Kensington and Chelsea. That these areas would succumb to brick and mortar is inevitable. But the stately nature of these developments can be traced back to Jermyn.

Not for nothing has Jermyn been hailed as 'the founder of the West End'.

Finally, on the sunny evening of Wednesday 28 September 2011, we came back, descendants of Jermyn's heirs, writers whom he had inspired, and residents of the area he had created, to the corner of St James's Square and Duke of York Street, to witness the unveiling of a plaque, by the young Marquess of Bristol, Jermyn's senior ancestral nephew, on the wall of Chatham House, home of The Royal Institute of International Affairs, which stands on the site of the house in which Jermyn died. It reads:

> Look left to St James's Square, and right to St James's Church in Jermyn Street. All this was the inspiration of one man: HENRY JERMYN, EARL OF ST ALBANS, K.G., 1605-1684, diplomat, favourite of Queen Henrietta Maria and 'Founder of the West End', who died in his house on this site.

The wording, like the plaque itself, was my idea, a thankful nod to the man who had proved such a rich and fascinating subject for research throughout my adult life.

For me, the unveiling of the plaque was full of resonance of that first, previous commemoration of his life, back in 1685. A small green plaque, to tell passers-by a little of who Jermyn was, and what he had achieved.

I felt it was the least he deserved.

The Westminster green plaque commemorating Henry Jermyn.

ELEGY

January 1684

By thee, St Albans, living we did learn
The art of life, and by thy light discern
The truth which men dispute; but by thee dead
Were taught upon the world's gay pride to tread
And that way sooner master it than he
To whom both Indies tributary be.
Anon, *An elegy on the death of the most illustrious lord,*
the Earl of St Albans.

In spring 1684, before the Glorious Revolution had set
Europe on such a different course to the one Jermyn had
intended, Mr Deacon the bookseller put a pamphlet on sale at
his shop at the sign of the Angel in 'Guilt-spur Street-
Without-Newgate'.

It was entitled *An elegy on the death of the most illustrious lord,*
the Earl of St Albans and included an epitaph:

> Hail! sacred house in which his relics sleep;
> Blest marble, give me leave t'approach and weep.
> Unto thy self, great spirit, I will repeat
> Thy own brave story; tell thy self how great
> Thou were in Mind's empires, and how all
> Who out-live thee see but the funeral of glory;
> And if yet some virtuous be,
> They but the apparitions are of thee.

The *Elegy* included some curious lines:

Let us contemplate thee (brave soul), and though
We cannot track the way which thou didst go
In thy celestial journey, and our heart
Expansion wants to think what now thou art,
How bright and wide thy glories, yet we may
Remember thee as thou went in thy clay;
Great without title, in thy self alone
A mighty lord, thou stood obliged to none
....

And now my sorrows follow thee, I tread the milky
way
And see the snowy head of Atlas far below, while
all the high-
Swollen buildings seem but atoms to my eye.
How small seems greatness here! how not a span
His empire who commands the Ocean,
Both that which boasts so much its mighty ore,
And th' other which with pearl hath paved its
shore!

The elegy was anonymous but the style is remarkably similar
to D'Avenant's. It may have been written as a parting gift, in
anticipation of Jermyn's inevitable demise, before the poet felt
the chill embrace of death in 1668. Only D'Avenant, after all,
could have had the temerity to follow Jermyn's soul beyond
death, just as his spirit had flown in pursuit of the dreams
Jermyn had shared with Rupert and Endymion Porter half a
century earlier.

The day after New Years' day 1684 dawned bitter and clear. In
Jermyn's bedchamber in St James' Square the fire blazed

bright. Outside, the hoar frost bit deep an
frozen solid.

We can dare imagine the final scene.

Jermyn's old servant, Sarah Jamett, came in and stok
She turned to smile at Jermyn, but it was not her face that he sa
Pale as ice and framed by dense red curls, it was the face of
Elizabeth I, his little sister's putative godmother.

Sitting on his father's knee, enveloped happily in a sweet-smelling cloud of tobacco smoke, Jermyn listened now as the old man told him the sorrowful story of the little sister who died, on a bitterly cold day such as this, so soon before he was born.

The tobacco smoke lifted and with it the darkness. He found himself standing in sunlight. He sniffed the sneezy smell of the meadow grasses and saw the dog-roses that choked the hedgerows with their flower-burdened stems. Down to the Lark he ran, through the haze of golden pollen thrown up into the noonday air by his grandfather's munching cows. The cows lifted their heads to stare in surprise as he and his brothers, Robert and Thomas, dashed past, whooping with joy.

Calling after them, he tripped but felt gentle hands catching him. It was his mother, her face young again, now older, and now it was the face of Lord Bacon, his brows furrowed quizzically. Through the heady meadows they strolled and, while the woodpeckers drummed on the trees in the wood, Bacon talked to him of cows, of journeys to Venus and of the swift passage of souls through the heliocentric solar system.

The drumming was louder now, the beat of drums themselves, and Jermyn peeked eagerly round Bacon's legs to see the oak doors of the audience chamber at St James's Palace fly open.

ping down like a bejewelled wave, the double row of ...ers bowed low to James I and his fair-faced consort ...kingham, who tipped his sombrero jauntily at Jermyn as he swaggered past. Turning his head to follow him, Jermyn saw him pass through the archway of El Escorial and into the bright sunlight of the grand salon of the Louvre.

Jermyn followed Buckingham in, his entire frame trembling in anticipation of what might happen next.

The stately drums thudded louder as he approached the crowd of half-remembered courtiers. His heart racing, he ran through the throng, pushing people aside, searching everywhere.

At last he caught sight of her – again, again, after so many years. Tears welled up in his eyes as she turned to face him. Following Lord Kensington's lead, he swept a low bow, the drums thudding now in his own temples as he raised his head again. Her deep brown Tuscan eyes flashed bright as her gaze settled on him. Her brows furrowed, as if struggling to remember the details of some precious vision. Yet this vision was not some fragment of memory from the past, but a glimpse of the decades that stretched out before them.

He stood staring at her, his mouth half-open, trying to speak. 'The future...', he stammered.

'No', he heard Richelieu reply sharply, 'nothing is certain: it is for you to forge your own destiny'.

Now he and Henrietta Maria ran, her hand in his, through the flower gardens of St James's Palace and out onto the terraces of Saint-Germain. Together they stopped, breathless, gazing out over the valley of the Seine, their hands resting on the damp moss on the stone balustrade. In the forest, pheasants rasped their klaxon-mating calls. 'Wake! Wake!' they seemed to cry.

As the drumming continued, he turned to Henrietta Maria as they stepped out onto the balcony of the Queen's House and gazed with pride over the newly laid-out gardens of Greenwich. Henrietta Maria looked old now, grey hairs whisping around her temples and onto the pillows of her deathbed at Colombes.

He spoke softly: 'May God and the angels protect you'.

'Adieu', she whispered back.

The drumming was stately now, and more remote. He was alone, standing at the window of his house in St James's Square, gazing out across the rooftops to the crenelated towers of St James's Palace. Somewhere nearby, the voice of Saint-Évremond was repeating words from that memorable letter he once wrote to Jermyn, about love in old age. *'Monsieur des Yveteaux... He died at eighty years of age, causing a Saraband to be played to him, a little before he expired, that his soul, as he expressed himself, might slide away the easier. You'll not pitch upon music to soften the hardships of that voyage...'*

No music, then.

Below him, and silent in the rosy-fingered dawn, England lay peacefully under her blanket of snow. Villagers dragged what little firewood their lords had allowed them home to their dank cottages. Farmers sat by warm hearths in village alehouses complaining, as they had since time immemorial, about the weather. Young nobles, splendid in their plumed hats and long, richly-braided coats, admired the elegant spirals their sharp skates were carving on the frozen surfaces of lakes.

Jermyn glimpsed the glint of the Channel and saw the verdant hills of Albion spread out below him. About him, the silvery clouds were alive, as he had always imagined they would be, with cherubs. Above them smiled down Aphrodite and Dionysius, whilst Apollo's chariot described its stately arc through the broad heavens.

Speeding over France, he caught sight of the snow-capped peaks of the Pyrenees below his feet. At high noon he passed over Madrid and then the shimmering peaks of the Andalucian mountains and the dazzling expanse of the Mediterranean lay before him.

He turned, suddenly hesitant as the cool afternoon air brushed his cheek. D'Avenant hovered behind him, smiling.

'Go on', cried the poet. 'You know the way!'

Beyond the sea, the snowy head of Mount Atlas rose majestically above the North African coast. He crossed Africa, pink and brown, below him.

He reached the eastern coast at sunset and started to cross the narrow strip of ocean, glittering in the last rays of the sun.

There, before him, lay Madagascar.

And, turning, he saw her by his side again.

APPENDICES

THE CALENDAR IN THE SEVENTEENTH CENTURY.

Until 1752, the English legal year began on 25 March; thus, 24 March 1660 was recorded as 24 March 1659 or 24 March 1659/60. Until 1752, the English did not use Leap Years and were, in consequence, an increasing number of days behind the Continent.

When Jermyn was alive, there was a lapse of 10 days, and thus the date of Henrietta Maria's death, 31 August 1669 in England was 10 September 1669 in France. Confusing in itself, these discrepancies become yet more mentally-taxing when Englishmen on the Continent, writing to England, sometimes used the French calendar and on other occasions the English. A further layer of complexity is added when editors of printed letters correct dates to modern style without saying so, leading further writers to think they were original dates, and thus to correct them again.

Thus, although Henrietta Maria died on 10 September in France, which was 31 August in England, the ambiguous renderings of these dates have led some writers to re-correct, making her date of death, as it would have been in England, 21 August – which is wrong.

In the endnotes, the dates of documents are given as they were written in their original form. In the text, dates between 1 January and 24 March are corrected to the modern English year and are given from point of view of seventeenth century England, even when they took place (and thus were dated differently) on the Continent.

RED HERRINGS

There are three contemporary portraits of Henry Jermyn: a miniature in the Royal Collection at Windsor; one of Jermyn as a young cavalier by Van Dyck (the full-length original was at Rushbrook, and at least one copy, at Ickworth, and various engravings based on it exist) and Lely's 1674 portrait of Jermyn in his Garter Robes, copies of which are at Ickworth, Cirencester Park and Kedleston Hall. In addition, several cartoons of Jermyn appear in anti-Royalist propaganda news-sheets.

However, he also appears in John Singleton Copley's painting *Charles I Demanding the Five Impeached Members of the House of Commons*, now in Boston Public Library, Massachusetts. Working in the 1790s, Copley researched his painting meticulously, and based the depictions of each character on original sources, hence Jermyn is depicted faithfully from his portrait by Van Dyck. But Copley's research let him down on one point: on 4 January 1642, when this dramatic event took place, Jermyn was already in exile in Paris.

In the course of research I found two letters supposedly by Jermyn but which are not. The first is addressed to William Murray in 1642 and was printed by Parliament ('Three Letters of Dangerous Consequence' Harvard Library; Gay 642.1710). It stands out for its uncharacteristically florid style and was clearly composed by hostile propagandists. The second is an undated clerk's copy at Woburn Abbey (HMC 39(9)) of one from 'H. St Albans' to Lord Southampton in which the writer begs leave to attend Parliament after three years' disgrace. Between the Restoration and Southampton's death in 1667, the records of the House of Lords show that Jermyn was never absent for such a long period. Apart from the name at the bottom – which I believe the clerk simply got wrong – the letter seems to have nothing to do with Jermyn at all.

ACKNOWLEDGMENTS

Copious thanks go to the many people who have helped me in this work since it began in 1992, including my mother, who bought me my first word-processor to help me start working on this book, and also my father; the Earl Bathurst; Peter Beauclerk-Dewar; W. B. Bellinger; Edmund Berkeley jnr; Martin Biddle; Mary Billot; the Marquess of Bristol; Dean Bubier; Ian Burton; Sir Michael Bunbury; Janice H. Chadbourne; Alan Clark; Nick Crowe; Dan Cruickshank; Jane Cunningham; Elizabeth English; Aude Fitzsimons; Simon Fowler; Michael Gandy; Lita Garcia; Paul Gaskell; John German; Craig Goldman; Adam Green; J. M. Hamill; Mrs W.

H. for her great generosity; Dr Kate Harris; Dr Mary Hesse; Professor Ronald Hutton; Leslie Jermyn; David H. Johnson; Dr Henry Lancaster; Maggie Lewis; Cécile Maincion; Justin H. Martin; Rosalind K. Marshall; Christine Mason; Ann Mitchell; Dr Richard Mortimer; Dr Maureen Mulvihill (for her pioneering work on the Villiers clan); Pamela Palgrave; Jeremy Palmer; Dr N. Aubertin-Porter; Vincent Quesniaux; Mary Robertson; A.M.J. Rothschild; Chris Schofield; Dr Malcolm Smuts; Chris Stanton; Gillian Tindall; S.R. Tomlinson; Cliff Webb; David Williams; Dr Louise Yeoman: and also the staff at the Beaney Institute, Canterbury, the British Library and the Bodleian Library.

I would like to acknowledge the advice and encouragement of Tony Bentley; Paul Sidey; Michael Alcock; Anna Power and Andrew Lownie. James Essinger, author of *Jacquard's Web*, *Spellbound* and *Cantia*, gave me an enormous quantity of enthusiastic encouragement and advice on the text. Without him, this book may never have emerged from its chrysalis, nor taken the form it has now. The novelist Fiona Mountain also provided this book with an extraordinary boost, when she decided to base her novel *Cavalier Queen* on it, turning the real Jermyn into an admirably believable, and enormously likeable romantic fictional hero. My great thanks go to the Canterbury Literary Agency for representing this boom so successfully, and to Martin Rynja of Gibson Square, for having the vision to accept and publish it. Finally, though any remaining faults are entirely mine, Scott Crowley has expended much time checking and proof reading the manuscript at various stages of its existence – and encouraging me, unfalteringly, throughout.

BIBLIOGRAPHY

MANUSCRIPT SOURCES

Bibliothèque Nationale, Paris, Archives des Affaires Etrangères (AAE), Correspondence politique, sous-serie Angletèrre, vol.130.

British Library: Add. Ms 15,856; 18,981; 18,982; 21,506; 21,947; 22,062; 22,063; 22,067; 33,596; 37, 047; 37,998; Add Ch 70,760 Add. Rot. 13,586; Egerton Ms 2,550 ff. 1, 36-7; 2,542 ff. 335-41; 3,349 f. 2; 3351 f.127; Stowe Ms 185 f. 111; 201, f.9; 202 f. 231; 204 f. 9; 207 f. 422.

Guildford Muniment Room, 129/45/7; 3/1/22.

History of Parliament, manuscript essays on Sir Thomas and Henry Jermyn.

Longleat Muniment Room, Longleat Mss, Coventry Papers, vol. 81 p.1 et seq.

National Library of Ireland, Dublin, Ormonde Mss vol. 45 no. 379; Carte Mss, vol. 60 no. 400.

The National Archives: Audit Office, bundle 307, roll 1202; C10/224/29; LC 5/132 p. 3; L.R.R.O. 63/5 p. 318; L.L.R.O. 63/11 p. 197; PC2/54 ff.27 34; PROB11 – will of Elinor Villiers, written 26 September 1681, proved Prerogative Court of Canterbury, 30 July 1685 f.94; will of Mrs Eleanor Dakins, written 20 April 1689, proved Prerogative Court of Canterbury 129, 1694, 152; S.P. (France) 78/127 ff. 85-90.

PRINTED SOURCES

———— Acts of the Privy Council of England 1582-1628, HMSO.

———— Adair, John, By the Sword Divided: Eyewitness accounts of the English Civil War, Sutton Publishing, 1998.

———— Adams, Index Villaris, 1671.

———— Adamson, D. & Dewar, P. de Vere Beauclerk; The House of Nell Gwyn, London, Kimber.

———— Airy, Osmund (ed.), The Lauderdale Papers, vol. I 1639-1667, Camden Society 1884.

———— Albion, Cannon Gordon. Charles I and the Court of Rome, London, Burns Oates and Washbourne Ltd, 1935.

———— Anderson, Dr James, The New Book of Constitutions of the Antient and Honourable Fraternity of Free and Accepted Masons containing Their History, Charges, Regulations, &c collected and digested by order of the Grand Lodge from their old Records, faithful Traditions and Lodge Books, For the use of the Lodges, London, 1738, reprinted in Quator Coronati Reprints vol. 7, 1978.

———— Ashmole, Elias, The Institutions, Laws & Ceremonies of the Most Noble Order of the Garter, London, J. Macock for Nathaneal Brooke, 1672.

———— Aubrey, John, The Natural History and Antiquities of Surrey, 1718/9.

———— Aubrey, Philip, Mr Secretary Thurloe, Cromwell's Secretary of State 1652-1660. The Athlone Press, London.

———— Aulanier, Christaine, 'Le Pavillon du Roi', Histoire du palais et du Musée du Louvre, Éditions des Musées Nationaux, Paris, 1958.

———— Bacon, Francis, The Essays, George Routledge and Sons, London, 1884.

———— Barbour, Violet; Henry Bennet Earl of Arlington, Secretary of State to Charles II. Washington: A.H.S, London: Humphrey Milford and Oxford University Press 1914.

———— Beauclerk-Dewar, Peter and Powell, Roger, Right Royal Bastards: The Fruits of Passion, Peter Beauclerk-Dewar and Roger Powell, Burke's Peerage & Gentry, 2006.

———— Berkeley's Memoirs, printed in appendix to A Narrative by John Ashburnham..., London, Payne and Foss, Pall Mall; Baldwin and Cradock, Paternoster-Row, 1830.

———— Betham, Rev. William, Baronetage of England, 1803.

——— Birch, Thomas, *The Court and Times of Charles I*, 1848.

——— Birch, Thomas; *A Collection of the State Papers of John Thurloe Esq., &c*; London, Gyles, Woodward and Davis, 1762, 7 vols.

——— *Bishop Burnett's History of His Own Time with Notes by the Earls of Dartmouth and Hardwicke, Speaker Onslow and Dean Swift*. 6 Vols, Oxford University Press 2nd edn 1833.

——— Bray, William (ed.), *Memoirs Illustrative of the Life and Writings of John Evelyn Esq., F.R.S.*, London, Alex. Murray & son 1871.

——— Brenan, *A History of the House of Percy.*

——— Browning, Andrew; *Thomas Osborne, Earl of Danby and Duke of Leeds 1632-1712*; Glasgow, Jackson Spon & Co. 1951.

——— Berghclere, Lady; *The Life of James First Duke of Ormonde 1610-1688*. London, John Murray, Albemarle Street, W. 1912.

——— *Bishop Burnett's History of His Own Time with Notes by the Earls of Dartmouth and Hardwicke, Speaker Onslow and Dean Swift*. 6 vols, Oxford University Press 2nd edn 1833.

——— Brandon; 'Letters in the possession of His Grace the Duke of Hamilton and Brandon relating to the years 1638-1650'. *Camden Society*, 1880.

——— Brinckmann, C.; 'The Relations between England and Germany 1660-88', *English Historical Review*, no. 24, 1909.

——— Browning, Andrew, M.A. &c, (ed.); *Memoirs of Sir John Reresby, the complete text and a selection from his letters*. Jackson, Son & Co., Glasgow, 1936.

——— Bruce, John Esq. F.S.A.(ed.); 'Charles I in 1646. Letters of King Charles the First to Henrietta Maria'. *Camden Society*, 1856. Bryant, Sir Arthur (ed.), *The Letters, Speeches and Declarations of King Charles II*. Cassell & Co. Ltd, London, Toronto, Melbourne and Sydney. Newcastle, 1935.

——— Burke, John and John Bernard, *A Genealogical and Heraldic History of the Extinct and Dormant Baronetcies of England, Ireland and Scotland*, London, 1841.

——— Burke, Sir Bernard, *A Genealogical History of the Dormant, Abeyant, Forfeited and Extinct Peerages of the British Empire*, London, 1866.

Burke, Sir B., *A Genealogical and Heraldic History of the Landed Gentry of Great Britain and Ireland*, various editions.

Burke's Genealogical and Heraldic History of the Peerage, Baronetage and Knightage, various editions.

——— *Cabala, sive Scrinia Sacra: Mysteries of State & Government in letters of Illustrious Persons & Great Ministers of State*. Printed for Tho. Sawbridge in Little-Britain, Mat. Gillyflower in Westminster-Hall, Ric. Bentley in Covent-Garden, Mat. Wootton in Fleet-Street & Geo. Conniers in Little-Britain, May 1691.

——— *Calendar of state papers and manuscripts relating to English affairs, existing in the archives and collections of Venice, and in other libraries of northern Italy* (S.P.Ven.), 1603-1675.

——— *Calendar of state papers, colonial series, preserved in her Majesty's Public Record Office, America and West Indies*, 1574-1692.

——— *Calendar of state papers, domestic series, preserved in her Majesty's Public Record Office*, (S.P.Dom.) 1547-1704.

——— *Calendar of the Clarendon state papers preserved in the Bodleian Library* (Clar. S.P.); vol. 1 to January 1649, ed. Rev. O. Ogle and W.H. Bliss under Rev. H. Coxe, Oxford, Clarendon Press, 1872; vol. 2, death of Charles I to end of 1654, ed. Rev. W. Dunn Macray and Rev. H. O. Cox, Oxford, Clarendon Press, 1869 (sic); vol. 3, 1655-1657, ed. Rev. W. Dunn Macray and Rev. H. O. Coxe, Oxford, Clarendon Press, 1876; vol. 4, 1657-1660 ed. F.J. Routledge MA B.Litt. Oxford, Clarendon Press, 1932; vol. 5, 1660-1726, ed. F.J. Routledge, Oxford. Clarendon Press, 1970.

——— *Calendar of treasury books preserved in her Majesty's Public Record Office*, prepared by William A. Shaw, 1-9 (1666-92).

——— *Calendar of treasury papers preserved in her Majesty's Public Record Office*, prepared by Joseph Redington, 1, (1557-1696).

——— Carman, Harry J. and Syrett, Harold C.; *A History of the American People*. Alfred A. Knopf, New York, 1954.

——— Carte, Thomas; *The Life of James Duke of Ormond; containing an account of the most remarkable affairs of his time and particularly of Ireland under his government with an appendix and collection of letters serving to verify the most material facts in the said history* (first published 1735); new edition, 6 vols, Oxford, University Press, 1851.

────── Cartwright, Julia; *Madame – A Life of Henrietta, Daughter of Charles I and Duchess of Orleans*. London, Seeley and Co. Ltd, 1900.

────── Castells, W. Bro. the Rev. F. de P. *English Freemasonry in its Period of Transition A.D. 1600-1700*, Rider & Co., London, 1931.

────── Cherniak, Warren L; *The Poet's Time – politics and religion in the work of Andrew Marvell.* Cambridge University Press.

────── Christie, W.D (ed.), introductory notes in 'Letters addressed from London to Sir Joseph Williamson while plenipotentiary at the congress of Cologne in the years 1673 and 1674', *Camden Society* 8, 1874.

────── Christ, Yvan, *Plan historié du Louvre*, 1958.

────── Clark, Andrew (ed.), *The Life and Times of Anthony Wood, Antiquary of Oxford 1632-1695*, Clarendon Press, 1892.

────── Clark, Andrew (ed.), *Brief Lives, Chiefly of Contemporaries, set down by John Aubrey between the years 1655 & 1696*, Clarendon Press, 1898.

────── Coates, Mary (ed.); 'The Letter-Book of John Viscount Mordaunt 1658-1660', *Camden Society* 3rd Series, vol. 69, 1945.

────── Cohn-Sherbok, Dan, *The Jewish Heritage*, Basil Blackwell, Oxford, 1988.

────── Cokayne, G.E. ('G.E.C.'), *Complete Baronetage*, Allan Sutton, 1983.

────── Cokayne, G.E. ('G.E.C.'), *The Complete Peerage of England, Scotland, Ireland, Great Britain and the United Kingdom*, 1929.

────── Colvin, H.M. (ed.); *The History of the King's Works*. H.M.S.O. London 1976.

────── Conder, Edward, junior, *Records of the Hole Craft and Fellowship of Masons*, Swan Sonnenschein & Co., 1894.

────── Cooper, John, *The Queen's Agent: Francis Walsingham at the Court of Elizabeth I*, Faber & Faber, 2011.

────── *Court Mercurie, The*, no. 3, 10 July-20 July 1645, B.L. Pamphlets, Thomason Tracts E93.

────── Cronin, Vincent, *Louis XIV*, The Reprint Society Ltd, 1965.

────── Cunningham, P., *Letters of Horace Walpole*, London, 1857-9.

────── Dalrymple, Sir John, *Memoirs of Great Britain and Ireland*.

────── Dasent, Arthur Irwin; *The History of St James's Square, and the foundation of the West End of London, With a glimpse of Whitehall in the Reign of Charles the Second*. Macmillan & Co., London, 1895.

────── Daufresne, J.C., *Le Louvre et les Tuileries. Architectures de fête et d'apparat*, Paris, Manges, 1994.

────── D'Aulnoy, Marie Catherine, Baronne; *Memoirs of the Court of England in 1675*; translated by Mrs William Henry Arthur, edited by George David Gilbert, London, John Lane The Bodley Head N.Y; John Lane & Co. Toronto; Bell and Cockburn, 1913.

────── D'Avenant, Sir William; *Madagascar and Other Poems*. Printed by John Haviland for Thomas Walkly, 1638, Imprim. Matth. Clay, Feb 26 1637.

────── D'Avenant, Sir William; *The Preface to Gondibert and the Answer to the Preface by Thomas Hobbes*; Mattieu Guillemot, rue Saint-Jacques, 1650.

────── D'Avenant, Sir William, *The Siege of Rhodes*, London, 1656.

────── D'Avenel, *Lettres de Cardinal Mazarin*, (1906).

────── Dethan, Georges; *The Young Mazarin*, Thames and Hudson, London, 1977.

────── *Dictionary of National Biography*, Oxford University Press.

────── Downes, Kerry; *Christopher Wren*; Allen Lane and Penguin Press, London, 1971.

────── Downes, Kerry, *Sir Christopher Wren* (exhibition catalogue), Trefoil Books for Whitechapel Art Gallery, 1982.

────── Dugdale, William, Norroy King of Arms; *The Baronage of England or, An Historical Account of Our English Nobility &c.* London, 1676, vol. 2.

────── Elliott, J.H., *The Count-Duke of Olivares: the Statesman in an Age of Decline*, Yale's U.P., 1986.

────── Ellis, M.F.H., 'The Channel Islands and the Great Rebellion', *Ann. Bull. Soc. Jersiaise*, vol. 13 1937.

────── Evelyn, John, introduction to *A Parallel of the Ancient Architecture with the Modern... written in French by Roland Fréart, Sieur de Chambray; made English* London, (August) 1664.

────── Evelyn, John, *Fumifugium, or the Inconvenience of the aer, and smocke of London dissipated*. London, W. Godbid for Gabriel Bedel and Thomas Collins, 1661.

—— Farrer, Rev. Edmund, *Portraits in Suffolk Houses*, 1908.

—— Feiling, Keith; *British Foreign Policy 1660-1672*. Macmillan & Co. Ltd, London, 1930.

—— 'Five Letters of King Charles II' communicated to *The Camden Miscellany* by The Most Honourable the Marquess of Bristol, President of the Camden Society, Camden Society 1864.

—— Firth, C.H. (ed.); *Memoirs of Edmund Ludlow, Lieutenant General of the Horse & c. 1625-1672*. Oxford, Clarendon Press, 1894.

—— Fraser, Antonia, *King Charles II*, Book Club Associates, London, 1979.

—— Fry, Edw. Alexander (ed.), *Index to the Chancery Proceedings (Reynardson's Division)*. London, British Record Society, 1903.

—— Gardiner, Samuel R. (ed.) 'Hamilton Papers'. Addenda. *Camden Society* 1893.

—— Gardiner, Samuel R., History of England from the accession of James I. to the outbreak of the Civil War, 1603-1642, vol. 7, AMS Press, New York, 1965.

—— Geyl, Pieter, *History of the Low Countries*, Macmillan, London, 1964.

—— Gerbier d'Ouvilly, Sir Balthazar, *A Briefe Discourse Concerning the Three Chief Principles of Magnificent Building, viz, Solidity, Conveniency and Ornament*, London, 1662.

—— Gillow, J. *Biographical Dictionary of the English Catholics.*

—— Girouard, Mark, *Cities & People*, Yale University Press, 1985.

—— Gladish, David F.; *Introduction to Gondibert*. Oxford, Clarendon Press 1971.

—— Gould, Robert Freke, *The History of Freemasonry, its Antiquities, Symbols, Constitutions, Customs &c*, Caxton, London.

—— Gosse, E., *From Shakespeare to Pope: an enquiry into the causes and phenomena of the rise of classical poetry in England*. Cambridge University Press, 1885.

—— Green, Mary Anne Everett (ed.), *Calendar of the Proceedings of the Committee for Advance of Money, 1642-1656, preserved in the State Paper Office of Her Majesty's Public Record Office*, 1888. Green, Mary Anne Everett (ed.), *Calendar of the Proceedings of the Committee for Compounding, etc, 1643-1660, preserved in the State Paper Office of Her Majesty's Public Record Office*, 1889-92.

—— Green, Mary Anne Everett, *Letters of Henrietta Maria including her private correspondence with Charles the First collected from the Public Archives and Private Libraries of France and England*. London, Richard Bentley, 1857. Green, Mary Anne Everett, *Lives of the Princesses of England*. London, Hurst & Blackett for Henry Colburn, vols 5 & 6, 1855-6.

—— Grosart, Rev. Alexander B.; *The Complete Works in Verse and Prose of Abraham Cowley, now for the first time collected and edited; with memorial-introduction and notes and illustrations, Portraits &c*. Chertsey Worthies' Library, first published 1881, reprinted by AMS Press Inc., New York, 1967.

—— Grose, Clyde L.; 'Louis XIV's Financial Relations with Charles II and the English Parliament', *The Journal of Modern History*, vol. 1 June 1929 no. 2.

—— Guillim, John, *A Display of Heraldry*, S. Rycroft and R. Blome, London, 1679.

—— Halliwell, J.O., (ed.)., *Sir Symonds D'Ewes' Diary*, 1845.

—— Hamilton, A. *Memoirs of the Comte de Gramont*, trans. Quennell, P, Routledge & sons, London, 1930.

—— Harris, F.R.; *The Life of Edward Montague K.G. First Earl of Sandwich 1625-1672*. John Murray, London 1912.

—— Harris, John, *The Artist and the Country House*, Philip Wilson Publishers, London, 1979.

—— Harris, John, Orgel, Stephen and Strong, Roy; *The King's Arcadia: Inigo Jones and the Stuart Court*. Lund Humphries, London, 1973.

—— Hartmann, Cyril Hughes; *The King's Friend, A Life of Charles Berkeley Viscount Fitzhardinge, Earl of Falmouth 1630-1665*. Heinemann Ltd 1951.

—— *Haydn's Book of Dignities*, London, W.H. Allen & Co, 3rd edn, 1894. Harbage, Alfred; *Sir William Davenant, Poet Venturer, 1606-1668*. University of Pennsylvania Press, Philadelphia, 1935.

—— Herford C.H., and Simpson, P. and E. (eds.), *Ben Jonson*, Oxford, Clarendon Press, 1947.

—— Hervey, Rev. Sydenham A.H.; *Little Saxham Registers... 1559 to 1850*. George Booth, Woodbridge, 1901.

—— Hervey, Rev. Sydenham H.A.; *Rushbrook Parish Registers 1567 to 1850. With Jermyn and Davers Annals*. George Booth, Woodbridge, 1903.

—— Heywood, John (ed.); *Letters of Saint-Évremond*. Routledge, London, 1930.

BIBLIOGRAPHY 341

——— Hill, Christopher, *Intellectual origins of the English Revolution revisited,* Oxford, Clarendon Press, 1997.

——— Hillairet, J., *Dictionnaire Historique des rues de Paris.*

——— H.M.C.: Reports of the Royal Commission on Historical Manuscripts (H.M.C.): manuscript collections of: Bankes; Duke of Beaufort; 10 Lord Braye; 2 Journal of Jean Chevallier; Coke; 4, Earl of Denbigh; Earl of Egremont; 71 Finch 1; Miss C. Griffiths; Hastings 2; 6, House of Lords; 77 De L'Isle and Dudley; 6 P. Wykeham-Martin; 10 ns Maskelyne; 2 Montrose; 9, Alfred Morrison; 3, Duke of Northumberland; 7 Ormonde; Ormonde ns 1; Pepys 70; 7, Lord Preston's letter book in Sir F. Graham's Mss; 9 Marquess of Salisbury 22; Capt. Stewart; 5 Sutherland; Dawson Turner; 7, Sir Henry Verney; 4, Earl de la Warr's Mss and Lismore Papers 2nd ser. 4.

——— Hobbes, Thomas, *Leviathan,* Dent, n.d.(Everyman's Library series), n.d.

——— Hore, J.P., *Sporting and Rural Records of the Cheveley Estate.* Priv. pr. 1899.

——— Hubert, Elie, 'Letters of Charles II...'; *Ann. Bull. Soc. Jersiaise* vol 3. 1891.

——— Hutton, Ronald, *Charles the Second: King of England, Scotland, and Ireland,* Oxford University Press, 1991 (1989).

——— Huxley, Aldous; *Grey Eminence; A study in religion and politics,* Chatto & Windus, London, 1941.

——— Hyde, Edward, Earl of Clarendon, *The History of the Rebellion and Civil Wars in England, 1641-1660,* Oxford, The Theatre, 1703, 2 vols.

——— Hyde, Edward, Earl of Clarendon, *The Life of Edward Earl of Clarendon... written by himself.* Oxford, Clarendon Printing House, 1756 1 vol., written c. 1668-9.

——— Hyde, Edward, Earl of Clarendon, *Brief View and Survey of the Dangerous and Pernicious Errors to Church and State in Mr Hobbes's Book Entitled 'Leviathan'* 1676.

——— Jermyn, Rev. George Bitton, 'Pedigree of the Family of Jermyn', *The Herald and Genealogist,* 5 (1870).

——— Jesse, John Heneage; *Memorials of the Court of England during the reign of the Stuarts including the Protectorate,* Bentley, London, 1840.

——— *Journals of the House of Lords* (1660-1684).

——— Jusserand, J.J.(ed.), *Recueil des instructions donnees aux ambassadeurs et ministres de France depuis les traites Westphalie jusqu'a la Revolution francaise,* vol. 25, Angleterre, tome 2: 1660-1690, Paris, E. Boccard. 1929

——— Jusserand, J.J., *French Ambassador at the Court of Charles the Second – Le Comte de Cominges from his unpublished correspondence.* London, T. Fisher Unwin, 1892.

——— Kaufman, H.A.; *Conscientious Cavalier. Col. Bullen Reymes M.P., F.R.S., 1613-1672, The Man and His Times.* Jonathan Cape, London, 1962.

——— Kennett, White, *History of the Life and Reign of King Charles I.*

——— Kenyon, J.P. *Robert Spencer Earl of Sunderland 1641-1702,* Longmans Greek & Co. London 1958.

——— Kingston, Alfred, *East Anglia and the Civil War,* Elliot Stock. London, 1897.

——— Knachel, Philip A.; *England and the Fronde; The impact of the English Civil War and Revolution on France.* Cornel University Press for the Folger Shakespeare Library.

——— Knoop, D, and Jones, A.P.G., *The London Mason in the Seventeenth Century,* Mancester University Press and the Quator Coronati Lodge, 1935.

——— La Fayette, Madame, *Histoire de Madame Henriette.*

——— Lescure, de (ed.), *Memoires of the Abbé Choisy,* Paris, 1883.

——— Lambert, J., *Guide to St James's Church; Piccadilly,* 1958.

——— 'Letters of King Charles II', *Ann. Bull. Soc. Jersiaise,* vol.11, 1929.

——— *Life and Death of Henrietta Maria de Bourbon, Queen to That Blessed King and Martyr Charles I, The,* London, 1685.

——— Lindsay, Lord, *Lives of the Lindsays, or, a Memoir of the Houses of Crawford and Balcarres.* London, John Murray,1849.

——— Lister, T.H.; *Life and Administration of Edward Earl of Clarendon with original correspondence and authentic papers never before published,* Longman, Orme, Brown, Green and Longmans, 3 vols, London, 1837.

——— Lockyer, Roger; *Buckingham, The Life and Political Career of George Villiers, First Duke of Buckingham 1592-1628.* Longman, London and New York

——— Loftis, John (ed.) *The Memoirs of Anne, Lady Halkett and Ann, Lady Fanshawe.* Clarendon Press, Oxford, 1979.

———— Logan, W.H. & Maidment J.(eds.); *The Dramatic Works of Sir William D'Avenant.* William Paterson, Edinburgh and H. Southeran & Co., London, 1872.

———— Long, Charles Edward, M.A.(ed.); *Diary of the Marches of the Royal Army During the Great Civil War; kept by Richard Symonds.* Camden Society 1859.

———— Loomie S.J., Albert J. (ed.); *Ceremonies of Charles I; the note-books of John Finet 1628-1641.* New York, Fordham University Press, 1987.

———— Manley, Delarivierre, *The New Atlantis,* 1709.

———— Marshall, Rosalind K.; *Henrietta Maria The Intrepid Queen.* London, H.M.S.O., 1990.

———— Martin, D.C., 'Sir Robert Moray F.R.S. (1608?-1673)', *Notes and Records of the Royal Society of London,* vol. 15, 1960.

———— Martin, L.C.; *Abraham Cowley Poetry & Prose with Sprat's Life and Observations by Dryden, Addison, Johnson and others.* Oxford, Clarendon Press.

———— Megalotti, Count Lorenzo, *Travels of Cosmo the Third Grand Duke of Tuscany through England 1669,* London, 1821.

———— *Mercurius Aulicus,* 19 September 1644 et seq., B.L.Pamphlets.

———— *Mercurius Britannicus,* 15-22 July 1644, 19-26 September 1644 et seq., B.L. Pamphlets.

———— Messervy, Rev. J.A.; 'Liste des Gouveneurs, Lieut.-Gouveneurs et Deputes Gouveneurs de L'isle de Jersey 1461-1749'. *Ann. Bull. Soc. Jersiaise,* vol. 4, 1901. Miller. John, *James II: A study in Kingship,* Watland, 1977.

———— *Miscellanea Aulica: or, a Collection of State-Treatises, Never before published.* Ed. T Brown. London, Hartley, Gibson and Hodgson, 1702.

———— Montagu-Smith, Patrick and Montgommery-Massingberd, Hugh, *The Country Life Book of Royal Palaces Castles & Homes,* Country Life Books, 1981.

———— Montpensier, Mademoiselle de., *Memoirs,* edited from the French, Henry Colburn, London, 1848.

———— Morel, Bernard, *The French Crown Jewels,* Fonds Mercator, Antwerp, 1989.

———— Morrah, Patrick. *Prince Rupert of the Rhine.* London, Constable, 1976.

———— Motteville; *Memoires de Mme de Motteville, Pour servir a l'histoire d'Anne d'Austriche.* Nouvelle edition, Paris, 1822.

———— Mountain, Fiona, *Cavalier Queen,* Preface, 2011.

———— *A Narrative by John Ashburnham of his Attendance on King Charles the First from Oxford to the Scottish Army and from Hampton Court to the Isle of Wight; never before printed. To which is prefixed a Vindication of his character and conduct, from the misrepresentations of Lord Clarendon, by his   lineal descendant and representative.* London, Payne and Foss, Pall Mall; Baldwin and Cradock, Paternoster-Row. 1830.

———— Nethercot, Arthur H; Abraham Cowley, *The Muse's Hannibal,* New York, Russell & Russell.

———— Nethercot, Arthur H.; *Sir William D'Avenant.* New York, Russell and Russell, 1938.

———— *New Discoverie of Mr Jermyns Conspiracy Being the coppie of a letter sent from France from the said Mr Jermyn, to a Nobleman in the North, with Divers other passages from Yorke. Published by a true copie, A,* London, by T.F. for D.C. July 21 1642; B.L. Thomason Tracts E 107 (35).

———— Newman, *Royalist Officers in England and Wales, 1642-1660,* Garland reference library of social science, v. 72, 1981.

———— Nichol Smith, David, *Characters from the Histories & Memoirs of the Seventeenth Century,* Oxford, Clarendon Press, 1918 (1953).

———— Nicholas, Nicholas Harris, *History of the Orders of Knighthood of the British Empire &c,* London, John Hunter, 1842.

———— *Notes and Queries,* 11th ser. 9, 14 February 1914, p. 126.

———— 'Notes of Proceedings in the Long Parliament by Sir Ralph Verney', *Camden Society,* 1845.

———— Oakeshott, Michael (ed.); *Leviathan or the Matter, Forme and Power of a Commonwealth Ecclesiastical and Civil, by Thomas Hobbes,* Basil Blackwell, Oxford, 1946.

———— Ollard, Richard, *Clarendon's Four Portraits,* Hamish Hamilton, London, 1989.

———— Oman, Carola; *Henrietta Maria.* Hodder and Stoughton, St Paul's House, London.

———— Platts, Beryl; *A History of Greenwich.* 2nd edn; Procter Press, London, 1986.

———— Prinsterer, G.G. van, *Archives de la Maison d'Orange-Nassau,* 2nd series 1584-1688, 5 vols, Leyden and Utrecht, 1857-1861.

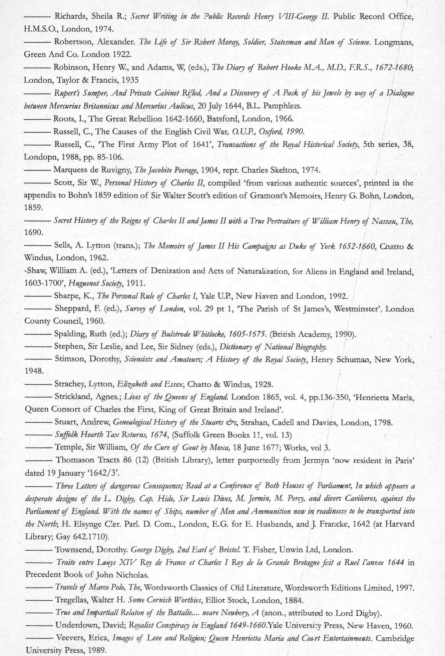

—— Richards, Sheila R.; *Secret Writing in the Public Records Henry VIII-George II*. Public Record Office, H.M.S.O., London, 1974.

—— Robertson, Alexander. *The Life of Sir Robert Moray, Soldier, Statesman and Man of Science*. Longmans, Green And Co. London 1922.

—— Robinson, Henry W., and Adams, W, (eds.), *The Diary of Robert Hooke M.A., M.D., F.R.S., 1672-1680*; London, Taylor & Francis, 1935

—— *Rupert's Sumper, And Private Cabinet Rifled, And a Discovery of A Pack of his Jewels by way of a Dialogue between Mercurius Britannicus and Mercurius Aulicus*, 20 July 1644, B.L. Pamphlets.

—— Roots, I., The Great Rebellion 1642-1660, Batsford, London, 1966.

—— Russell, C., The Causes of the English Civil War, *O.U.P., Oxford, 1990*.

—— Russell, C., 'The First Army Plot of 1641', *Transactions of the Royal Historical Society*, 5th series, 38, Londopn, 1988, pp. 85-106.

—— Marquess de Ruvigny, *The Jacobite Peerage*, 1904, repr. Charles Skelton, 1974.

—— Scott, Sir W., *Personal History of Charles II*, compiled 'from various authentic sources', printed in the appendix to Bohn's 1859 edition of Sir Walter Scott's edition of Gramont's Memoirs, Henry G. Bohn, London, 1859.

—— *Secret History of the Reigns of Charles II and James II with a True Portraiture of William Henry of Nassau, The*, 1690.

—— Sells, A. Lytton (trans.); *The Memoirs of James II His Campaigns as Duke of York 1652-1660*, Chatto & Windus, London, 1962.

-Shaw, William A. (ed.), 'Letters of Denization and Acts of Naturalization, for Aliens in England and Ireland, 1603-1700', *Huguenot Society*, 1911.

—— Sharpe, K., *The Personal Rule of Charles I*, Yale U.P., New Haven and London, 1992.

—— Sheppard, F. (ed.), *Survey of London*, vol. 29 pt 1, 'The Parish of St James's, Westminster', London County Council, 1960.

—— Spalding, Ruth (ed.); *Diary of Bulstrode Whitlocke, 1605-1575*. (British Academy, 1990).

—— Stephen, Sir Leslie, and Lee, Sir Sidney (eds.), *Dictionary of National Biography*.

—— Stimson, Dorothy, *Scientists and Amateurs; A History of the Royal Society*, Henry Schuman, New York, 1948.

—— Strachey, Lytton, *Elizabeth and Essex*, Chatto & Windus, 1928.

—— Strickland, Agnes.; *Lives of the Queens of England*. London 1865, vol. 4, pp.136-350, 'Henrietta Maria, Queen Consort of Charles the First, King of Great Britain and Ireland'.

—— Stuart, Andrew, *Genealogical History of the Stuarts &c*, Strahan, Cadell and Davies, London, 1798.

—— *Suffolk Hearth Tax Returns, 1674*, (Suffolk Green Books 11, vol. 13)

—— Temple, Sir William, *Of the Cure of Gout by Moxa*, 18 June 1677; Works, vol 3.

—— Thomason Tracts 86 (12) (British Library), letter purportedly from Jermyn 'now resident in Paris' dated 19 January '1642/3'.

—— *Three Letters of dangerous Consequence; Read at a Conference of Both Houses of Parliament, In which appears a desperate designe of the L. Digby, Cap. Hide, Sir Lewis Dives, M. Jermin, M. Percy, and divers Cavileeres, against the Parliament of England. With the names of Ships, number of Men and Ammunition now in readinesss to be transported into the North*; H. Elsynge Cler. Parl. D. Com., London, E.G. for E. Husbands, and J. Francke, 1642 (at Harvard Library; Gay 642.1710).

—— Townsend, Dorothy. *George Digby, 2nd Earl of Bristol*. T. Fisher, Unwin Ltd, London.

—— *Traite entre Louys XIV Roy de France et Charles I Roy de la Grande Bretagne fcit a Ruel l'annee 1644* in Precedent Book of John Nicholas.

—— *Travels of Marco Polo, The*, Wordsworth Classics of Old Literature, Wordsworth Editions Limited, 1997.

—— Tregellas, Walter H. *Some Cornish Worthies*, Elliot Stock, London, 1884.

—— *True and Impartiall Relaton of the Battaile.... neare Newbery, A* (anon., attributed to Lord Digby).

—— Underdown, David; *Royalist Conspiracy in England 1649-1660*.Yale University Press, New Haven, 1960.

—— Veevers, Erica, *Images of Love and Religion; Queen Henrietta Maria and Court Entertainments*. Cambridge University Press, 1989.

—— Veith, David M. (ed.), *The Complete Poems of John Wilmot, Earl of Rochester*, New Haven and London,

Yale University Press, 1968.

———— Virgil, *The Eclogues. The Georgics*, translated by C. Day Lewis, Oxford University Press, (1966, 2009).

———— Williamson, Hugh Ross; *Four Stuart Portraits*. Evans Brothers Ltd, London, 1949.

———— Warburton, Bartholemew E.G., *Memoirs of Prince Rupert & the Cavaliers, with their Private Correspondence*, 1851.

———— Warner, George F. (ed.); 'The Nicholas Papers; Correspondence of Sir Edward Nicholas Secretary of State', vol. 1 1641-1652. *Camden Society* 1886; vol. 2 January 1653 – June 1655. *Camden Society* 1892; vol. 3 July 1655 – December 1656. *Camden Society* 1897; vol. 4 1657-1660, *Camden Society* 3rd Series vol. 31, 1920.

———— Warrant to Jermyn of January 1675, S.P.Dom., Channel Islands 9, no. 27, draft, printed in *Ann. Bull. Soc. Jersiaise,* vol. 6, 1909.

———— Wedgewood, C.V., *The King's War 1641-1647*, Classic Penguin, 2001.

———— Wezel, G.W.C. van, *Het paleis van Hendrik III graaf van Nassau te Breda*, Rijksdienst voor de Monumentenzorg, Zeit, 1999.

———— Wheatley, Henry B.; *The Diary of Samuel Pepys M.A., F.R.S..* London, G. Bell & Sons, 1918.

———— *Works of Sir William Temple, bart, The*; 4 vols, printed in Weybridge, S. Hamilton for F.C. and J. Rivington et al., London, 1814.

———— Wren, Christopher, junior, *Parentalia, or Memoirs of the Family of the Wrens... Chiefly of Sir Christopher Wren, Late Surveyor General of the Royal Buildings, President of the Royal Society.* London, for T. Osborn, Grey's Inn & R. Dodsey, Pall Mall, 1750.

———— Wright, Dudley, *England's Masonic Pioneers*, George Kening & Co., London, 1925.

NOTES ON SOURCES

FOREWORD

'a soul composed of the eagle and the dove…' Abraham Cowley, *The Civil War* (1643).
'his agents were his own servants…', John Cooper, *The Queen's Agent*, p. 163.

PRELUDE – THE GREAT COACH Thursday, 12 September 1678

Thursday, 12 September 1678. The gates of Windsor Castle are thrown wide open…' The Prelude is a fiction-alised account of his visit to the French Ambassador. The visit really took place that day. The ongoing negotia-tions for the French subsidy were discussed and the ambassador did, when reporting the meeting back to Paris, express his surprise that someone who held no ministerial office should have been so closely involved with such sensitive negotiations. Jermyn's world-view is extrapolated from his Freemasonry and a careful study of how 17th Century Britons saw their past, and his views on international politics are extrapolated from letters he wrote from the Restoration onwards. The purported savagery shown by the Spanish to the Incas was much reported. Jermyn's appearance is taken from the portrait painted of him by Lely some six years earlier and knowledge of his health extracted from his and other people's letters.
'recalling prolific tales' Nathaniel Angelo of Eton, a friend of Milton's, raged that all of Henrietta Maria's children 'were Jermyn's bastards', 13 August 1660, Captain Francis Robinson to Nicholas, S.P.Dom., 10.
'had entrusted these incredibly sensitive negotiations…' The letter in which Barillon described Jermyn's visit to his lodgings in Windsor on 12 September 1678 is in *Correspondence politique, sous-serie Angleterre*, vol.130, f. 281-282v, including his comment 'qu'un homme si esloigne du ministere ne devroit estre'.

EDUCATION OF A COURTIER 1605-1622

'he has long used it and finds no hurt…' quoted without source in the *History of Parliament's* article on Sir Thomas Jermyn.
'They found her sweating and shivering violently…' Elizabeth Jermyn's death is described in a letter of J. Packer to Winwood dated 31 January 1604/5, which related that Lady Jermyn 'has forsaken Hanworth till time efface the memory of the lamentable accident to Sir Thomas Germayne's only daughter (a child), who was poisoned by eating a piece of bread and butter spread with rat's bane. One of Sir Maurice Berkley's sons was also in danger from the same cause' (Buccleugh MSS at Montagu House, quoted in Hervey, Rushbrook p. 344). The opening of this chapter is an imaginative reconstruction of the events that surrounded this event. The precise time that Jermyn was taken to Rushbrook is not recorded.
'Brutus's temple of Apollo, where Brutus's body lay…'. John Hardynge's *Chronicle*, ch. xvi.
'too short to read all sorts of books…' Gramont's Memoirs, 1859 edition, p. 353.

THE MADRID EMBASSY 1622-3

'On Friday, 7 March 1623, there was a sharp knock…' This story is told in Lockyer, Roger; *Buckingham, The Life and Political Career of George Villiers, First Duke of Buckingham 1592-1628*. Longman, London and New York, citing the Denmilne Mss 33.1.10.21; Harl. Ms 1581.352 and Harl. Ms 3638 f. 125; HMC 8 Pt 1 Appendix, Digby Mss.

COURTING THE LOUVRE 1624-8

'Little Madame…' Cabala.
'a soul composed of the eagle and the dove…' Abraham Cowley, *The Civil War* (1643).
'saw him gladly…' Paris, 5 August 1627, Venetian Ambassador to Doge and Senate, S.P. Ven.
'to set Buckingham's party by the ears…' August 1627, Venetian Ambassador, S.P. Ven.

TWO DISPUTED CASES OF PATERNITY 1628 – 1635

Tom Killigrew was performing this task…' The story of Tom Killigrew is in Cunningham, P., *Letters of Horace Walpole*, London, 1857-9.
'There are several other stories of similar incidents…' Other stories referred to here are one recorded by Sir John Percival and heard by him from George Clarke, who became a Page to the King on 20 March 1627/8 (H.M.C. vol.

7 p. 244, Earl of Egremont's Mss); by Lord Dartmouth (in a footnote to Burnett), who had it in turn from Sir Francis Compton, whose mother heard it from Mrs Seymour who claimed to have witnessed the event; and one by Peyton, quoted in Jesse.

'as to faith, or sin of the flesh...' 25 August 1636, Gregory Panzani to Rome, repeating the words of her confessor, Fr Phillip's words, in Vatican Papers vol. 39 p. 96 qu. Green, Letters.

'he is so dark that I am ashamed of him...' Henrietta Maria to Mme de St George, Bethune MS 9293 f. 5, Bib. Du Roi, quoted in Strickland, p. 187.

'His size and fatness supply the want of beauty...' 1630, Henrietta Maria to Mme de St George, Imperial Library, St Petersburg quoted in Strickland, p. 187.

'he is so fat and so tall...' 1630, Henrietta Maria to Mme de St George, Bethune MS 9293 f. 5, Bib. Du Roi, quoted in Strickland, p. 187.

'Had the Prince ever stood as a fully-grown man...' Charles II's startling dissimilarity to his parents is discussed by Antonia Fraser in *King Charles II*, pp. 9-12.

'the King was a bastard and his mother was Jermyn's whore...' 4 August 1660, imputed to one John Wilson of Newcastle on Tyne, S.P. Dom., vol. 10.

'all the royal children were Jermyn's bastards...' 13 August 1660, Captain Francis Robinson to Nicholas relating Nicholas Angelo's allegations, S.P. Dom., vol. 10.

'Had so wholly made over...' Thomas Carew, Gentlemen of the bedchamber, S.P. Dom, 1628-9, p. 393, quoted in Sharpe, *Charles I*, p. 171.

'petulant and fleering...' March 1633, S.P. Dom. 'Fleering' means sniffy or sneering.

'I liked Eleanor well enough...', Fiona Mountain, *Cavalier Queen*, Preface, 2011, p. 268.

'there never passed one word between us touching marriage...' c. May 1633, Jermyn to Charles I. H.M.C., Coke MSS.

'she hath herself confessed to me...' c. May 1633, Jermyn to Charles I. H.M.C., Coke MSS.

'ever after [be]... reputed to have forfeited their modesty...' Hastings MS, Legal Box 5, quoted on Sharpe, p. 190.

'with deep oaths...' Quoted without source in Oman.

'my cousin...' P.C.C. will of Mrs Eleanor Dakin, written 20 April 1689, proved 129, 1694, 152.

'When Jermyn stepped ashore there [in Jersey] in 1634...' I analysed the Jermyn family's very patchy relations with the inhabitants of their governorship of Jersey in 'Henry Jermyn, (1605-1684), Earl of St Alban, K.G., Governor of Jersey', *Société Jersiaise, Annual Bulletin for 2000*, 27(4), pp. 636-652.

SIR WILLIAM D'AVENANT'S DREAM OF MADAGASCAR 1635 –1637

'valiant in a strange bed...' Nethercot, D'Avenant.

'Turtle shells... dragons' blood and diverse sorts of other gums...' Richard Boothby, *A Briefe Discovery... of... Madagascar*, 1646.

'may well be compared to the Land of Canaan...' Richard Boothby, *A Briefe Discovery... of... Madagascar*, published in 1646.

'romance some would put into Rupert's head...' 4 April 1636, Elizabeth of Bohemia to Sir Thomas Roe, S.P. Dom. Car. I, 16, 317 no. 12: 6 April 1637, S.P. German.

'they may be for Madagascar...' Paris, 15 January 1655, Jermyn to Charles II, Clar. S.P. no. 22. In fact, Penn's fleet sailed to America.

'In 1640, Jermyn and Henrietta organised a survey...'. The appointment of the commissioners to perform this are c. 1640 appears in S.P. Dom., vol. 470.

'SPEAK WITH MR JERMYN ABOUT IT' 1637-1640

'full of soup and gold', *Last Instructions to a Painter* (1681), attributed to Andrew Marvell.

'had engaged her...' 16 January 1639, Castle to Bridgewater, Ellesmere MS 7818.

'How shall I recognise her?...' Quoted in Marshall p. 78.

'Such beggarly snakes...' quoted from Dalrymple by Roots, p. 26.

'are not so settled as was to be wished...' London, 19 July 1639, Jermyn to Captain George Carteret, S.P. Dom. vol. 426.

'spoke much, and appeared to be the most leading man...' Hyde, *Rebellion*, quoted in Nichol Smith, pp. 132-6.

'Appointed to the lucrative position...' Sharpe p. 839, quoting from 9 June 1640 Ellesmere MS 7837 and 7819.

'After supper they would lock themselves away with Jermyn...' Jermyn was 'now so great with the King as he and the Queen are locked up alone with him many hours together. It is not unlikely, if our affaires settle, but that he may prove a great favourite. He hath laid a shrewd foundation, and, in my judgement, advances apace towards it, holding secret intelligence with the new officer that shall be made' (January 1641, HMC 77 Sir John Temple to Leicester).

'looked upon by the whole court...' May 1641, Robert Browne to Sir Francis Ottley, Ottley Papers p. 30.

'speak with Mr Jermyn about it...' Paris, 26 February/ 8 March 1641, Robert Reade to Thomas Windebank, S.P. Dom., vol. 477.

'he does with great dexterity bring all his pieces together...' 4 March 1641, Sir John Temple to the Earl of Leicester, H.M.C., 77.

'he planned a new government incorporating staunch Royalists...' Jermyn's proposed 'cabinet reshuffle' is described in Temple's letter to Leicester, 21 January 1640/1, HMC 77.

'by making him a Secretary of State...' On 24 December 1640 the Earl of Northumberland wrote to Lord Leicester 'Your Lordship makes a right use and judgment of H. Jermyn, for certainly he both believes and wishes some person Secretary, over whom he hopes to have more power and interest then he can expect from the Earl of Leicester': his proposal for Nicholas' appointment is noted in his 'cabinet reshuffle'.

'DO SOMETHING EXTRAORDINARY' 1637 – 1641

'do something extraordinary...'1641, *A Copy of a Letter found in the Privy Lodgings at Whitehall.*

'For several months Jermyn waited...' This period of indecision is described in great detail in Temple's letters to Leicester, HMC 77.

'a plot to bring the northern army...' The main sources for the Army Plot are (1) Nathaniel Fiennes's report of the depositions of the conspirators to the Commons Close Committee, 14 June 1641, published in 1642; (2) notes made by Verney on a letter of confession written by Harry Percy, 'Notes of Proceedings in the Long Parliament by Sir Ralph Verney, *Camden Society*, 1845 and (3) Percy's confession, printed version SP 16/481/41 and MS version (Alnwick Castle MSS 15, f 223a-b).

'a matter of greater consequence...', Chudleigh's deposition, Braye MSS 2, 147v, House of Lords Record Office.

'the parliament was so in love with the Scots...', Chudleigh's deposition in Fiennes's report.

'...if the army merely declared its open support for the King...', specifically, in terms of preserving the bishop's votes in the Lords, maintaining the army in Ireland and allowing the King his much needed finance.

'desired Goring and Jermyn...' Percy's confession in Brenan, *A History of the House of Percy*, p. 247.

'set my army into a good posture...' This and the preceding incidents are from Fiennes's interrogation of Goring, Marquis of Salisbury's Mss, H.M.C. 9 pt 22, London, H.M.S.O. 1971 pp. 356-9 and Brenan, *A History of the House of Percy*, p. 247.

'Jermyn then revealed...' In Fiennes's report, Pollard asserted that 'There were propositions made by Goring and Jermyn about bringing up the army hither' but Goring made the more plausible assertion that 'Jermyn first proposed the bringing up of the army'.

'We disliked...' Pollard's account, in Fiennes's report.

'vain and foolish...' Percy's confession, SP 16/481/41 and Brenan, *A History of the House of Percy*, p. 247.

'Professor Russell has argued...' Russell, 'Army Plot', p. 101.

'The day set for the plot was May Day...' Besides the records of the interrogation of the plotters, the foregoing paragraphs also rely on Samuel Gardner's article in the *English Historical Review*, in which he discusses to Rossetti's account in Nunziatura di Colonia vol. 21.

'Jermyn toyed briefly with the idea of staying in Portsmouth...' According to Sir Symonds D'Ewes's diary, the King excused himself to Parliament by claiming that Jermyn's warrant to leave England had been made prior to 4 May. The warrant for Jermyn's arrest at Portsmouth was issued on 6 May (H.M.C., Miss C. Griffiths' Mss). The often-quoted reference to Jermyn escaping in his black satin suit and white boots is from an attributed quote in the old D.N.B.

COLONEL LORD JERMYN 1641 – 1643

'that the fortunes of the most exalted...' d'Aulnoy.

'The people who are faithful to our service...' Strickland.

'poor traitors...' 6/16 July 1642, Henrietta Maria to Charles I, Harl. Ms 3797 f. 83b, qu. Green, Letters.

'I have nobody in the world...' 2 June 1642, Henrietta Maria to Charles I, qu. Green, Letters.

'the Queen's coach clattered down the Staedt-Straat...' *Three Letters of dangerous Consequence; Read at a Conference of Both Houses of Parliament, In which appears a desperate design of the L. Digby, Cap. Hide, Sir Lewis Dives, M. Jermyn, M. Percy, and divers Cavaliers, against the Parliament of England. With the names of Ships, number of Men and Ammunition now in readiness to be transported into the North*; H. Elsynge Cler. Parl. D. Com., London, E.G. for E. Husbands, and J. Francke, 1642 (at Harvard Library; Gay 642.1710); first letter, the Hague 20 June/1 July 1642 states that they came seven nights ago. Interestingly, Wilmot in York wrote to William Crofts in the Hague on 12/22 June, 'Pray if Master Jermyn be with you, present my most humble service to him', indicating that Jermyn's arrival there was known to Charles I.

'It is a great trouble to me...' 13/23 July 1642, Henrietta Maria to Charles I, Harl. Ms. 7379 p. 47 qu. Green, Letters.

'Live still, the pleasure of each other's sight...' D'Avenant, 'To The Lord D.L.', *Madagascar, with Other Poems.*

'They settled down to sleep...' Their adventures at sea and at Bridlington are described by Henrietta Maria herself in her letters to her husband, though the incident involving Mitte she kept back, only telling it years later to her friend Madame de Motteville.

'she-majesty generalissima...' 27 June 1643, Henrietta Maria to Charles I, Harl. Ms 7379.

'Generalissima...' *King's Cabinet, Opened* p. 33 qu. Green, Letters.

'and at Nottingham...' 27 June 1643, Henrietta Maria to Charles I, Harl. Ms 7379.

'It is not a great matter...' 25 June 1643, Henrietta Maria to Newcastle, Harl. Ms 6988 f. 46 qu. Green, Letters.

'graceful and beautiful...' Hyde, *Life*, quoted in Nichol Smith p. 120.

'the excellent temper of his arms...' Hyde, Rebellion.

'he charged it through...' Abraham Cowley, *The Civil War*, part 3 (Cowley, Works).

'my troopes...' 1 September 1645, Saint-Germain, Jermyn to Digby, State Papers Foreign, Ciphers (S.P.106) 10, no 6, deciphered by Richards.

'THE STRONGEST PILLAR IN THE LAND' 1644

'There is a story that exists in several incarnations...' 29 January 1672, 'Dr Edward Lake's Diary', *Camden Miscellany*, vol. 1.

'for if a person [like Percy] speaks to you boldly...' 27 May 1643, Henrietta Maria to Charles I, Harl. Ms 7379 f. 62b.

'This of more trouble to me...' February 1644, Trevor to Rupert, qu. Morrah.

'I find prince Rupert...' Oxford, 19 February 1644, Arthur Trevor to Ormond, Carte, vol. 6 p 38.

'most violent ambition to have her husband created a Baron...' Holles, Gervase, 'Memorials of the Holles Family', *Camden Society* 1937; the warrant was dated 6 April 1644.

'I was never more against any thing...' Oxford, 12 March 1643/4, Jermyn to Rupert, B.L. Add. Ms 18,981 f. 86.

'there being provisions and ammunition...' Exeter, 14 June 1644, Jermyn to Rupert, B.L. Add. Ms 21,506 f. 29.

'it was not possible...' Exeter, 30 June 1644, Jermyn to Digby, S.P. Dom., vol. 502.

'riding by her, and upon every stop...' 10 July-20 July, *The Court Mercury* no. 3, B.L. Pamphlets, Tomason Tracts E.93; it also mistakenly reported that the Cornish had forced them to turn back to Exeter.

'Here is the woefullest spectacle...' Francis Basset's account, qu. Marshall.

'Clinging to the sides of their ship's longboats...' The story of their journey and its surprising conclusion is based on Bossuet's *Vie de Reine Henriette*, as related in Strickland but this, rather like a lot of literature about Henrietta Maria, takes no account of the fact that the Queen was surrounded by her servants – 'the queen, exhausted as she was, was forced to explain to them who she really was'. But Queens tended not to do such things when they had loyal Lord Chamberlains to do so for them.

'SOME SUCCOUR FOR ENGLAND' 1644 – 1645

'But to this end your Highness...' Jermyn to Frederick Henry, Prince of Orange, 6/16 August 1644, S.P. Dom., 502.

'country air...' Paris, 2/12 May 1645, Jermyn to Charles I, H.M.C. 6, House of Lords Mss – see H.M.C. 1, Appx 6.

'is gone from Dunkirk three weeks since...' Paris, 9/19 May 1645, Jermyn to Digby, S.P. Dom., vol. 507.

'too much levity...' Burnet's *History of his own Times*, 1 pp. 94-5.

'You will make an inconsiderable contemptible benefit...' Saint-Germain, 19 August 1645, Jermyn to Hyde, Clar. Mss 1940.

'withal commanded [me] to make overture...' 6/16 August 1644, Jermyn to Prince of Orange, S.P. Dom., vol. 502.

'it might happen that before this campaign...' 6/16 August 1644, Jermyn to Prince of Orange, S.P. Dom., vol. 502.

'He dares not offend the Cardinal's dog...' Paris, 23 March 1655, Hatton to Nicholas, Nicholas Papers 2 pp. 228-230.

'You must call him *my cousin*...' Paris, 3 December 1644, Jermyn and Henrietta Maria, Harl. Ms 7379 f. 45 qu. Green, Letters.

THE 'GREAT HELL-CAT' 1645 – 1646

'The torment of misfortunes...' Cardiff, 5 August 1645, George Digby to Jermyn, B.L. Add. Ms 33,596 f. 11.

'his linen was plain, not very clean...' Sir Philip Warwick, *Memories of the Reigne of King Charles I*, 1707, pp. 247-8, quoted in Nichol Smith, p. 141.

'with great torment and agony...' Hyde, *Rebellion*, quoted in Nichol Smith, pp. 132-6.

'great Hell-cat...' Paris, 29 March 1661, Venetian Ambassador to Doge and Senate, S.P. Ven., reporting a conversation he had just had with Jermyn.

'I can say this of Naseby...' quoted without reference in Adair, J. (ed.), *By the Sword Divided*, pp. 192-4. The original says 'smite out', which I have interpreted as 'cry out'.

'for the insensible engaging...' Saint-Germain, 26 July/5 August 1645, Jermyn to Lord Digby. S.P. Dom., Vol. 510.

'Mazarin also paid for Moray...' The machinations of Moray, Montereuil, Jermyn and the others involved in this episode are extremely hard to fathom from contemporary correspondence: the best attempt, from which I took my lead here, was made by Robertson in his biography of Moray.

'My Dear Cousin Harry',... n.d., c. June 1646, Jermyn to Sir Henry Killigrew, qu. Tregellas, Walter H. *Some Cornish Worthies*, Elliot Stock, London, 1884.

'send mine and thine...' Charles I to Henrietta Maria, Clar. S.P. vol. 2 p. 230.

' tell Jermyn, from me...' 23 July 1646, Charles I to Henrietta Maria, Bruce.

'THE LOUVRE PRESBYTER' 1646 – 1649

'the Louvre Presbyter...' 5/15 January 1650, Hatton to Nicholas, Nicholas Papers.

'If he were ever affected with melancholy...' Clar. MS 122, qu. Ollard, who argues effectively (and I agree with him) that Hyde's biographical sketch originally to have been about Arlington was really about Jermyn.

'Lord Jermyn kept an excellent table...' Clarendon, 13, 129.

'Harry, this is chiefly to chide you...' Droitwich, 14 May 1645, Charles I to Jermyn, H.M.C. 6, House of Lords Mss.

'Jermyn had a furious argument...' 7 October 1645, Sir Robert Honeywood to Sir Harry Vane, S.P. Dom. 511.

'Lord Jermyn knows nothing about religion!...' Hyde, Rebellion.

'a king of Presbytery, or no king at all...' Saint-Germain, 18/28 September 1646, Jermyn and Colepeper to Charles I, Clar. S.P. no. 2313, endorsed, 'Recd 5/15 Oct'.

'From Paris, they sent Jack Ashburnham and Jermyn's own cousin Sir John Berkeley...' Berkeley and Ashburnham's memoirs.

'We must look upon your endeavours that are abroad...' Kilkenny, 24 January 1648/9, Ormond to Jermyn, Carte vol. 6 p. 598-9.

'OUR OWN CONDITION IS LIKE TO BE VERY SAD' 1649 – 1656

'Jermyn in whom united doth remain...' Abraham Cowley, *The Civil War*, part 3 (Cowley, Works).

'Our own condition is likely to be very sad...' Paris, 8 January 1648/9, Cowley to Arlington, Cowley, Works.

'*Lord Jermyn took this opportunity...*' Gamache. 'Jermyn' has been substituted here for 'Lord St Albans'.

'*le Favori...*' Motteville.

'shameful attachment...' *Le caduée d'état* (1652) qu. Knachel.

'made a clandestine marriage...' Mme Baviere's memoirs.

'her being married to my lord...' 22 November 1662, Pepys' Diary.

'Cowley witnessed the wedding...' *The Life and Death of Henrietta Maria de Bourbon, Queen to That Blessed King and Martyr Charles I*, London, 1685.

'signatures were subsequently – and most conveniently – cut off...' In 1820, the antiquarian George Smeeton, in a footnote to his reprint of *The Life and Death of Henrietta Maria de Bourbon*, claimed that "the late Mr. Coram, the printseller, purchased of Yardly (a dealer in waste paper and parchment) a deed of settlement of an estate, from Henry Jermyn, Earl of St Albans, to Henrietta Maria as a marriage dower; which besides the signature of the Earl, was subscribed by Cowley the Poet, and other persons as witnesses. Mr. Coram sold the deed to the Rev. Mr. Brand for five guineas, who cut off many of the names on the deed to enrich his collection of autographs; at the sale of this gentleman's effects, they passed into the hands of the late Mr. Bindley".

'solemnly married together...' *The Secret History of the Reigns of Charles II and James II with a True Portraiture of William Henry of Nassau*, 1690.

'Historians remain divided over whether Jermyn and Henrietta Maria became husband and wife...' Amongst the books which record the marriage as a statement of fact are Rev. William Betham (*Baronetage of England*, 1803); W.D. Christie's notes to *Letters of Sir Joseph Williamson* (Camden Society) and Sir Philip Francis (1740-1818) in his manuscript notes to Hyde's Rebellion, in which he wrote – inaccurately – of the Queen's desire that Hyde should call on Jermyn before she accepted Anne's marriage to James and commented, 'No man can read it without believing that this vain bedlam, who makes such a rout about her son's marriage and mesalliance, was married to St. Alban's. On what other grounds than his being the husband of the queen-mother could the Earl of Clarendon, Lord High Chancellor of England, be called on to pay the first visit to that upstart?'; Adamson and Dewar (Adamson, D. & Dewar, P. de Vere Beauclerk; *The House of Nell Gwyn*, London, Kimber) infer that the mere couple of days which elapsed between Jermyn's death and the creation of Charles II's son Charles Beauclerk as Duke of St Albans implied a family tie. On the other hand Strickland and also Gillow in his *Biographical Dictionary of the English Catholics*, believed firmly there was no marriage, founding their belief in their perception of the flawless morality of the Queen.

'I had read the history of France'... Montpensier 3 p. 15.

'employed and trusted...' 1/11 December 1653 n.s., Nicholas to Hyde, Nicholas Papers.

'the Shield from Heaven...' Abraham Cowley, *Pindarique Odes*, "To Mr Hobs".

'the Louvre Presbyter...' 5/15 January 1650, Hatton to Nicholas, Nicholas Papers.

'It was not until spring 1652 that he was even appointed to the Privy Council...' Hyde, *Rebellion*. The date is unknown. The *History of Parliament* says 1651, not 1652.

'you must never think to see me again...' Cologne, 31 October/10 November 1654, Charles II to Jermyn, Clar. S.P. no. 2063.

'Get out!', she reportedly shrieked' ... 'Allez, allez; vous este une impertinent!'. 1 January 1655, Hatton to Nicholas, Nicholas Papers.

'all's well...' about early December 1654, Charles II to Jermyn, draft, Clar. S.P. no. 2096, 2.

'You are not to judge of the queen's affections...' Paris, 21 January 1656, Jermyn to Charles II, Thurloe S.P., vol. 1 p. 691.

THE CHÂTEAU OF COLOMBES 1656 – 1660

'I cannot chose but embrace...' Jermyn to Sir Marmaduke Langdale; Senlis, France, 22 November 1654, Holme Hall MSS, H.M.C. Various II, which catalogues it in 1653: the tone strongly suggests that it was written after the 1654 rising had failed.

'Lord Jermyn', the English ambassador reported...' 2/12 January 1655/6, Rene Angier to Cromwell, Thurloe S.P. vol. 4 p. 375.

'Mr Jackson...' February 1655, Charles II to Jermyn, Clar. S.P. no. 64.

'used by the King...' 3 April 1655, Hyde to Nicholas, Clar. S.P. no. 87, stating that 'Mr Jackson stays at Dusseldorp'.

'Mr Juxley...' London, 8 March 1655, O'Neill to Nicholas, Nicholas Papers vol. 2 p. 219.

'Mr Welworth...' 2 September/12 October 1649 (sic), Hatton to Nicholas, Nicholas Papers. The Clarendon Society's transcription of this letter includes a footnote attached to Jermyn's name which is not entirely clear; "'Mr Welworth', a pseudonym, in Nicholas's summary on the back of the letter". This means either that Mr Welworth was a pseudonym used by Nicholas and Hatton of Jermyn, or a pseudonym used by Jermyn himself.

'Nemo...' 30 August/ 9 September 1659, probably from Walter Montagu to Bellings, Clar. S.P.

'Lord Clancarrl...' Clar. S.P. vol. 62 f. 52.

'conversations with Jermyn...', Paris, 18/28 April 1657, Bampfield to Sir John Hobart, Clar. S.P. no. 843 1; 18/28 April 1657, Bampfield to Thurloe, S.P. Dom., 154 and Clar. S.P. 543 2.

'Hyde had picked up on Bampfield's unreliability...', 3/13 March 1653, Nicholas to Hyde, Nicholas Papers vol. 2 p. 7.

'Cromwell's prospective treaty with Spain..', Madrid, 13 July 1657, Bennet to Hyde, Clar. S.P. no. 979.

'the engagements contracted with the dead monster...' 10/20 September 1658, Jermyn to Charles II, Clar. S.P. vol. 58 f. 352-3, see Clar. S.P. 3, p 415.

'I see we carry our lousy fate...' 22 October 1659, Colepeper to Nicholas, Nicholas Papers.

'Mazarin agreed to draw up a special agreement...' That, at least, is what is stated in *The Life and Death of... Henrietta Maria de Bourbon*, published 10 years later, which tells us that Jermyn managed to have private articles agreed between the Spanish and French, independent of the treaty. Presumably, this was achieved by the meeting with Mazarin at Saint-Vincent.

'with mighty joy...' Paris, 19-20/29-30 November 1659, Nicholas Armorer to Lady Mordaunt, Coates.

'the best quartered of anybody...' Colombes, 26 November/6 December 1659, Mordaunt to Lady Mordaunt, Coates.

'with him among his papers...' Kingstone's report of what Jermyn had told Lord Aubigny, 29 March/8 April 1660, Kingstone to Thurloe, Thurloe S.P. vol. 7 p. 891; Kingstone to Hyde, 8 April 1660, Clar. S.P. vol. 71 f. 71-2.

'it was to the English Freemasons that Jermyn may now have looked for support...' Reasons for believing this are stated in the next chapter.

'implacably bitter...' London, 18 April 1660, Morley to Hyde, Clar. S.P. vol. 71 f. 295-6.

'the Lord Chancellor cannot be put out...' London, 13 April 1660, Dr Morley to Hyde, Clar. S.P. vol. 71 f. 233-4.

'with all the marks of joy imaginable' Reresby's diary.

'you may judge of my joy...' Colombes, 29 May/9 June 1660, Henrietta Maria to Charles II, qu. Cartwright.

RESTORATION! 1660 – 1662

'Closer Union...' 25 March/4 April 1661, Jermyn to Charles II, Clar. S.P. vol. 74, 288-9.

'They will be preserved so very much...' Paris, 19 July 1662, Jermyn to Winchelsea (in Pera), H.M.C. 71, Finch 1.

'pleased with Harry Jermyn's love...' 10/20 May and 24 May/3 June 1658, Daniel O'Neil to Hyde, Clar. S.P. 60, 517-20 and 61, 19-20.

'beating his toy drum...' Cronin, p. 35.

'Comte de St Alban...' 23 June 1661, S.P., qu. Lister 2, p 410.

'a new tie which will draw still closer...' 1 April 1661, Louis XIV to Charles II, Œevre de Louis XIV, 1806.

'According to some sources, the Portuguese marriage'... Carte and Lister (p.126) agreed that the idea of the Portuguese marriage originated with Jermyn and Henrietta Maria, who certainly wanted her son to marry a Catholic princess. However, Robert Southwell, in his biography of Ormonde, wrote that the idea had been proposed by Melo to Monck and Morice before Restoration. Even if the plan had originated with Melo, there is no reason to disbelieve that Jermyn was the first to advocate it in France.

'GRAND MASTER OF THE FREEMASONS' 1662

'We are graciously pleased at the humble...' Charles II's confirmation of the grant of what would become St James's Square, 1662, S.P. Dom., Warrant Book 7, 1662, September 1662.

'High Steward of Greenwich...' My arguments for Jermyn's pivotal role here are stated in 'Henry Jermyn and the Creation of Greenwich', Bygone Kent 19 no. 10 pp. 613-617.

'poor Cowley...' Colombes, 7/17 August 1667, Jermyn to Hyde, Clar. S.P. vol. 85 f. 398-9.

'but according to his usual humanity...' Thomas Spratt to Martin Clifford, 1668, in introduction to Spratt's edition of Cowley's Complete Works (Cowley, Works).

'Anderson's Constitutions...' this topic was first broached in my article "Henry Jermyn, Grand Master of the Freemasons?", Freemasonry Today, issue 6, Autumn 1998 p. 46.

'Shortly after the Restoration, Jermyn and Charles were talking in a chamber at Whitehall...' Scott, Sir W., Personal History of Charles II, compiled 'from various authentic sources', printed in the appendix to Bohn's 1859 edition of Sir Walter Scott's edition of Gramont's Memoirs, Henry G. Bohn, London, 1859.

'Antrim had granted Jermyn a share of the estates' revenue...' The entire Antrim affair caused a vast amount of back-biting, misconceptions and downright lies, which I attempted to untangle in 'The Earl of St Alban's, The Marquis of Antrim and the Irish Acts of Settlement and Explanation, 1660-1684', The Irish Genealogist, vol. 10, no. 2, 1999, pp 234-240.

'In 1640, Jermyn and Henrietta Maria had organised a survey of St James's'... Jermyn's development of St James's is outlined more fully in my article 'Founder of the West End? Henry Jermyn and the Development of St James's', Westminster, Westminster History Review, no. 2, 1999, pp. 13-18.

'The beauty of this great town...' 14 August 1663, Jermyn to Charles II, S.P. Dom. 340, p. 239. It is gratifying to note that this quote now heads the Museum of London's display on the growth of Stuart London.

'Ours is the crowning era...' Virgil, Eclogues IV, lines 4-6.

SOMERSET HOUSE 1662 – 1663

'the sponge that sucked in...' Clar. MS 122, qu. Ollard.

'The design aims higher...' Whitehall, 7 and 11 October 1662, Nicholas to Ormonde, Clar. S.P. qu. Lister 3, pp. 223-5.

'planned to replace Hyde's friend, Lord Treasurer Southampton, with Jermyn himself...' This, at least, is the story reported in Pepys' Diary for 17 October and 22 November 1662.

'for courting Lady Castlemaine...' 30 December 1662, Sir George Fletcher to Daniel le Fleming, H.M.C., Le Fleming Mss.

'he suffered the great belly...' Mrs Delarivierre Manley, The New Atlantis.

'The King hath declared...' 29 July 1667, Pepys' Diary.

'The King hesitated...' Old D.N.B., sub. Grafton.

'rudely bred...' *Complete Peerage* 6 p. 44 n.(a).
'exceedingly handsome...' 6 September 1679, Evelyn's Diary.
'Including Baron Ipswich...' Ruvigny, *sub* Dover.
'a large fit of the gout...' Whitehall, 4 January 1672/3, Jermyn to Essex, Lord Lieutenant of Ireland, B.L. Stowe MS 201, f.9.

THE SECOND ANGLO-DUTCH WAR 1664 – 1666

'Lionne, 'who hath...' Paris, 10 May 1661, Jermyn to Hyde, Clar. S.P., Bodleian Library, qu. Lister 3 pp. 124-128.

THE ROAD TO BREDA 1664 – 1667

'thirteen or fourteen great and good houses...' 14 August 1663, petition for freehold and Patent Roll 17 Car. II 1665, Part 6, no. 3077, membrane 17, qu. in full by Dasent.
'hung with gilded leather containing tapestry...' 9 September 1676, Duke of Norfolk's Deeds, Arundel Castle, cited in Dasent.
'Charles had recently started copying Jermyn's habit...' 17 October 1666, Pepys' Diary.
'he heard that Henrietta Maria had died. Then... robbers lept out...' The false report of the Queen's death is in John Carlisle's letter to Williamson, 28 January 1667 (S.P. Dom., vol. 189, 1667) and the true report of Jermyn's robbery is in a letter of 22 February/4 March 1666/7 from Sir Heneage Finch to John Finch (H.M.C., 71, Finch I).
'Pray be pleased to tell me...' Paris, 16/26 March 1667, Jermyn to Hyde, Clar S.P. vol. 85 f. 143-4; Lister 3 pp. 450-2.
'fell into flames of passion...' Paris, 10/20 April 1667, Jermyn to Hyde, Clar S.P. vol. 85 f. 197-8; Lister 3 pp. 459-60.
'open-faced...' 20/30 April 1667, Jermyn to Hyde, Clar. S.P. vol. 85 f. 225-6.
'We are so amazed with the number...' Brussels, 3/13 May 1667, Sir William Temple to Jermyn, Temple, Works 1, p. 268-9.
'But when he reached the market town of Arras he could go no further...' The principal sources for Jermyn's peace negotiations are Jermyn's correspondence with Charles II, Hyde and Arlington in the Clarendon State Papers in the Bodleian Library, and with Holles and Coventry in the Longleat collection, with much useful commentary too from the Venetian ambassadors (S.P. Ven) and Hyde's autobiography. His own correspondence tells clearly what happened on his ill-fated trip to Arras, whilst the false story of his ignominious expulsion from the French court at Douai seems to have originated with Col. Bullen Reames, who stated that a letter (which was, in fact, non-existent) had arrived from Jermyn about 24 or 25 June 'wherein he says that the King of France did lately fall out with him, giving him ill names, saying that he had belied him to our king by saying he had promised to assist our King and to forward the peace, saying that indeed he had offered to forward the peace at such a time, but it was not accepted of, or so he thinks himself not obliged, and would do what was fit for him; and so made him go out of his sight in great displeasure', a story repeated at once in Pepys' Diary on 26 June 1667 and the following day by Charles Bertie (London, 27 June 1667, Charles Bertie to Sir Thomas Osborne, H.M.C., Lindsey Mss), 'our correspondence with France is very bad, my Lord St Albans being banished [from] the French army and the Court'. Jermyn's own letters show that none of this was true.
'repeated on gilt-edged paper...' Feiling, Keith; *British Foreign Policy 1660-1672*. Macmillan & Co. Ltd, London, 1930.

THE GRAND DESIGN 1667 – 1668

'author of these misfortunes...' Paris, 26 June/6 July 1667, Jermyn to Hyde, Clar. S.P. vol. 85 f. 346-7.
'St Alban's writ to, that he may bewail...' Anon, *Last Instructions to a painter, about the Dutch Wars, 1667*, (printed 1681).
'the King's service and your own quiet...' Colombes, 10/20 July 1667, Jermyn to Hyde, Clar. S.P. vol. 85 f. 357-8.
'if he dies without some very signal calamity...' Clar. MS 122, qu. Ollard.
'Charles now agreed to follow a new version of Jermyn's Closer Alliance – the Grand Design...' All discussion of Grand Design is rendered difficult for historians because the letters of Charles II to Madame, at the AAE, which provide most information about it, only survive up to June 1669. We know, therefore, that James; Arlington; Clifford; Arundell (Henrietta Maria's Master of the Horse) and, possibly Belasyse (Feiling) – all Catholics, with the possible exception at that stage of Arlington – were told of the plan in January 1669. Later, Turenne, Buckingham, Lionne, Louvois and Colbert de Croissy were informed of everything except for the conversion clause. Historians

have argued – somewhat half-heartedly – over the point at which Jermyn was admitted to the secret, minus the conversion clause. Some argue that it was as late as June 1669 (Mignet), whilst a letter from Charles II to Madame refers to someone, decoded variously as Arlington (Cartwright) or Jermyn (Bryant), who 'does believe there is some business with France, which he knows nothing of' (Whitehall, 25 May 1669, Charles II to Madame). Even if the code-name used in the letter was Jermyn's – which is not known at all – there is no evidence that 'some business' was definitely the Grand Design. Jermyn's complicity in the plan as early as March 1669 is certainly indicated by Charles II's instructions to him to brief Arundell when he arrived in Paris that month on a mission to reaffirm to Louis the King's desire for the Grand Design (7 March 1669, Charles to Madame, Cartwright). The simplest explanation is that no specific record exists of Jermyn's admission to the Grand Design because it never happened. On the contrary: what everyone else seems to have missed are the repeated proposals for just such a plan, albeit without the conversion clause, in Jermyn's correspondence going right back to before the Restoration – and who is more likely to have dreamed up the conversion clause, and convinced Jermyn about it too on the grounds that it would usher in religious freedom for all – than Henrietta Maria herself?
'my ministers are anything but what I will have them...' 8 July 1668, Charles II to Madame, qu. Bryant.

SAINT-DENIS 1669

'she is not yet near so well as we wish to see her...' 10 April 1669, Jermyn to Arlington, S.P. France, qu. Green, Letters.
'she coughs not much...' 17 April 1669, Jermyn to Arlington, S.P. France, qu. Green, Letters.
'You cannot imagine what a noise Lord St Albans...' 6 May 1669, Charles II to Madame, qu. Bryant.
'If that which hath happened here...' Colombes Sep: 10 [16]69', i.e. 30 August/10 September, S.P. (France) 78/127 f 85-6.
'I am sure without this...' 1/11 September 1669, Ralph Montagu to Arlington, qu. Hervey, Rushbrook p. 284.
'the easiest way of carrying on things here with decency... you ought to pity me...' Colombes, 1/11 September 1669 (morning), Jermyn to Arlington, S.P. (France) 78/127 ff 91-94v.
'At ten o'clock that morning, the congregation began to proceed...' The account of Henrietta Maria's funeral is from the *Rélation de la pompe funèbre, faite en l'Eglise de S. Denys en France, pour la Reyne Mère d'Angleterre* (Brussels, n.d.), quoted in Marshall.

THE SECRET TREATY OF DOVER 1669 – 1678

'You will believe me easily...' Colombes, 30 August/10 September 1669, Jermyn to Arlington. S.P. (France) 78/127 f. 87-90.
'I have no tears in reserve'... D'Aulnoy.
'he became obsessed with the much younger 'Miledy'...' The Baroness d'Aulnoy referred to the object of Jermyn's desires as 'Miledy', and proceeded to describe her affair with Buckingham's nephew Lord Arran. This was clearly Richard Butler, Earl of Arran, the widower of Buckingham's niece. He was Earl of Arran in Ireland, but James Douglas, later 4th Duke of Hamilton, was Earl of Arran in Scotland. This caused confusion at court and, because Des Maizeux wrote that Jermyn withdrew his attentions from Katherine Crofts when she was courted by 'The Earl of Arran, afterwards Duke of Hamilton', some writers have made the mistake of assuming that d'Aulnoy's (Irish) Arran was Hamilton, the Scottish Arran and that, ergo, Miledy was Katherine Crofts. In fact, the identities of both men are perfectly clear, and, in any case, d'Aulnoy indicates that Miledy's status was of higher rank to Katherine, who was a baron's sister. My identification of Miledy as Elizabeth Bagot, widow of Lord Falmouth, is conjectural. Like Miledy, Lady Falmouth was a renowned beauty and a great favorite of the King, and Gramont referred to her as "your Miledi" in a letter to Falmouth in 1664 (23 November 1664, Gramont to Charles, Earl of Falmouth, Hartmann). It is appreciated that 'Miledy' was used as frequently as 'Milord', but Gramont's use of the term indicates he may have been using a particular nickname. This idea led me to look at David Loggan's engraving of 'Miledy' dressed as Britannia, which appears at the front of the publications of the Sheldonian Theatre, Oxford. The girl depicted bears a remarkable similarity to Sir Peter Lely's portrait of Lady Falmouth at Althorpe, though I would be the first to admit that many of Lely's portraits of young women are pretty similar. Lady Falmouth certainly socialised with the Jermyns – in 1667, Pepys even reported a rumour that she was going to marry Harry Jermyn.
'St Albans, with wrinkles and smiles in his face...' 'Signor Dildo', in Veith, David M. (ed.), *The Complete Poems of John Wilmot, Earl of Rochester*, New Haven and London, Yale University Press, 1968. Borgo was near Modena; Rochester may have been alluding to Jermyn's approval of James' marriage, unless the word in fact reads 'pergo', i.e. Purgatory.
'At this age all the springs of ambition leave us...' Saint-Evremond, Letter no. 66, nd (c.1670-5), *To Monsieur—*

who could not endure that the Earl of Saint Albans should be in love in his old age.

'it is true that I have greatly loved this lady...' d'Aulnoy.

'I admire their Beauty, without any design...' Saint-Évremond, Letter no. 66 (c. 1670-5), *To Monsieur—. who could not endure that the Earl of Saint Albans should be in love in his old age.*

'including one she said she owed Jermyn...' Orléans, beside himself with jealousy when he discovered Jermyn's complicity in his wife's secret correspondence with Charles, refused to allow Ralph Montagu to give the money to Jermyn.

'joining together to surpass all others...' 24 May 1669, S.P. Ven.; 'On the assumption that the division of the Spanish Netherlands between these two kingdoms would be easy, it is stated that St Albans has authority to offer money to the king here to pay all his debts provided he detaches himself from the triple alliance. With this knot undone the Spaniards would no longer have a safeguard for their marts. With their own left free, Holland would be greatly weakened and so France and England would be able to think of conquests in the north and of joining together to surpass all others in the trade of America and the East Indies'.

'The Earl of St Albans is grown young again... 13 May 1671, Henshaw to Sir Robert Paston, H.M.C. 6, Ingilsby Mss.

'Knight of the Garter...' Charles II's intention to make Jermyn a Garter knight is first referred to in 1650 (God forbid!' exclaimed Hyde: Madrid, 26 April 1650 Hyde to Nicholas Clar. S.P. no. 290). Most sources give the date of the investiture at St George's Chapel, Windsor – as opposed to the appointment – as 3 June 1671. This is either a typesetting error, or the *intended* date, if the ceremony was clearly put off because of the naval engagement with the Dutch. The actual date, inscribed deliberately on Jermyn's tomb at Rushbrook, was 'Pridie Kalends Julias' – 30 June.

'a poor old man such as I...' d'Aulnoy.

'to give you a little account of my self'... 'Cheevlye nr Newmarket', 2 January 1674/5, Jermyn to Ormonde. National Library of Ireland, Dublin, Carte MSS, vol. 60 (16 Sept 1674-2 Jan 1674/5) no. 400, 2 sheets, yellow paper, noticed in H.M.C. VI, Ormonde MSS.

'Where there are Mayernes...' This is a Court in-joke: Theodore Mayerne had been Charles I and Henrietta Maria's principal doctor.

'JOINING TOGETHER TO SURPASS ALL OTHERS' 1678 – 1685

'we contemn/Gyges wealthy diadem...' 'contemn' means to dispise. Gyges was a king of Lydia, who was rather too concerned with worldly wealth.

'Fill the Bowl with rosy Wine...' Cowley, 'The Epicure', *Anacreontiques*, 8.

'By 1678, Wren had become Deputy Grand Master...' see chapter sixteen.

'large and magnificent structures...' John Evelyn's introduction to *A Parallel of the Ancient Architecture with the Modern... written in French by Roland Fréart, Sieur de Chambray; made English*, London, (August) 1664.

'for the conveniency of the Nobility and Gentry...' June 1663, petition of Jermyn's builders, S.P. Dom., 29/75 no. 27.

'If it please God to continue those beginnings...' Paris, 19 July 1662, Jermyn to Winchelsea, H.M.C., 71, Finch 1.

'a diamond studded box, worth 1,500 *livres*...' Jermyn's role in these final negotiations is described in Sir John Dalrymple, *Memoirs of Great Britain and Ireland*, vol. 2 p. 319, quoting from Barillon's correspondence in AAE.

'to whom', Saint-Évremond had written in 1677, 'you yielded the title of the first gouty Man in England...' 1677, second letter, Saint-Évremond to Jermyn, Saint-Évremond.

'an extraordinary appetite...' 18 September 1683, Evelyn's Diary.

'Henry, Duke of Grafton, one of Barbara Villiers' sons...' The case for Harry Jermyn being the 1st Duke of Grafton's son is set out in detail in the Appendix.

'As for news, what is from foreign parts...' Hervey, Rushbrook, p. 289.

'decent Christian burial amongst my ancestors in the church of Rushbrook...' Jermyn's will.

'THE FUNERAL OF GLORY'? 1685 – present

'If it belongs to Henry Jermyn's first governorship...' *Jersey Evening Post*, 30 May 2007, and communication from Prof. Biddle to author.

'the founder of the West End...' *Survey of London* 29, introduction and Dasent p.5

INDEX